Analyzing Novell® Networks

Analyzing Novell® Networks

Carl Malamud

VNR Van Nostrand Reinhold
New York

Copyright © 1992 by Van Nostrand Reinhold.

Library of Congress Catalog Card Number 90-12495
ISBN 0-442-00364-1
ISBN 0-442-01302-7 (paperback)

All rights reserved. No part of this work covered by the copyright hereon may be reproduced or used in any form or by any means—graphic, electronic, or mechanical, including photocopying, recording, taping, or information storage and retrieval systems—without written permission of the publisher.

Printed in the United States of America

Van Nostrand Reinhold
115 Fifth Avenue
New York, New York 10011

Van Nostrand Reinhold International Company Limited
11 New Fetter Lane
London EC4P 4EE, England

Van Nostrand Reinhold
480 La Trobe Street
Melbourne, Victoria 3000, Australia

Nelson Canada
1120 Birchmount Road
Scarborough, Ontario MIK 5G4, Canada

16 15 14 13 12 11 10 9 8 7 6 5 4 3 2 1

Cover based on an original perspective drawing by Jan Vredeman de Vries (1527–1604), reprinted in *Perspective*, Dover Pictorial Archive Series (Dover Publications, 1968). Color was added without the participation of the original artist.

Library of Congress Cataloging-in-Publication Data

Malamud, Carl, 1959
  Analyzing Novell® networks / Carl Malamud.
      p. cm.
  Includes index.
  ISBN 0-442-00364-1
  ISBN 0-442-01302-7 (paperback)
  1. Local area networks (Computer networks) 2. NetWare (Computer operating system) 3. Computer network architectures. I. Title.
TK5105.7.M35 1990
621.39'81—dc20   90-12495
                                                         CIP

To Ernie

Contents

Preface	xi
A Note on Trademarks	xiii
Acknowledgments	xv
1. Analyzing Networks	**1**
Network Architectures	3
Protocol Stacks and the NetWare Architecture	6
NetWare Core Protocols	10
Gateways	16
The Sniffer Network Analyzer	18
Analyzing Networks	22
Getting the Software	24
Using This Book	24

PART I: NETWORKS

2. Data Links and LLC	**27**
The Data Link Layer	29
Ethernet and IEEE 802.3	31
Thickwire Networks	38
Repeaters	40
Cheapernet Networks	42
Other Media	43
Bridges	43
Novell and Ethernet	48
Key Points in This Chapter	49
3. Token Ring and ARCNET	**51**
Other Data Links	53
Datapoint's ARCNET	54
ARCNET Wiring and Hubs	54
ARCNET Packets	58

The Fragmentation Header	62
ISO/IEEE Token Ring Standard	64
Active and Standby Monitors	70
Error Recovery and Initialization	71
Token Ring Extensions: 16 Mbps and FDDI	74
Integrating Different Subnetworks	74
Key Points in This Chapter	76

4. IPX and SPX — 77

The Network and Transport Layers	79
XNS and Novell	81
IPX	82
RIP and the Internet	89
The Error and Echo Protocols	93
NetWare Core Protocols	94
SPX	100
The Service Advertisement Protocol	102
IPX and SPX Clients	105
Key Points in This Chapter	106

PART II: NetWare

5. NetWare Core Protocols — 109

NetWare and Servers	111
NetWare Operating system	113
The Bindery	115
Communications Utilities	120
File Access	121
Locking and Synchronization	133
Print Services	140
Job Servers	141
Accounting Services	143
Key Points in This Chapter	144

6. Message Handling Service — 145

Message Handling Services	147
MHS Message Structure	148
The User Interface	152
The Message Transfer Agent	153
Gateways	158
X.400 and MHS	161
Directory Services	165
Key Points in This Chapter	165

7. Data Access   167
      Flat Versus Structured Data Access   169
      The Btree File Structure   170
      Novell's Btrieve   173
      SQL and Databases   174
      Novell's XQL   176
      Other Database Systems   181
      Key Points in This Chapter   182

8. Remote Procedure Calls   183
      Upper Layers   185
      Interprocess Communication   187
      Netwise RPC Tool   189
      Procedure Declarations   191
      Process Binding   193
      The Client Stub   195
      Server Control Procedure   196
      Custom Procedures   197
      ISO and Sun RPC Mechanisms   200
      Role of the RPC Tool   201
      Key Points in This Chapter   202

PART III: GATEWAYS

9. STREAMS and Protocol Stacks   205
      Protocol Stacks and the Operating System   207
      Character I/O Mechanisms   208
      The STREAMS Multiplexor   213
      Transport Level Interface   215
      Link Support Layer   217
      Named Pipes and STREAMS   219
      STREAMS and NetWare Environments   221
      Key Points in This Chapter   221

10. AppleTalk   223
      Novell and AppleTalk   225
      Lower-Level Protocols   227
      AppleTalk Filing Protocol   230
      Printer Access Protocol   235
      Other Features   237
      Key Points in This Chapter   237

11. DECnet and Portable NetWare   239
      Portable NetWare   241
      NetWare for VMS   244

DECnet	245
LAT Protocol	248
VAX Clusters	251
Novell and DECnet	251
Key Points in This Chapter	253

12. X.25 and Wide Area Networks — **255**

Wide Area Networks	257
Asynchronous Bridges	257
Asynchronous Gateways	259
X.25 Bridges	261
Novell X.25 Gateway	261
Integrating Novell and WANs	263
Key Points in This Chapter	264

13. Gateways to Other Networks — **267**

Gateways	269
TCP/IP	269
Network File System	272
IBM and SNA	276
NetBIOS	278
OSI	280
Key Points in This Chapter	281

Bibliography — **283**

Glossary — **291**

Index — **335**

Ordering the Software — **344**

Preface

This book is a description of the architecture of Novell's NetWare. An architecture is a design—it explains what the pieces are and how they fit together. A network architecture is the design that enables products to work together in a distributed environment.

A network is made up of many pieces—computers, controller cards, disk drives, and cables. The architecture builds this collection of pieces up into a coherent whole. The goal of a network is to provide services—access to files, exchange of messages, access to databases, and printing. This book explains how Novell provides those services.

The book, after an overview chapter, starts with a description of what makes up the local area network—the cables, protocols, and controllers that allow different computers to exchange data. ARCNET, Ethernet, and token ring are three of the main local area networks (LANs) supported by Novell.

Next, the network protocols—IPX and SPX—are discussed. These basic Novell protocols enable several networks to be connected together into an internet. They define how data from one user is delivered to another and guarantee that data won't be lost in transit.

At this point, the beginnings of a network are in place: data can be delivered from one user to another. The book then discusses the NetWare Core Protocols (NCP). NCP defines the basic services found in a Novell network—access to remote data, security services, or printing, for example. The function of NCP is to make the network transparent to the user. A remote disk drive should look just like a local disk drive. A remote printer should be accessible in the same way when it is remote as when it is local.

Further levels of transparency are built by messaging and database services. The Action Technology Message Handling Service allows different programs to send messages to each other. While this service can be as simple as electronic mail, it can also include automatic updates to remote databases. Database services are provided through a variety of Novell software tools that make data access more powerful than standard file management techniques.

To many, a Novell network is simply a platform for important applications to run on. The network administrator can buy a variety of third-party utilities and use NetWare to make them accessible to users. Two chapters discuss STREAMS and remote procedure calls, mechanisms that allow programs from a wide variety of vendors to easily take their place on the network.

The book continues by discussing the coexistence of Novell NetWare with other computers. First, the Apple Macintosh is integrated into the network. Next, different kinds of servers running operating systems like Unix or DEC's VMS are integrated.

Finally, the book discusses how other kinds of networks can coexist with Novell's NetWare. DECnet, AppleTalk, TCP/IP, and IBM's SNA are all architectures that can, to some degree, provide interoperability with workstations running the NetWare software.

By building up the network piece by piece, the reader gains an appreciation for the overall design—the architecture of Novell NetWare. From the architecture comes specific products—new releases of NetWare, new controller cards or peripherals, or different pieces of software.

This book is not a handbook. It's not something you keep next to your monitor, unless you're trying to block the glare from a light. This book is for the reader who wants a technical overview of Novell NetWare.

The overview shows what a Novell network can do. People developing programs for NetWare, buying networks, comparing networks, or trying to plan networks are all intended readers.

Nor do we ignore that ubiquitous creature in computer science literature, "the user." By showing the architecture, we attempt to give intelligent users an understanding of what is happening on their networks.

A Note on Trademarks

Conversation Manager and MHS by Action Technologies are trademarks and Action Technologies, MacAccess, and The Coordinator are registered trademarks of Action Technologies, Inc.

PostScript is a trademark of Adobe Systems.

Apple, AppleShare, AppleTalk, Finder, ImageWriter, LaserWriter, LocalTalk, Macintosh, and Quickdraw are trademarks of Apple Computer.

dBase IV and Framework are trademarks of Ashton-Tate.

Ashton-Tate/Microsoft SQL Server is a trademark of Ashton-Tate and Microsoft.

STREAMS, Transport Layer Interface, Unix, and Unix System V Release 4 are trademarks of AT&T.

Banyan and VINES are trademarks of Banyan.

Sidekick is a trademark of Borland.

FaxPress is a trademark of Castelle.

cc:Mail is a trademark of cc:Mail.

CompuServe is a trademark of CompuServe.

Convex is a trademark of Convex.

Cray is a trademark of Cray Computer.

CEO is a trademark of Data General.

ARCNET, ARCNET Plus, Attached Resource Computer, and DATAPOINT are registered trademarks of DATAPOINT Corporation.

DaVinci is a trademark of DaVinci Systems.

All-In-One, DEC, DECnet, LAT, LAVC, MAILbus, Message Router, MicroVAX, MOP, Rdb, ThinWire, Ultrix, VAX, VAX Cluster, VMS, and VMS Mail are trademarks of Digital Equipment Corporation.

pcAnywhere is a trademark of Dynamic Microprocessor Associates.

SQLBase Server is a trademark of Gupta Technologies.

HP DeskManager, Hewlett-Packard Laserjet, and PCL are trademarks of Hewlett-Packard.

Informix is a trademark of Informix.

Ingres is a trademark of the Ingres Corporation.

Hijaak is a trademark of Inset Systems.

AS/400, DISOSS, IBM, IBM PC LAN, PC/AT, PC/XT, PROFS, SNA, SNADS, System/370, System/38, and 3270 Display Station are trademarks of International Business Machines, Inc.

Agenda and Lotus 1-2-3 are trademarks of Lotus.

REM and MCI Mail are trademarks of MCI.

MS-DOS, Microsoft, Microsoft Excel, Microsoft Windows, and Microsoft Word are trademarks of Microsoft.

NCR is a trademark of NCR.

Netwise and RPC Tool are trademarks of Netwise.

Network General and Sniffer Analyzer are trademarks of Network General Corporation.

C Network Compiler, C Network Compiler/386, IPX, NACS, NetWare, NetWare C Interface for DOS, NetWare for VMS, NetWare MHS, NetWare RPC, NetWare SQL, NetWare System Call for DOS, NetWare 386, NLM, Novell, Portable NetWare, RX-Net, SFT, SPX, VAP, and Xtrieve PLUS are trademarks and Btrieve and XQL are registered trademarks of Novell.

M-Bridge MCI Mail Gateway is a trademark of On-Site Communications.

Oracle is a trademark of Oracle Corporation.

Paradox is a trademark of Paradox.

Prime is a trademark of Prime.

DESQview 386 is a trademark of Quarterdeck Office Systems.

Retix is a trademark of Retix.

MAILbridge Server/MHS and Softswitch are trademarks of Softswitch.

Network File System, Open Network Computing, SPARC, Sun, SunOS, and TOPS are trademarks of Sun Microsystems, Inc.

Tandem is a trademark of Tandem.

3Com and 3+ are trademarks of 3Com.

Touch Communications is a trademark of Touch Communications.

TransLAN and Vitalink are trademarks of Vitalink.

Wang Office is a trademark of Wang.

WordPerfect and WordPerfect Office are trademarks of WordPerfect Corporation.

Clearinghouse, Interpress, Interscript, NS, and XNS are trademarks and Xerox is a registered trademark of Xerox Corporation.

Carl Malamud is a trademark of Carl Malamud.

Acknowledgments

I would like to thank Network General for their generous help in making this book possible. Their contributions, including careful reviews of the manuscript in draft form, were quite useful. In particular, I would like to thank Christopher Poda, Harry Saal, Jay Weil, Valerie Lasker, and Len Shustek. Bill Alderson of Pine Mountain Group also reviewed sections of the book.

Several other companies were also quite helpful in giving me access to documentation, software, and other resource materials. Don Thompson and Anne Theriault of Netwise were particularly helpful on remote procedure calls and STREAMS. Art Sabsevitz of AT&T reviewed the STREAMS chapter. Barry Sadler and anonymous reviewers at Datapoint Corporation helped on ARCNET. R. Flores of Action Technologies reviewed the chapter on Message Handling Systems. Richard Ozer of Berkeley, California provided a careful technical review of the entire manuscript.

Novell was helpful in giving me access to materials and information. My contact points at the corporation were Patty Heisser, Robert R. Northrup, and Kyle Humphries. I would also like to thank the anonymous reviewers at Novell who made comments on the manuscript when it was in draft form. Novell asked me to point out that their review of the book does not constitute an endorsement. The reader should also note that the reverse is true—my writing a book on NetWare should not be taken as an endorsement of their products.

As always, despite the contributions of my many reviewers, any errors that remain are of course my own.

CHAPTER 1

Analyzing Networks

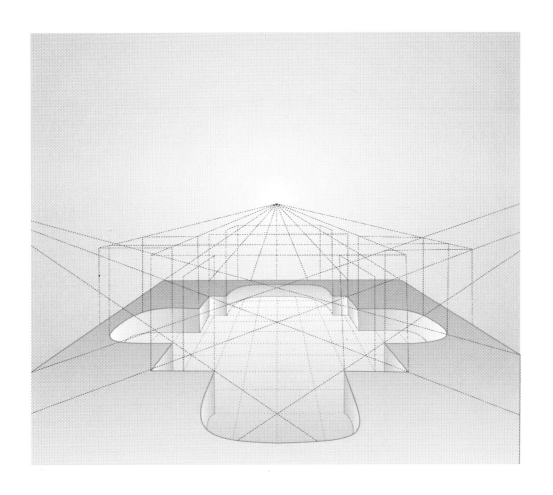

CHAPTER 1

Analyzing Networks

Network Architectures

There are two ways to write a book about Novell networks. One is as a hands-on, troubleshooting guide—a book you keep near you if you're responsible for administering a Novell network. In theory, that hands-on guide is the manual you get with the software, but companies such as Novell are not known for the clarity and precision of their manuals, hence the need for books and other information to supplement that available directly from the vendor.

Another approach is to step back from the day-to-day details of running a network and look at how it is designed: the network architecture. This book adopts an architectural approach that shows how different kinds of pieces in a network work together. This is not to say that we will not be concerned with the realities of day-to-day work on a network. After all, what good is a design if it doesn't work?

The concept of an architecture is a slippery one to describe. In theory, you can take a given architecture and implement it in a number of different ways. In a building, this would be equivalent to specifying a wall but not specifying the materials. Or, one could specify the material as brick but leave the exact method of installing brick to the bricklayer.

The line between an architecture and its implementation is difficult to find. This is particularly true in the case of a proprietary product like Novell's NetWare—they don't publish their design, but they do, however, have to publish what their networks do. With this information we can infer their architecture.

One help in looking at the architecture of NetWare is that Novell, like many other companies, builds on existing standards and technologies. Once we've identified which specific technologies are in NetWare, we have a pretty good idea of how they are using it.

Why concentrate on a relatively abstract concept of an architecture instead of just explaining in a straightforward manner what the different products are and what they do? A knowledge of the architecture lets the reader look at any product and quickly understand what the product is doing. The architecture provides a framework for analysis.

Just as the Novell products conform to an architecture, any computing environment has an architecture. A given user environment has a network architecture, although in many cases it is more implied than explicit.

The Novell architectures provided in this book are both a subset and a superset of the functions that users will need in their own architectures. It is a superset in that no one computing environment will use all the aspects of the Novell architecture. Even if you bought all products made by Novell and Novell-compatible vendors, there would still be unused aspects.

The Novell architecture is a subset of the user architecture in that most computing environments need to use more than just network services. Even in a Novell-only environment, the user will still need an operating system (DOS, OS/2, Macintosh) and applications (Microsoft Excel, WordPerfect, for example). Many environments use several kinds of network services: a Novell network for the departments and an IBM mainframe for data processing, for example.

In computer networks, it is becoming increasingly common for vendors to tout the flexibility of their products—all your applications, computers, and network media will interconnect, both now and forever. The only problem is, they don't usually tell you how they accomplish this feat.

This book attempts to remedy that problem by explaining what a Novell network is. A network can be thought of as a machine (or several interrelated machines) that accomplishes work. The work can be simple, such as sending a message from one computer to another, or complex, such as sending electronic mail from one user to another. In this use of the word, the network is more than just the wire—it is a collection of computers acting as if they were a single, integrated computing system.

One can look at such a machine from a variety of perspectives. Much of the literature on networks is intended for people who are either buying networks or designing them. The literature for the buyer tends to be at an extremely high level—the equivalent of a TV advertisement for a new car. Conversely, the literature for the maker of the machine is at an extremely low level—the equivalent of the design specifications for making the new car.

This book is aimed at a third group—those who use the machine. It explains how the network works without necessarily delving into the level of detail necessary for designing the hardware or coding the software.

Clients and Servers

When people knock on your office door, they are usually there because they want something. You are performing a service, and your visitor is a client. With a few exceptions, most people don't just wander the halls aimlessly—they have a purpose in mind.

Computer networks work the same way. When one computer wishes to use the network, it is for the purpose of getting some work done—of obtaining a service. A server might provide printing services, electronic mail, database management, statistical computing, or remote storage of data.

In the Novell view of the world, the user is on a workstation, a client of the network. In addition to the workstation, there are servers; possibly one, possibly a great many. The combination of the software for the workstation and the software for servers is known as Novell NetWare.

NetWare consists of two pieces of software. First, there is an operating system for a PC-based system that acts as a server for the rest of the network. Attached to the server are a variety of disk drives, communications devices, and output devices such as printers. The NetWare operating system allows many different remote users to access these peripheral devices.

The second part of NetWare is the workstation software, known as a NetWare shell, which makes remote resources appear local. For example, users should be able to print on a remote printer the same way they would if the printer were locally attached to the LPT port on the PC.

This basic NetWare system consists entirely of PCs. Novell takes a PC-centric view of the world—most of their energies are invested in software for this particular platform. We will see later how the Apple Macintosh and other systems can be integrated into the network.

Users and the Protocol Stack

Clients request services and servers furnish them. Yet these two software programs are located on different computers. How do they communicate? A network architecture specifies how two programs can communicate with each other.

Remote access to a printer is an example of a service. The server is a print server on the NetWare operating system. The client is a word processing program. The word processing program, the user, does not communicate directly with the print server. Instead, it simply attempts to print the data to the local LPT port on the PC.

The data going to the LPT port is intercepted by the NetWare shell on the workstation. The word processing program is not really communicating with the print server. Instead, it asks the NetWare shell to take data going to the local LPT port and deliver it to the print server on the network.

The print server and the NetWare shell work together. The responsibility of the shell is to take the data and put it into a series of packets, labeling each one as being destined for the print server program on a particular computer.

The shell, in turn, will take each of these packets and submit it to another program on the workstation, IPX. IPX doesn't know anything about printing, but it does know how to take a labeled packet and get it to the destination computer. IPX is responsible for routing the packet to its appropriate destination. It takes the envelope it received from the shell and puts it into another envelope with routing directions on it.

IPX then hands the packet down to another module, the Ethernet driver. The Ethernet is responsible for actually getting the data over the cable to the destination. There, it hands the data up to IPX. IPX in turn hands the data up to the print server.

Data keeps getting packaged into envelopes and sealed. The envelopes are handed to the next module, which puts its own instructions on them. At each layer, the tasks become more and more specialized. By the time the last module on the workstation is reached, the instructions are quite simple—transmit a string of bytes over a wire.

Data is going down a protocol stack—a collection of software modules on a computer that, working together, provide network services. Each layer of the protocol stack is communicating with its peer through the instructions on each envelope; it ignores the information sealed inside the envelope. Each layer communicates with three entities: its peer on the remote computer, its user on the local computer, and a module for which it is the user on the local computer.

This highly simplistic view of what happens on a network is an example of an architecture—defining tasks and isolating them in a software module that provides clearly defined services and expects clearly defined services from other modules.

Protocol Stacks and the NetWare Architecture

The best way to look at network architectures is to use the seven-layer model developed by the International Standards Organization (ISO). The model divides up the tasks performed on a network into seven categories, each building on the services of the lower layer (see Fig. 1-1).

It is possible for several different protocols to be resident at one layer of the network. At the data link layer, for example, Novell supports at least three different protocols: Ethernet, ARCNET, and token ring. By using the ISO model, we can categorize all the different pieces of a Novell network and see what service each piece provides and how it compares to the other components in the network.

At the bottom of the network are the data link and physical layers. Ethernet, token ring, ARCNET, and X.25 are all examples of standards that provide a data link service—the transfer of a packet of data from one node to another on the same network.

Figure 1-2 shows a simple example of a data link, based on the Ethernet protocols. A piece of coaxial cable has several computers attached to it. A special device is the multiport transceiver (MPT), which allows several computers to share a single connection to the coaxial cable. The data link layer, which in this case is the Ethernet, is responsible for accepting a packet of data from its client and sending it out over the physical medium.

The intended destination node, also connected to the Ethernet, is listening to the physical medium. When it detects a packet with its address on it, it copies the packet off the cable and into the computer. It then sends the packet up to its client, the network layer of the network.

A variety of different data links exist. Each of these different types of networks has different characteristics, such as the maximum number of nodes, the maximum distance between nodes, and the transmission speed of the medium. Chapters 2 and 3 discuss three of the important data links used for local area networks in a Novell network.

No one data link is ideal—most organizations will have at least two different kinds. For example, Ethernet is often used as a local area network. Even if an

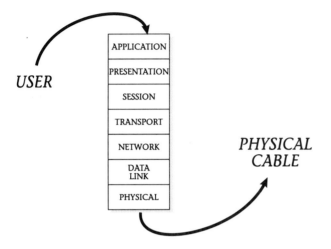

Fig. 1-1 The ISO Reference Model

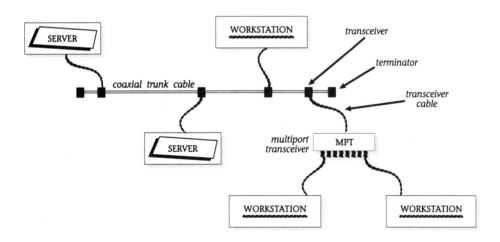

Fig. 1-2 A Simple Ethernet Configuration

organization standardizes on Ethernet as a local area network protocol, another data link mechanism will usually be needed for the wide area network.

Even in a local environment, organizations may wish to have several different types of data links. Ethernet may be used to connect Unix-based minicomputers together. The token ring could be used for workstations and IBM equipment. ARCNET could be used for small clumps of workstations in outlying offices.

Network Layer

It is the responsibility of the network layer of the network to draw all these different data links together into a coherent network environment (see Fig. 1-3). In the illustration, the top portion is an Ethernet, the middle is a token ring, and the bottom is an ARCNET.

Notice that there are servers that connect the data links together. These servers are actually members of both data links, and they can provide NetWare services to workstations on both of them. In addition, the servers act as a router between the two data links.

If a workstation wishes to send data, it submits the packet to its network layer, which then looks at the destination address and determines if it is on the local network. If so, it sends the packet directly. If not, it sends the packet to the closest router, which determines where the destination node is.

The router then forwards the packet to another router. If that router is directly connected to the destination network, it then sends the packet to its final destination. Otherwise, it sends the packet to another router. The network layer thus collects several data links together and forms an internetwork.

In the Novell environment, a network is a single data link. An internetwork is the collection of one or more data links, connected together with routers. The word *network* is also used to refer to the collection of services and data links that make up a networking environment. A router is the computer used to connect two or more data links together; Novell literature calls it a bridge.

Generally, a bridge is a device that connects two similar data links, that is, two Ethernets, together. The bridge, known as a MAC-layer bridge (explained in Chapter 2), makes the two Ethernets appear as one to its client—the network layer. Novell calls the router a bridge, as in a network-layer bridge.

Throughout the book, the word *router* will be used unless the name of a specific Novell product is being discussed. Even there, pains will be taken to point out that which term is being used—the MAC-layer bridge or network-layer router. This issue will become clearer to the reader after reading Chapter 2 on MAC-layer bridges and Chapter 4 on the network layer functionality.

Transport Layer

The network layer is responsible for making a packet reach the eventual destination. However, for a variety of reasons to be examined later, it is not practical to have the network layer guarantee that the data has reached its eventual destination.

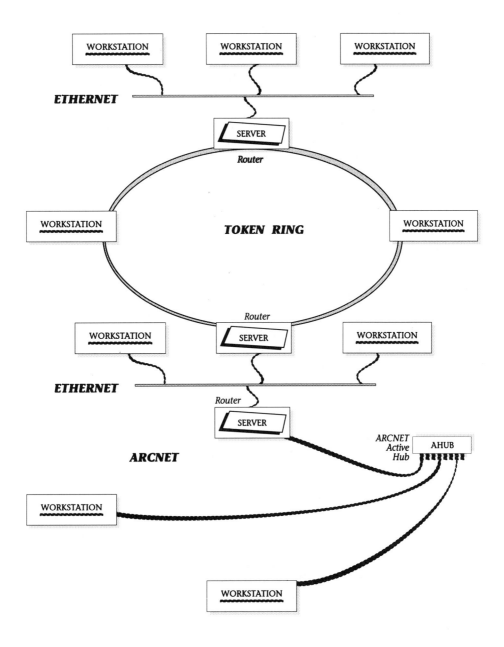

Fig. 1-3 A Collection of Data Links

The guaranteed delivery of data is the responsibility of the transport layer of the network. The transport layer assigns each outgoing message a sequence number. The transport layer on the remote end of the network checks each incoming packet and makes sure that nothing is missing.

The user of the transport layer sees a virtual circuit (see Fig. 1-4). The virtual circuit means that the user doesn't have to worry about how the data made it through the network. The user of a reliable transport service is able to assume that all data it receives is the data that was transmitted, in the correct order.

In Figure 1-4, we see the software modules that help provide the virtual circuit. IPX is the NetWare network-level protocol. The transport layer here is the Sequenced Packet Exchange, one of two different transport protocols used in NetWare.

In Chapter 4, we will look in more detail at the various protocols that Novell offers at the network and transport layers of the network. Figure 1-5 shows a more complete stack for the Novell architecture. Notice that in addition to IPX and SPX, there are a variety of other protocols. RIP, for example, is the Routing Information Protocol, which is used by the network layer to find out about changes in the network topology.

In addition to SPX, notice that there is a protocol called PEP, the Packet Exchange Protocol. SPX and PEP are the two transport layer providers in a Novell network. The other protocols shown in the diagram, Error, Echo, and SAP, are used for services such as service advertisement or error detection and are discussed in Chapter 5.

NetWare Core Protocols

The basic services in a Novell network are a collection of functions provided by a file server, labeled the NetWare Core Protocols (NCP) in Figure 1-5. NCP allows a workstation to use computing resources on a file server. It consists of two pieces—the NetWare shell on the workstation and the software on the server—that can interpret and respond to incoming requests.

The main resource provided by the file server is access to disk drives. The workstation is able to access remote data transparently, as if it were on a local disk drive. On the PC, the user sees different disk drives, each labeled by a letter of the alphabet. Remote data can be "mounted" as a local disk drive.

When a user refers to a disk drive in a data request (i.e., copying a file from one drive to another), the NetWare shell on the workstation intercepts the incoming request. If the data is located on a server, the NetWare shell will hand the request off to the NetWare Core Protocols portion of the shell, which will package the request as a proper NCP request.

The NCP request is submitted to PEP, which guarantees that the message will be received at the file server. PEP, in turn, submits the request to IPX, which decides how to route the packet to the destination node. IPX uses a data link, or series of data links, to move the packet to the final destination.

At the remote node, the request, if accepted, will be handed off to the NetWare operating system, which will do the operation. Any resulting information

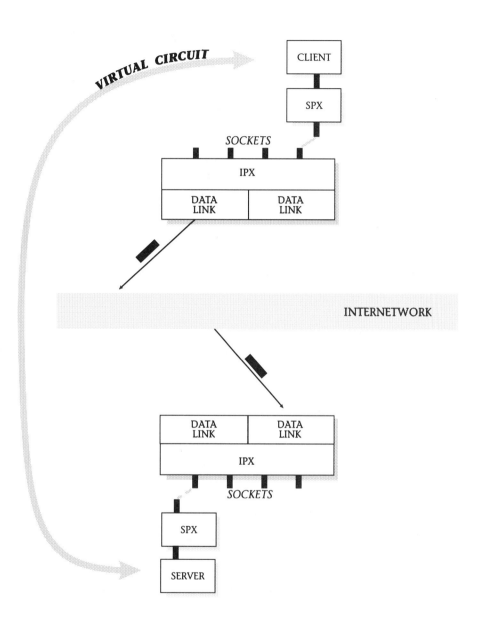

Fig. 1-4 A Transport Layer Virtual Circuit

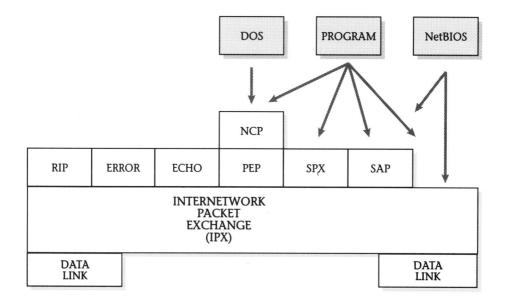

Fig. 1-5 Portions of the Novell Protocol Stack

will be handed back to the NCP program on the server, which will package the data for transmission back over the network.

To supplement the basic file operations, the file server provides two other services, security and synchronization. Security ensures that a user is only able to access certain types of files and to perform operations on those files.

Synchronization ensures that two users will not perform incompatible actions on a file or a portion of a file. For example, if a user is in the middle of changing data, a read operation should not be permitted because the data might be half in the old state and half in the new state.

In addition to file access, NCP provides a variety of other services. For example, a user may print files on a printer attached to the file server. This is done in a manner that is transparent to the workstation by "capturing" data intended for a local communications port.

The transparency of printing and file operations is a crucial aspect of the NetWare Core Protocols, allowing software designed for a stand-alone environment to function effectively on the network. A word processing program, for example, can store files on the server and use its printer in a transparent fashion. Both the disk drive and the printer appear to be locally attached.

Other programs are specially designed to run on the network, particularly server-based programs. For example, a database management system can be designed to service multiple requests from different users simultaneously.

To help develop these services, the operating system on the file server, NetWare, provides a variety of support services. For example, the server maintains a queue management program. A program can use the queue management services as a way of staging incoming requests so they are serviced in the order received.

In addition to the basic NetWare Core Protocols, there are some advanced services that are available for the NetWare operating system. These advanced services allow structured access to data and message exchange.

Structured access to data, discussed in Chapter 7, is used in database-type applications. Rather than requiring the programmer to search a file for the relevant information, the structured access allows the program to specify exactly which portion of the file is needed.

The advanced data manipulation capabilities are provided at two levels. First, the Btrieve utilities allow a file to be structured for direct access. A file can have one or more indexes. The programmer requests data based on an index value.

For example, a Btrieve file might contain the last name in columns 1 through 10 of the file. This last name field would form the basis for the index. The programmer could then request all records in the file that have the index field with a specific value or range of values.

Without Btrieve, the programmer would have two strategies to get the required data. First, the programmer could search the whole file. This means moving the whole file across the network, including a great deal of unneeded data. The second strategy is for the programmer to develop an indexing method. Btrieve provides a value-added service to basic data access—a ready-made method for indexed retrieval of data.

Built on top of Btrieve is a further level of transparency, SQL-based data access. The Structured Query Language (SQL) is a standard method for communicating with databases. Novell's XQL product and NetWare SQL server allow a collection of Btrieve files to be designated as a database.

Included in the database definition are names for all of the columns and files contained in it. The programmer is then able to ask for data by name, without having to know in which file a particular piece of data is contained. In this way SQL permits the programmer to deal with data in a logical fashion and not have to know exactly how to get the data.

The Message Handling Service, developed by Action Technologies, is another type of data exchange (this product is known as NetWare MHS when resold by Novell). MHS allows users to exchange messages. The messages can be sent to multiple users and can have return receipts requested; there are a variety of other value-added services for message exchange.

MHS, discussed in Chapter 6, provides a method of moving messages from one user to another. The messages can be programs, text messages, or any other form of data. A variety of different programs, or user interfaces, have been written that can access these messages.

A typical user interface is an electronic mail program. The program allows the user to compose messages, helps maintain mailing lists and old mail, and allows the user to send out messages. The electronic mail program will package the message in the appropriate MHS format, then hand it off to MHS for delivery.

MHS, in turn, will use the services of the network, the transport and network layers, to have the message moved to the destination node. There, MHS will place the message in a mailbox, where the user's electronic mail program will be used to read the message.

One important feature of MHS is that many different user interfaces are allowed. Users can have different electronic mail programs and still exchange messages as long as they are both compatible with MHS. Other programs, such as for databases or word processing, are also compatible with MHS and can use the service for exchanging documents or data.

MHS is a technology that works on both NetWare and other kinds of networks. For example, MHS could be used to move messages between Novell and 3Com networks. In addition, MHS has gateways to other message handling environments.

An example of another message handling environment is the SNA Distribution Services (SNADS), used for message exchange on large IBM computers. DEC has their own message handling environment, called Message Router or MAILbus.

MHS gateways allow a message to be sent from a user with an MHS user interface to a user in another message handling environment. MHS moves the message up to the gateway. There, the message is repackaged into a new format and sent over the remote message handling environment to the eventual destination.

A Novell network can consist of a variety of basic services: data access, remote printing, structured database access, and message handling. These services can all reside on a single file server or can be distributed across the network.

The Service Advertisement Protocol (SAP) is used to inform users about the location of a particular service. This distribution of tasks on the network provides important flexibility for network expansion. When a new service is added to the network, the network manager can put that service on a dedicated PC or on an existing server. If a particular service is overused, the manager simply adds a new server. In this case, there are multiple providers of a particular service. SAP is again used to inform the workstations of the providers of that service.

Supplements to NetWare

The basic services offer a set of predefined functions. A more general mechanism is needed for a highly distributed environment, where programs use several different computers to accomplish their task.

A product from Netwise, the Remote Procedure Call (RPC) Tool, discussed in Chapter 8, is used to allow one program to request another to perform a task for it (when Novell sells this product, it is known as NetWare RPC). In a single computer, a program is segmented into a series of procedures. A procedure calls another procedure, passing it data and reading the returned values.

The RPC Tool allows these procedures to be distributed across a network in a fashion that is transparent to the programmer. The programmer designs the program in a logical fashion as a series of procedures. Then, the RPC Tool is used to prepare the program for operation in a networked environment.

When a program that has been compiled with the RPC Tool calls a remote procedure, the request is handed off to a program that appears to be the called procedure. Instead of directly executing the request locally, the network library packages that request into a message and hands it off to the transport layer to send over the network.

At the remote end the message will be reformatted as if it were the original calling procedure. The appropriate data is passed to the remote procedure and the results read. The results are then repackaged in a message and sent back to the original computer. There the results are unpacked and handed back to the calling procedure.

The RPC thus supplements the basic transport service by providing a way that a procedure can request other procedures to perform a task for it—a session layer service. The advantage of the Netwise RPC Tool is that it is available for a wide variety of different networks and computing systems.

Because the RPC Tool works on many different computers, operating systems, and network architectures, it allows the programmer to design a program without regard to the differences among the different systems and then later deploy it over different computing platforms. The distribution is transparent to the program, and therefore the program can be redistributed to other computers at a later time by simply recompiling it.

The fact that many networks and computing systems might be running programs means that the NetWare protocols by themselves are not enough. Many organizations have several different sets of transport protocols running in addition to NetWare, such as TCP/IP, DECnet, or IBM's SNA.

A Novell workstation thus needs to be able to use non-NetWare transport protocols in order to function effectively on a network. The NetWare protocols are used to access the NetWare Core Protocols; other stacks are used to access non-Novell services. Many data link drivers, such as Ethernet or token ring, are able to service many different network and transport layers simultaneously, allowing the workstation to participate in two or more networking architectures simultaneously.

Novell has adopted a standard interface to the transport service, AT&T's Transport Level Interface (TLI). The TLI interface allows a program, such as a database, to access transport services in a transparent fashion. This means that the program doesn't have to be rewritten to operate on a different kind of network.

To allow different transport stacks to be used in a dynamic fashion, there has to be a way of connecting the program and the transport stack. This is done using the AT&T STREAMS mechanism, discussed in Chapter 9, which passes data from one module to another.

The beginning of the stream is the Transport Level Interface. Next, there is a transport module, which inserts sequence numbers and control information into the message. The data is then sent to the network layer, which routes the message.

At the end of the stream is a driver for the data link level. The driver takes the message and sends it out the data link. At the other end, the data link layer will take the message and send it upstream to the network layer, transport layer, transport interface, and finally the program.

In addition to the Transport Level Interface, Novell advocates another interface between the data link and network layers, known as the Link Support Layer (LSL). If a network interface card and a network layer program are both written to this standard interface, they will be able to use each other's services.

The LSL allows flexibility in the configuration of a computer on a network. As long as the transport stacks (the transport and network layers) are written to the LSL interface, they can use any network interface card that is also written to that interface. We will see later that LSL is only one of several ways of assuring that this happens (the IEEE 802.2 standards do the same thing).

The Link Support Layer and the Transport Level Interface provide the ability to use different combinations of protocol stacks. TLI provides a standard interface to the user. In many cases, that user is the RPC Tool, which in turn provides a transparent interface to the user.

Gateways

The STREAMS mechanism forms the basis for connecting to other types of networks. The last part of the book discusses these different forms of networks and the specific types of connectivity that Novell offers. The level of connectivity is an important consideration. It is one thing to allow a user to send bits of data to another computer; it is quite another to provide a value-added service such as message exchange between dissimilar systems.

One of the network architectures most highly integrated with Novell is AppleTalk, discussed in Chapter 10. An Apple workstation does not use the NetWare protocols to communicate with a NetWare file server; instead it uses the standard Apple networking protocols.

The NetWare file server accepts requests using the AppleTalk protocols and translates those requests into native calls for the NetWare file system. This translation allows the NetWare server to appear just as any other Apple file server—providing data and printing services.

For other networks, Novell chose not to make the NetWare operating system emulate other types of computers. Instead, the basic NetWare services were repackaged and ported to other computers' operating systems. This is known as Portable NetWare, discussed in Chapter 11.

Portable NetWare is a program that is run on a non-PC host but looks to the workstation just like a PC-based file server. It supports the IPX and PEP protocols, as well as the basic services such as file access, security, and synchronization.

An example of Portable NetWare is the NetWare for VMS product. This software allows a DEC VAX minicomputer running the VMS operating system to act as a PC file server. Since the VAX can be significantly more powerful than a PC, this allows the workstation access to these expanded capabilities.

In addition, NetWare for VMS serves as a gateway to the DECnet network. DECnet is used to connect complex configurations of VAX and other computers into a network. Because the networks are typically larger than Novell networks, they have more sophisticated routing and transport layer capabilities.

A DECnet also has more sophisticated network-based services available. The NetWare for VMS product allows the Novell workstation to log onto a VAX as if it were a locally connected terminal. Then, the user can access these remote services just like any other user directly connected to that resource.

Gateways are also available to other major networking environments, such as TCP/IP or IBM's SNA. For example, a user could run TCP/IP on the workstation instead of NetWare. The reader can examine the level of functionality provided by a gateway and compare that to the native environment.

The gateway is often used to connect a particular department to an organizational backbone network, with many departments using NetWare as a local computing resource and using file servers, messaging systems, and other basic NetWare services.

Most of the work would be accomplished on this local network. Occasionally, however, access would be needed to the backbone network. The user might wish to send a message, access the corporate mainframe, or perform other tasks on the network. The gateway allows the user to have connectivity to the broader environment while still retaining the performance and functionality of the local NetWare workgroup.

As can be seen by the overview in this chapter, there are many different options available for configuring a network. Beginning at the data link layer, there is a choice of different access methods. Even within a particular type of data link, such as Ethernet, there are a variety of different wiring options.

At the transport and network layers there are several different options, including Novell's IPX and SPX protocols. Built on top of those protocols are some basic services. Each of the different networking environments has different services defined.

The gateway allows the user to combine different services together into an integrated network. The disadvantage of the gateway is often a loss of transparency and performance. The advantage is the ability to connect disparate resources together.

There are no easy answers on how to structure the computing resources in one environment. The more the reader learns, the more options open up. This flexibility can be considered a disadvantage because of all the different choices available.

A better way to look at this is that the flexibility opens up a set of possible solutions to the network manager. By carefully choosing an appropriate subset of networking options, the manager can ensure that new applications and equipment can be easily integrated into the network in a transparent manner.

The Sniffer Network Analyzer

An important tool used in this book is the Sniffer Network Analyzer, manufactured by Network General. The Sniffer Analyzer is a special-purpose computer that is attached to a particular network. The network analyzer captures traffic on the network, which can then be displayed in a variety of formats.

Throughout the book, the reader will see dumps from the Sniffer Analyzer's screen, used to illustrate particular protocols or issues in the operation of a network. The original function of the Sniffer Analyzer was troubleshooting—looking at a vendor's software to determine if it was running in a fashion incompatible with the network protocols of other vendors.

In this book, the Sniffer Analyzer is instead used as a teaching tool. Because it shows traffic on a network as a series of packets, and allows the user to zoom in and look at a particular packet, it is an ideal tool for explaining networks.

Figures 1-6 and 1-7 show two screens from the Sniffer Analyzer. The first is the main screen. Notice the options in the first column, such as generating data, capturing data, or displaying data. The highlighted option on Figure 1-6 is the one the user is currently looking at. Notice that the option in turn has more options available. When the user goes up and down the first columns, the options in the second column will change based on the particular item in the first column.

Figure 1-7 shows an example of this type of menu operation. It shows a user loading up a trace file, containing network traffic, from disk. This is how the reader would look at traffic from the demonstration software.

In addition to looking at previously captured data, the Sniffer Analyzer is able to capture new data, as shown in Figure 1-8. The illustration shows the number of packets received and also displays a skyline that shows the traffic versus time. The reader can perform this same operation by capturing data using an existing trace file. Instead of capturing data from the network, the user takes data already captured and uses that as a simulation of a real network.

After the data has been captured, or while being captured, it can be filtered. Notice in Figure 1-8 that the number of frames actually captured is less than the total number on the network, an indication that filtering occurred. A variety of different options are available to control which frames are captured (see Fig. 1-9).

One common type of filtering is by station address. If a particular computer is malfunctioning, for example, the user would filter traffic to and from that particular station.

Another way of filtering, used in this book quite often, is by the type of protocol. To understand how the NetWare Core Protocols work, the reader might look at only the NCP traffic between two stations on a network. This allows the user to isolate the traffic that pertains to one particular session.

Figures 1-10 and 1-11 show an example of examining a packet on a network. Figure 1-10 has two parts—a summary and a detail portion. The summary part shows a high-level view of many packets going through the network (subject to the filters that are defined). The detail part shows what is inside a single packet.

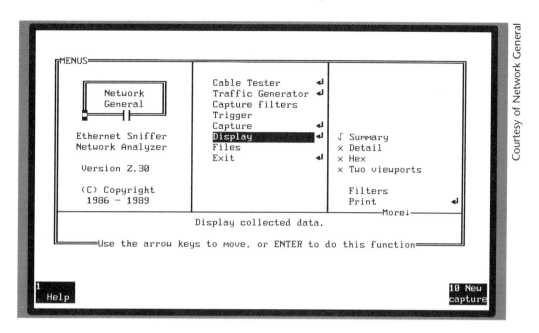

Fig. 1-6 The Sniffer Analyzer's Main Screen

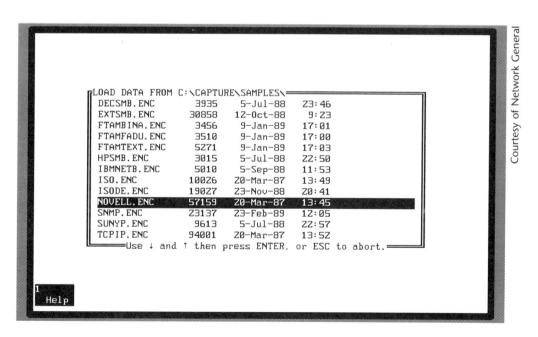

Fig. 1-7 Loading Captured Network Data

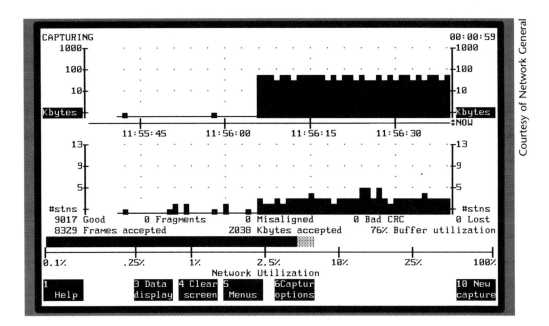

Fig. 1-8 Capturing New (or Old) Data

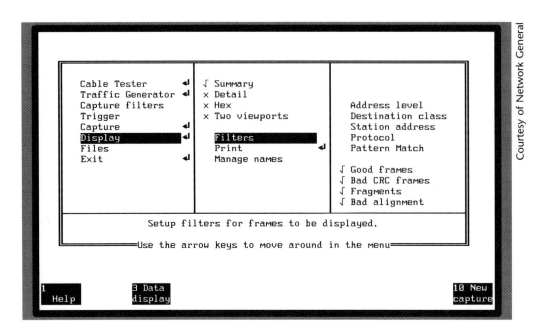

Fig. 1-9 Filtering Options

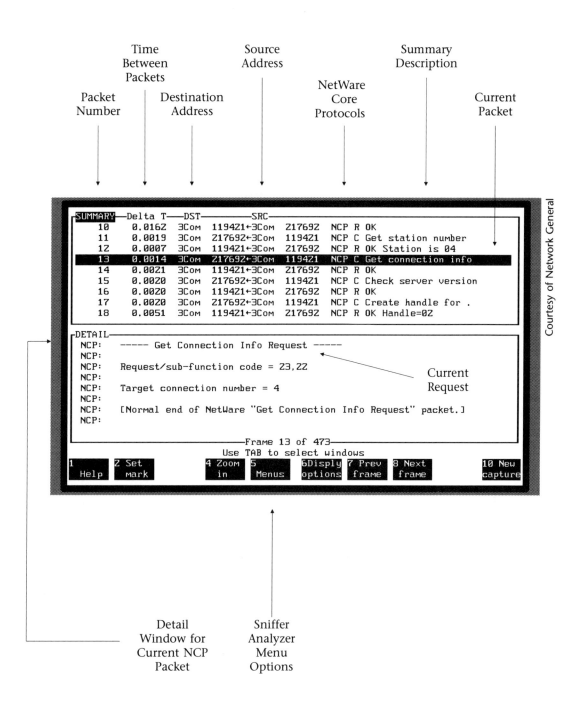

Fig. 1-10 Summary and Detail Windows

It is possible to zoom in on a particular packet, as shown in Figure 1-11. Notice that the packet has several parts. At the top of the screen, the word *XNS* denotes the Xerox Network System, which is the basic type of network layer that Novell uses.

The XNS portion of the screen, known as the XNS header, is in turn carrying data for its user, the NetWare Core Protocols. The reader can think of this packet as a series of envelopes. Each user of the network takes its incoming data and puts it into an envelope. That envelope is submitted to the next layer, which in turn puts it into an envelope.

The advantage of using an analyzer like the Sniffer Analyzer is that the user can peer into these envelopes and look at all the different address and other information used by the protocols. The Sniffer Analyzer is particularly useful because it displays the information in plain English instead of the internal coded format of the packets. The Sniffer Analyzer makes a wonderful way to understand exactly what is happening on a particular network.

Analyzing Networks

The title of this book is *Analyzing Novell Networks*. Network General's Sniffer Analyzer is a network analyzer. Often the term *analysis* denotes solving a specific problem. The Sniffer Analyzer, for example, can be used to find a specific problem with a particular version of a vendor's software. By looking at the data produced by that software, the analyst can very quickly determine if there is a problem.

In this book, analysis is used in a broader sense—understanding how a network works. Here, the Sniffer Network Analyzer becomes a teaching tool. The user can examine the screen dumps and see exactly how a particular type of packet is constructed and the sequence of messages on a network.

This type of analysis is also quite useful for the network manager attempting to plan out the growth of an existing network or the configuration of a new network. By analyzing the traffic on a network, and knowing how that traffic fits into the overall architecture, the network manager is in a position to determine the impact of any planned change.

For example, the manager might be trying to decide if the new electronic mail package should be provided as one central electronic mail hub or a series of distributed, smaller computers throughout the network. Analyzing the traffic produced by the hub will allow the manager to see the impact of adding one or more servers.

A programmer can also use this method of analysis. The Sniffer Analyzer allows the programmer to see how the underlying network treats a particular set of requests. For example, access to a particular file may be sent out by the transport and network layer as a series of 512-byte packets. The programmer can quickly spot this using the Sniffer Analyzer and, on an Ethernet, can instruct the network to use the maximum practical packet size of 1024 bytes. This means that half as many packets are needed to transport the data.

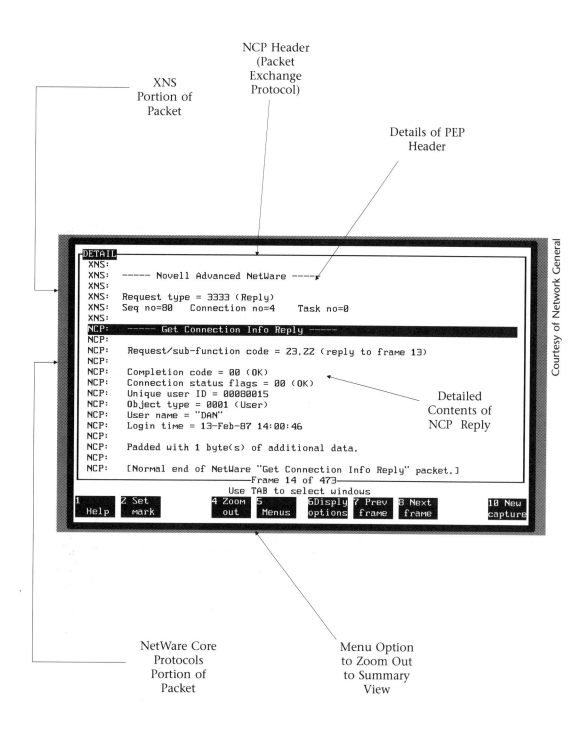

Fig. 1-11 Zooming in on a Packet

Getting the Software

There is an order form in the back of the book for obtaining the demonstration version of the Sniffer Network Analyzer from Network General. The demonstration software is self-explanatory and includes a tutorial and help files. The software includes a variety of trace files captured from real networks. The reader can load those trace files in and examine the different packets associated with the network traffic.

The software requires a standard IBM-compatible PC. The mail-order version of the software comes on 5.25-inch, 1.2-Mbyte disks.

Using This Book

This book provides a starting point to two important topics: using a network analyzer and analyzing Novell networks. It is intended to be used with a demonstration version of Network General's network analyzer but was written in a way that allows the use of the book without the software.

The starting point is obviously to read the book, which discusses the major issues in a Novell network, familiarizes the reader with the protocols that Novell uses, and shows how to configure a Novell network and connect the Novell network to other environments.

For further work, the reader is directed first to the demonstration software. Analyzing the network trace files contained in the software will provide a hands-on appreciation for how a Novell network works. Another form of hands-on work would be to log onto a real Novell network and look at the functionality provided by various services.

The next step would be to consult the bibliography for other, more detailed resources. For example, the reader might consult the IEEE documentation for different data link layers or the Xerox documentation for the network and transport layers. The bibliography also lists a variety of Novell and third-party manuals. These are the source documents that describe how to program a particular protocol. Even if the reader does not intend to program, the manual provides a good overview of exactly what services are provided at this layer.

PART I

NETWORKS

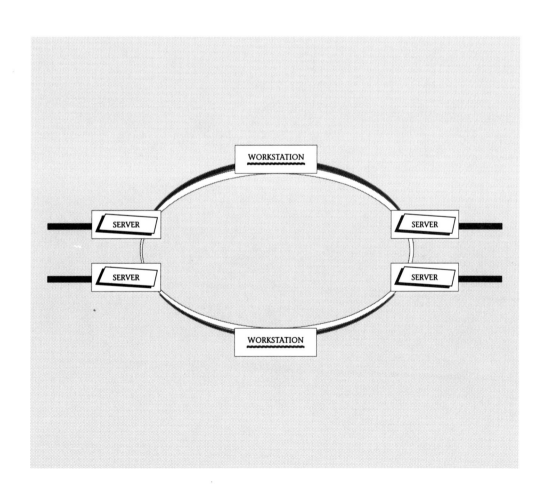

CHAPTER 2

Data Links and LLC

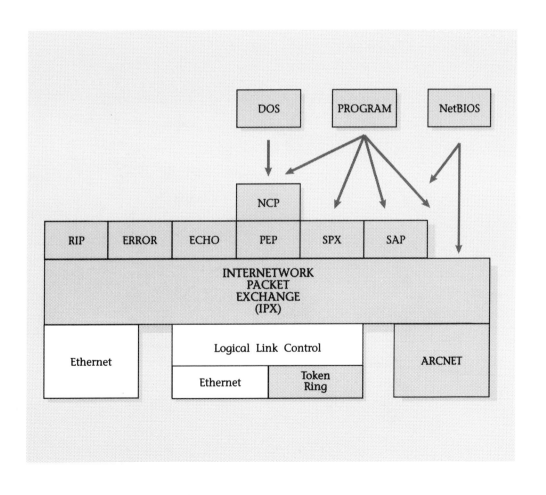

CHAPTER 2

Data Links and LLC

The Data Link Layer

This chapter begins a walk up Novell's protocol stack. We begin with the question of how to connect different computers together on a wire so they can exchange data. The service offered at this layer is conceptually quite simple—the transfer of a packet of data from one node, represented by a network address, to another node, represented by another address.

This chapter discusses one such type of network, the Ethernet, which transmits data at a gross rate of 10 million bits per second (Mbps). Ethernet is a standard that specifies the type of wire (the physical medium) and the devices used to connect computers to the medium. Ethernet also defines the protocol to be used on that wire so data can be transferred. One of the important aspects of this protocol is the method used to decide which node is allowed to transmit at any one time.

The next chapter discusses two alternatives to Ethernet, ARCNET and the token ring. Each of these networks uses a different method to physically connect computers together. They also have different protocols for access to the physical medium.

At this point, we are not really talking about a Novell network. All three networking methods can be used for a Novell network and can also be used for DECnet, TCP/IP, AppleTalk, or a variety of other architectures.

This chapter lays a foundation, the data link service, that will later be used by the Novell network. The network layer, IPX, will connect these different networks together, and then higher layers will begin to provide real services such as data access or printing.

MAC and LLC Sublayers

The data link layer is responsible for providing the service of transferring data from one node to another. This process is broken down into two sublayers, the Medium Access Control and the Logical Link Control (see Fig. 2-1).

The Logical Link Control provides the interface to the user of the network and may have several clients. Each client has a local service address. Well-known programs, such as IPX, the network layer of Novell, always have the same local service address.

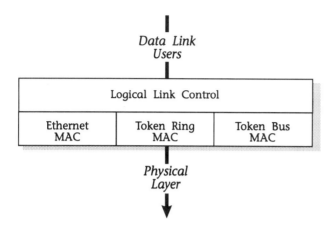

Fig. 2-1 MAC and LLC Sublayers

Each user on a computer has a local service address. Each computer then has a network address. For Ethernet, this address is a 48-bit number that is always unique. Numbers are assigned by the manufacturer of the Ethernet controller, who obtains blocks of unused numbers from the Institute of Electrical and Electronics Engineers (IEEE), a standards organization. The Logical Link Control has been defined by the IEEE as the 802.2 standard and subsequently adopted by the International Standards Organization (ISO) as an international standard. Similarly, Ethernet (originally developed by DEC, Intel, and Xerox) was redefined and adopted by the IEEE as the 802.3 standard and then adopted by ISO as an international standard.

A client of the data link layer, such as IPX, assembles a packet of data to send. IPX then submits that packet to the Logical Link Control, along with the network address of the remote computer and the service address of the remote program. The Logical Link Control hands this message down to the Medium Access Control sublayer.

The MAC sublayer is responsible for controlling the process of moving a packet of data across to the destination node. The MAC sublayer and the underlying physical layer of the network send the data to the MAC sublayer on the destination node, which then presents the packet to the Logical Link Control.

The LLC then sends the packet up to its client—in this case IPX. It may seem that most of the work is being done by the MAC and physical layer and that the Logical Link Control does not really add very much in the way of service. The Logical Link Control provides insulation, a standard interface to different MAC sublayers and different network layers. A company such as Novell can write one interface between their network layer and the Logical Link Control. When a new type of medium is provided, the client is insulated from the changes by the LLC layer.

There are also some networks that use an extended version of LLC, known as Class II operation. In Class II operation, LLC guarantees that data will be delivered. Novell networks use Class I operation, which is a best-effort delivery service.

This standard network interface (the Logical Link Control) and standard medium interface (the Medium Access Control) are the result of the standardization of Ethernet by the IEEE. This standard was subsequently adopted by the American National Standards Institute (ANSI) and ISO.

The version of the standard discussed in this chapter, Ethernet, is referred to as the IEEE 802.3 standard, after the third subcommittee of the 802 committee of the IEEE. The 802.3 subcommittee standardized the Medium Access Control and physical layer methods used in Ethernet. The Logical Link Control is sometimes referred to as the 802.2 standard. The token ring is defined as 802.5, and the token bus, a network methodology not discussed in this book, is 802.4.

Ethernet and IEEE 802.3

There are two versions of Ethernet currently in operation. The original Ethernet specification was a joint effort between DEC, Intel, and Xerox. That specification is currently at the second revision and is usually referred to as Ethernet Version 2.0.

Ethernet Version 2.0, in contrast to the IEEE version, does not use a Logical Link Control. All the information needed, including the destination network and service addresses, is embedded into one header. We will see later in this chapter that the differences between the two versions are slight and that both can coexist on the same network.

The fundamental difference between Ethernet and other MAC sublayers is the access method—the method used to determine which node is allowed to use the medium at any one time. All Ethernet nodes are connected to the same medium. If a node transmits data, that data is broadcast to the entire network. If two nodes start transmitting at once, the data from the two nodes will collide, resulting in gibberish on the network.

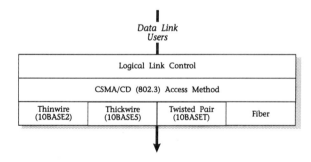

Fig. 2-2 MAC and Physical Layers

The access method used for Ethernet is the Carrier Sense–Multiple Access/Collision Detect, known as CSMA/CD (see Fig. 2-2). This methodology is embedded in the MAC layer of the network.

This methodology, in turn, has been implemented over a variety of different physical media. Many of the different physical variations of Ethernet have also been standardized by the IEEE. The twisted pair cable, for example, is the 10BASET substandard (for **10** Mbps using **Base**band signaling on **T**wisted pair). The 10BASE5 standard is a 10-Mbps baseband signaling method, with a 500-meter segment length (known as thickwire).

Thinwire is defined in the 10BASE2 standard. The 2 stands for a 200 meter maximum segment length, even though the limit is really 186 meters. We can consider ourselves lucky that the standard was not called 10BASE1.86.

Other media, such as fiber optics, are also available but have not been codified by a standards body—meaning that it is up to the vendor to come up with the methodology to be used. The 10BASET standard is an example of a medium that started as a vendor implementation and was later added to the standards.

All of these different physical media share the same basic CSMA/CD access method. Carrier Sense means that any node on an Ethernet is capable of sensing if the medium is being used at that time. It does so by listening for a period of time and determining if the signals on the network represent an idle cable or data being transmitted.

Multiple Access means that any node on the Ethernet can transmit at any time. No permission need be given by a network-wide controller or by receipt of a permission to send. There is one caveat, of course—the well-behaved Ethernet node does not transmit if another node is currently transmitting on the network.

It is still possible for data to collide under this methodology. If two nodes both begin listening at the same time, and both detect an unused network, they might both start transmitting at the same time. The data will propagate from the original starting points on the network and eventually collide. The resulting collision transmits itself through the wire, resulting in neither node being able to send data successfully.

If a collision does occur, the Ethernet standard specifies that each node will abort transmitting and back off for a random period of time. After this wait period, the node will again listen to the network and determine if it is able to transmit. It is still possible that the medium is still busy after the wait period.

Even if a node detects a collision, backs off, listens to the network, and then starts transmitting, there may be a second collision. The node will then back off one more time. The random period of time will be longer on the second back-off attempt. This procedure goes on for 10 retries, when the node finally gives up. In this case, the Ethernet will then tell its client that the transmission was unsuccessful.

The basic Ethernet service is shown in Figures 2-3 and 2-4. The address portion of the data link control (labeled *DLC* in the figures) corresponds to the Ethernet address. The packet is carrying data for IPX (listed as an *XNS Header* in

Courtesy of Network General

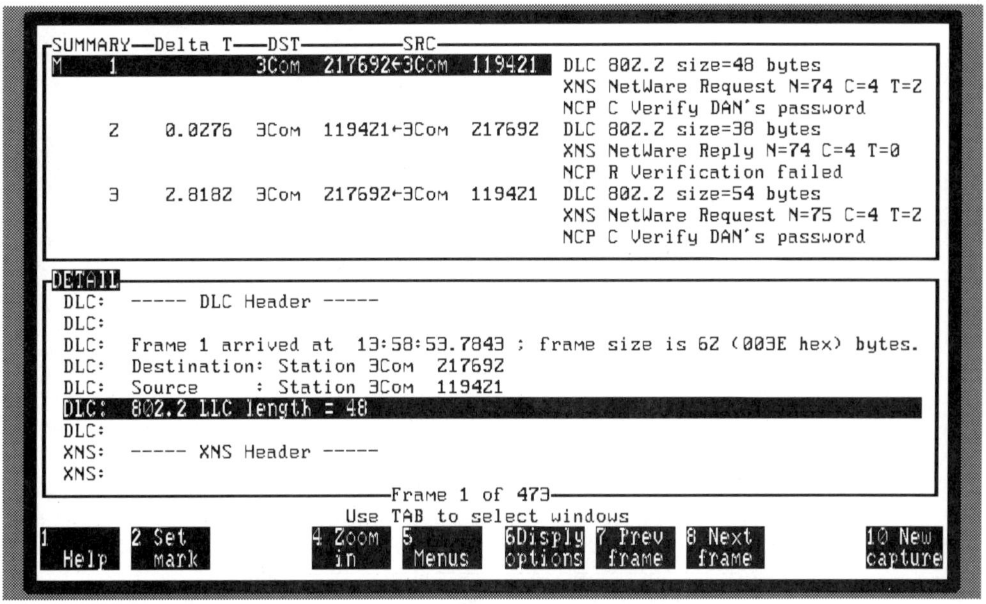

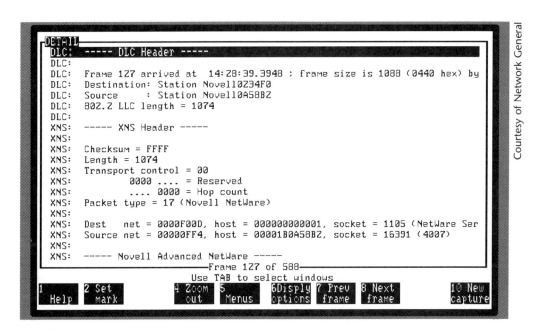

Fig. 2-3 Novell Traffic on an Ethernet

Courtesy of Network General

Fig. 2-4 Novell and 802.3 Headers in a Packet

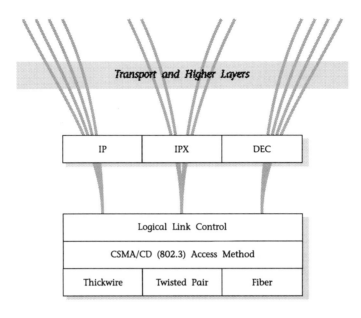

Fig. 2-5 Multiple LLC Users

Fig. 2-4), which in turn is carrying data for its client, the NetWare Core Protocols.

Both packets are being read by the Sniffer Analyzer as IEEE 802.3 format frames. In both figures there is the notation that there are roughly 40 bytes of Logical Link Control data in the packet. This information is part of the MAC sublayer—the Ethernet.

Normally, the packet would have an LLC header following the MAC header. The LLC header would contain information such as the type of client that the packet was being carried for. Instead, in both examples, we see that the Novell network layer, IPX, comes right after the MAC sublayer.

What is happening here is a result of a strange quirk in the way that Novell decided to configure their networks. Remember, there are two kinds of Ethernet formats—IEEE 802.3 and Ethernet Version 2.

In 802.3 operation, interaction with the user program (i.e., IPX) is handled by the Logical Link Control. In the MAC envelope, the field right after the address is a length indicator. The user of the service will be designated in the LLC address field. The MAC address is for the node; the LLC address is for the user within that node.

In Version 2, the field after the address is a type indicator—the user of the service. This is because there is no LLC in Version 2 and the Ethernet provides services directly to users such as IPX.

It is common for a single machine to receive packets in both formats. To tell the difference between the two formats, the Ethernet controller looks at the field right after the address. If the field is a length field, it must meet the rules

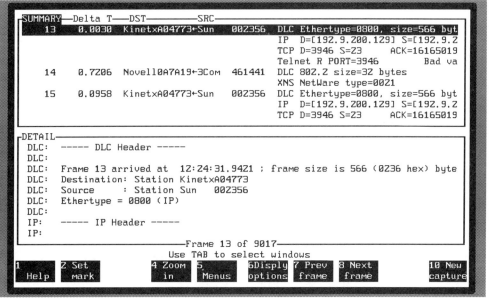

Fig. 2-6 IP and Novell on the Same Ethernet

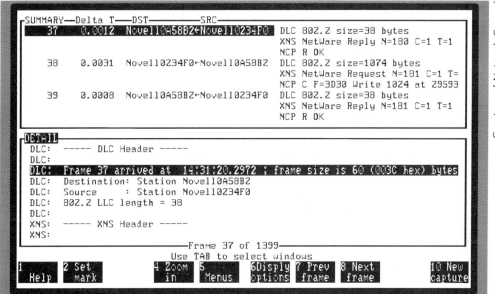

Fig. 2-7 A Padded Packet

for the length of an Ethernet packet—greater than 60 and less than 1518 bytes long.

Novell decided that they didn't need to share an Ethernet with other types of networks. So, they skipped the second address field, assuming that all packets coming in would be for IPX. In a shared environment, the controller would pass the data up to the Logical Link Control (since the number 1074 must be a length field, it must be an LLC packet). LLC in turn would look at the next fields and see that they didn't match the valid packet format it was expecting and signal an error.

In many environments, there will be more than just Novell nodes. For example, the network may consist of Novell, DEC, and TCP/IP clients (see Fig. 2-5). IP is the Internetwork Protocol, which is used for TCP/IP networks. The DEC clients are actually several different protocols, discussed in Chapter 11. Figure 2-5 shows this type of an environment; the 802.2 LLC layer is providing services to a variety of clients.

Figure 2-6 illustrates some traffic on a network that is carrying both TCP/IP traffic (the *IP* in the illustration) and Novell traffic. If a Novell node is sharing the data link with other nodes, a utility called ECONFIG is run, which makes the computer send out Novell packets in a standard format. Even if a network is envisioned just to carry Novell traffic, it is highly recommended that the ECONFIG utility be run, since this allows other nodes to be added in the future without changing the operation of all nodes on the existing network.

The basic operation of either 802.2 and 802.3 or Ethernet Level 2 (or even the Novell format) is to send a packet of data, which can be up to 1518 bytes long. Usually, in a Novell environment, the data portion of a packet is limited to 1024 bytes of data (which happens to correspond to two blocks of data returned from a disk drive on a file server).

To detect a collision, Ethernet requires that the packet be a minimum size, which ensures that a collision, should it occur, will be long enough for the other node to detect. Figure 2-7 shows a packet that has been padded. The frame size is 60 bytes, shown on the highlighted portion of the detail screen. Notice that the LLC data is less than that—38 bytes. Even if the bytes occupied by the MAC layer are added to the LLC data, this is still less than 60 bytes.

In Figure 2-7, the MAC layer padded the packet by adding enough data to bring it up to the minimum packet length. Most packets going through the network have at least 40 bytes of data—enough to hold the data link, network, and upper layer protocols. Even if a single character is being sent to the destination, the packet, in the case of an Ethernet, will still take 60 bytes of network bandwidth.

This may seem wasteful of network resources, particularly in the case of remote terminal access to a computer. This traffic is characterized by many single keystrokes, each occupying a single data packet. This is rarely the problem that it may seem at first glance. Most Ethernet networks, even the largest ones at major universities and research laboratories, are used at about 10 percent of their capacity, even during peak periods. The traffic represented by small data

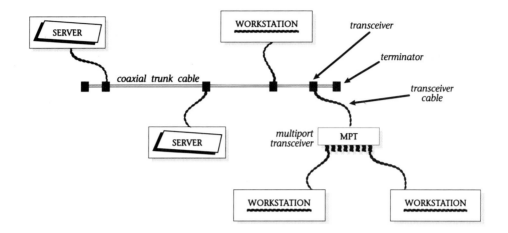

Fig. 2-8 Single-Segment Ethernet

packets is usually small enough, even in these large environments, to result in only a small performance drain on the network.

Where this does pose a problem, vendors use two strategies to more effectively use the bandwidth on the network. Some vendors, such as DEC, have a special protocol that bunches several requests into a single Ethernet packet. Although there have been rumors of a Novell "multiplexing protocol," no announcement had been made of one when this book went to press.

The second strategy, available in the Novell environment, is to segment the network using a MAC-layer bridge. The bridge allows traffic to be localized on one portion of the Ethernet, thus leaving the bandwidth available on other portions of the network. Bridges are discussed in more detail later in this chapter.

Packet formats, minimum and maximum size, and speed are issues that define the operation of an Ethernet regardless of the underlying physical medium. A twisted pair Ethernet will have the same speed and maximum packet size as one using fiber optics. The media differ on the configuration rules. The number of nodes on a piece of cable, the maximum length of the cable, or the combinations of different cable types are all configuration issues on which the media differ.

To illustrate the types of issues involved in configuration, the next section describes one particular medium, the thickwire form of coaxial cable. After that, the discussion will broaden to cover other media and the interconnection of different segments together.

Thickwire Networks

The basic Ethernet network is a piece of coaxial cable. The original heavily shielded coaxial cable is known as thickwire. This distinguishes it from the thinwire solution discussed in the next section.

Connected to the coaxial, or trunk, cable are various devices (see Fig. 2-8). A device, such as a workstation or server, has an Ethernet controller card in it. On the cable itself is a small box known as a transceiver. The transceiver connects to the cable and is responsible for physically sending and receiving data on the medium. A transceiver cable connects the transceiver and the Ethernet controller. The cable can be up to 50 meters long, allowing the device to be up to 50 meters from the trunk cable.

The trunk cable can be up to 500 meters long. Two nodes on an Ethernet can be separated by as much as 600 meters on this basic thickwire configuration: one 50 meter transceiver cable for each node and the 500 meters of trunk. Note that this is only the maximum separation for any two nodes: they could be closer. There is also a minimum separation of 2.5 meters of trunk cable for any two adjacent nodes.

The MPT device in Figure 2-8 is a multiport transceiver. This is a box, typically configured with eight transceivers built in. The multiport transceiver is then connected to the main trunk cable. Computers attach to this device using a transceiver cable just as they would a single-port transceiver. It is possible to use the multiport transceiver without laying any trunk cable. This is known as "Ethernet in a Can," since the multiport transceiver actually serves the same purpose as a small (very small) piece of cable.

The last piece of equipment is the terminator. Each end of the cable must be terminated to absorb the signals. Otherwise, the break at the end of the terminal will represent a large change in impedance, meaning that the signals bounce back on the medium and remain active forever (or at least a long time). The terminators prevent this echo chamber effect.

There are several configuration rules to the Ethernet in addition to the basic cable length limits for the trunk and transceiver cables. First, any devices connected to the main trunk (i.e., anything connected to a transceiver, such as a computer or MPT) must be multiples of 2.5 meters apart from each other. Usually, the coaxial cable is marked with a ring every 2.5 meters to simplify meeting this requirement.

The 2.5-meter separation rule is meant to minimize the buildup of reflections. Reflections, which end up distorting the real data, are minimized if nodes are multiples of 2.5 meters apart. A second limitation is that up to 100 devices may be connected to the 500-meter cable.

All of these limits are meant to ensure that a signal will propagate to the end of the network quickly without being distorted by noise and reflections, making the data unreadable. The 500-meter coaxial cable limit, for example, was fixed as the result of the propagation velocity of the medium and the rate at which signals became attenuated on this particular medium.

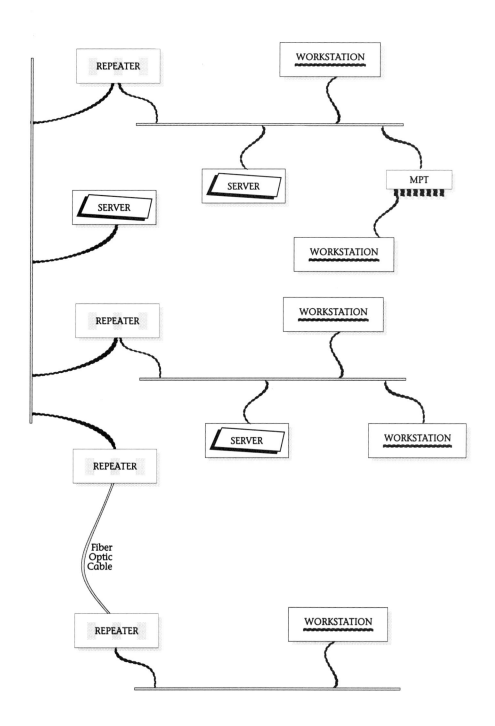

Fig. 2-9 A Multisegment Ethernet

Repeaters

Although an Ethernet can have up to 1024 nodes on it, we saw that the basic coaxial cable is limited to 100 nodes. A repeater is a device that connects several segments of an Ethernet together (see Fig. 2-9). Its function is to retime, reamplify, and retransmit a signal from one Ethernet segment to another, creating a multisegment Ethernet, to be distinguished from an extended Ethernet, discussed later.

The repeater counts as a node on an Ethernet segment. It uses a transceiver, may be up to 50 meters from the trunk cable, and must be a multiple of 2.5 meters from other nodes. No more than 100 nodes, including repeaters, may be on a single Ethernet segment.

An Ethernet node is different from a Novell node. Ethernet nodes include multiport transceivers, computers, and repeaters. The Ethernet limitation of 1024 nodes for a multisegment Ethernet applies to all the devices attached to the collection of cables connected by repeaters.

A Novell node is a different thing. It is a device, a computer, that runs the Novell IPX protocols. A Novell node might use Ethernet, ARCNET, or token ring as the data link. Likewise, it is possible to have Ethernet nodes that are not visible to the Novell environment, such as a repeater or a computer running other network protocols.

The repeater counts as a node on both segments of the Ethernet to which it is connected. The repeater counts against the 100-node limit on both of the segments. The repeater listens to both segments, rebroadcasting data to the other, thus connecting the segments together.

In Figure 2-9, one of the repeaters is a fiber optic repeater that has up to 1000 meters of fiber optic cable separating the two halves of the repeater. This device would be used, for example, to connect two buildings together into a single Ethernet. The two halves of the repeater (each one next to an Ethernet segment) count as a single full repeater. In Figure 2-9 there are several segments connected together into a multisegment Ethernet. The basic rule is that there can be no more than two repeaters in the path between any two nodes on the network.

The two-repeater limitation doesn't limit the network to three segments of coaxial cable, however. The rule says that between any two nodes, there can be two repeaters. In the illustration, there are actually four segments of cable. If any two nodes wish to communicate, they go through only two of the repeaters, hence over three segments of coaxial cable.

The rules are based on the path between any two nodes on the Ethernet because this is the distance that a signal will have to travel on the farthest path on the network. When one node begins transmitting, the signal will propagate to this far point of the network.

For a signal to propagate within the specified maximum propagation time in the Ethernet standard, there may be only two repeaters in their path. The repeaters, like coaxial or fiber optic cable, introduce delay into the network. Limiting the number of repeaters and the amount of cable ensures that the signal will propagate to the end in the specified time.

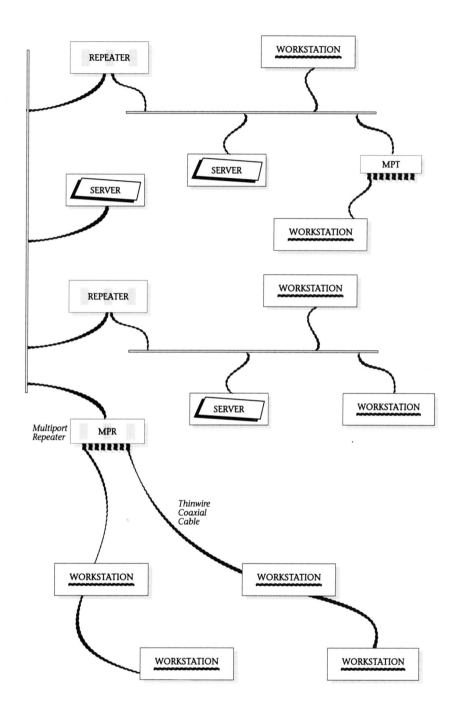

Fig. 2-10 Multimedia, Multisegment Ethernet

We are now in a position to calculate the maximum separation between two nodes on a multisegment Ethernet. A segment of coaxial cable is limited to 500 meters, a transceiver cable to 50 meters, and there can be up to 1000 meters total of fiber optic in the path.

We have three segments of coaxial cable in this maximum path, plus 1000 meters of fiber optic cable. In addition, there are six transceiver cables (one each for the two computers, plus four cables for the two repeaters), for a total length of 300 meters. The maximum separation between two nodes is thus 1500 (coax) + 1000 (fiber) + 300 (transceiver cables) for a total of 2800 meters. This limit, plus the maximum number of 1024 nodes, defines the limits of a single multisegment Ethernet.

Cheapernet Networks

The basic thickwire coaxial cable is a 0.4-inch-diameter, shielded coaxial cable. The cable is still and fairly thick, meaning that it is both fairly expensive and hard to handle. Another form of coaxial cable is thinwire (sometimes known as cheapernet) cable.

The cheapernet networks use a thinner cable with less shielding. This means that it is easier to handle and can be manufactured more cheaply. However, there is no free lunch. The thinner cable means that it loses the signal more quickly, which limits the maximum cable length.

Figure 2-10 shows cheapernet cable added to the multisegment Ethernet. A multiport repeater is used to connect the cheapernet segments to the coaxial trunk of the network. A multiport repeater can usually have up to eight segments of cheapernet attached. Like the multiport transceiver (which connects eight nodes, not eight segments), it can stand alone or be connected to a backbone cable.

Each segment of cheapernet can be up to 185 meters long and can have up to 30 nodes on it, of which the repeater counts as one. The nodes must be at least 0.5 meters apart on the cable. Since the cable loses a signal more quickly, the cable must run right next to the computer (the cable is usually 4 cm or less from the Ethernet controller).

Each of the segments on the cheapernet are governed by the same rules for the overall Ethernet. No two nodes may have more than three segments of coaxial cable, two repeaters, and 1000 meters of fiber between them. Because the insulation for a cheapernet coaxial segment is less than that of the thicker coaxial cable (hence the name thickwire), the maximum separation in this network will be less than in an exclusively thickwire network.

It is possible to splice thickwire and cheapernet together into a single piece of cable. This is done by connecting the two with a barrel connector. This solution is cheaper than a repeater and is used where there are many nodes close to each other and a few nodes separated throughout the rest of the building. Cheapernet would be used for the cluster of nodes and then is spliced to a piece of thickwire. Splicing can lead to many problems in calculating maximum lengths, not to mention problems from poor splicing. A multiport repeater is often a safer, if slightly more expensive, solution.

Many Ethernet controllers are able to handle both cheapernet and thickwire coaxial cable (and some can even handle twisted pair on the same controller). In the case of both cheapernet and thickwire, there are two ports on the Ethernet controller. One is a BNC port, used to connect to the cheapernet. The other port is the standard 15-pin connector used for thickwire. The user simply informs the board which port will be used, usually through either a software command or by physically moving a jumper.

Other Media

We saw that the basic access method, CSMA/CD, was built into the MAC layer of the Ethernet standard. Two different physical transmission media were described, both based on the coaxial cable. Neither the Ethernet nor the 802.3 standard is limited to the use of coaxial cable. Any physical medium that provides the appropriate propagation velocity and attenuation characteristics for the signals will work properly.

In addition to fiber and coaxial cables, many sites are using twisted pair wiring for their Ethernet configurations. Twisted pair is the same cable used for telephone systems. Since many buildings have extra twisted pair that was installed with the building, using this wire means that half the battle is already won for installing a network.

Actually laying cable from one room to another can be a complex task in many buildings. If the cable is already there and the user can avoid tearing up walls and climbing into elevator shafts, it becomes easier to convince management to allocate money for networking hardware. Even in new buildings, where the user typically has some input into the wiring available, twisted pair is being used because it is cheaper than coaxial cable.

An additional advantage of twisted pair is the ability to use a star configuration for wiring. It is typical for all offices to have a line to a satellite equipment closet in some central location. It is not as typical for each office to have wires connecting it to its neighbor, the requirement for coaxial cable.

This is not to say that coaxial cable has no place in a network. A very typical Ethernet configuration is to use coax as the backbone, running through the halls or the elevator shaft and down to the computer room. In the computer room, all the servers would be directly connected to the coaxial cable. In satellite wiring rooms, the user would install some form of a repeater that would form the transition to the twisted pair environment. Twisted pair wire would then be used from the satellite equipment room out to the individual offices.

Coaxial cable is also used in electrically noisy environments. The unshielded twisted pair is more susceptible to random disruptions caused by heavy machinery or other electrical noise. The additional shielding on the thickwire coaxial cable makes it more immune to these types of disturbances.

Bridges

The limits of a single multisegment Ethernet may be reached for a variety of reasons. First, the distance limitation may be reached because two nodes are

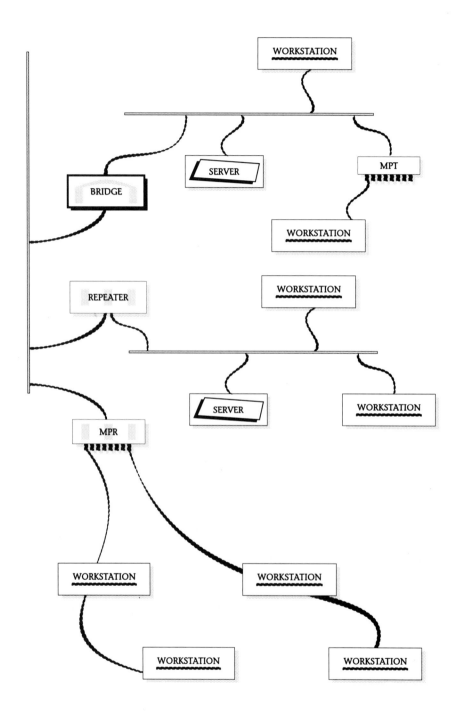

Fig. 2-11 An Extended Ethernet

too far apart. Second, the node limitation of 1024 nodes may be reached, prohibiting the use of a single Ethernet.

There are other reasons why nodes may not all be in a single Ethernet. Different departments in an organization may wish to control their own network resources, or may not be able to coordinate their activities. Requiring all departments in a building to coordinate their computing activities would be a fairly utopian undertaking in many organizations.

Aside from political and administrative reasons, there are performance considerations in segmenting a network into separate Ethernets. For example, one group of users may be performing extensive file transfers on the network. These file transfers would affect other users by limiting their access to the Ethernet.

There are many methods to connect separate Ethernets together. One is to use an upper layer, the network layer, to perform the process of forwarding a packet from one network to another. This has the advantage of allowing different kinds of data links to be connected together.

A disadvantage of using the network layer to forward packets between Ethernets is that there may be several kinds of network layer clients in a given network. Each of these clients, IP and IPX for example, would have to provide its own forwarding service. An additional disadvantage is that the network layer must make a routing decision. The network layer, such as IPX, is capable of routing data in a complex network topology. In the case of two Ethernets, the forwarding decision is quite simple, and the overhead of the more robust IPX is not necessary. The bridge, in this case, is not only cheaper but has higher performance. If the network layer is used, this will also involve the use of a computer, since IPX is a software program. This means that a computer must be dedicated to the task of connecting the networks together.

Figure 2-11 shows an example of a bridge configuration. Notice that the bridge is connected to two separate Ethernets. Each of those Ethernets could be a multisegment Ethernet, but for simplicity are shown as single-segment networks in the diagrams.

Unlike the repeater, the bridge does not repeat all data from one network to another. Instead, the bridge looks at the address of a packet on one Ethernet and decides if the destination address is on the other Ethernet. The bridge localizes traffic by only forwarding the packets that need to be forwarded. Each of the Ethernets connected by the bridge can be a full multisegment Ethernet with 1024 nodes and 2800 meters separation on each.

A bridge performs its task by learning the address of every node on each of the two networks that it is connecting. To do so, it listens to traffic on each network. When the bridge sees a packet on one network, it records the source address in its table as belonging to that network.

Every time the bridge sees a packet with a source address, it knows that the source lies on that side of it. However, it does not know at first which side the destination address lies on. Just to be safe, the bridge will forward the packet to the other side until it learns the location of the destination. Eventually, the destination address on the original packet will respond. The bridge will then

46 Analyzing Novell Networks

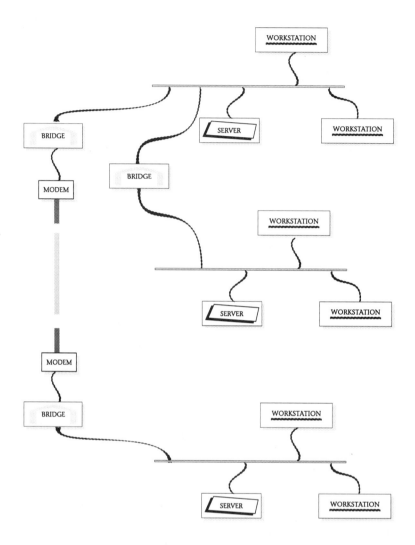

Fig. 2-12 Multiple Bridges

know which side that destination lies on and whether or not to forward future packets.

Many manufacturers offer a filtering capability on their bridges, allowing the manager to prevent certain types of packets from ever being forwarded. This firewall capability is useful in a multiple-architecture network as a security feature. For example, a bridge might be used to connect a public network to a special research-only network. The research network would use the TCP/IP protocols, while the public network would use both Novell and TCP/IP. By filtering out Novell traffic, the research network would be secured from unauthorized

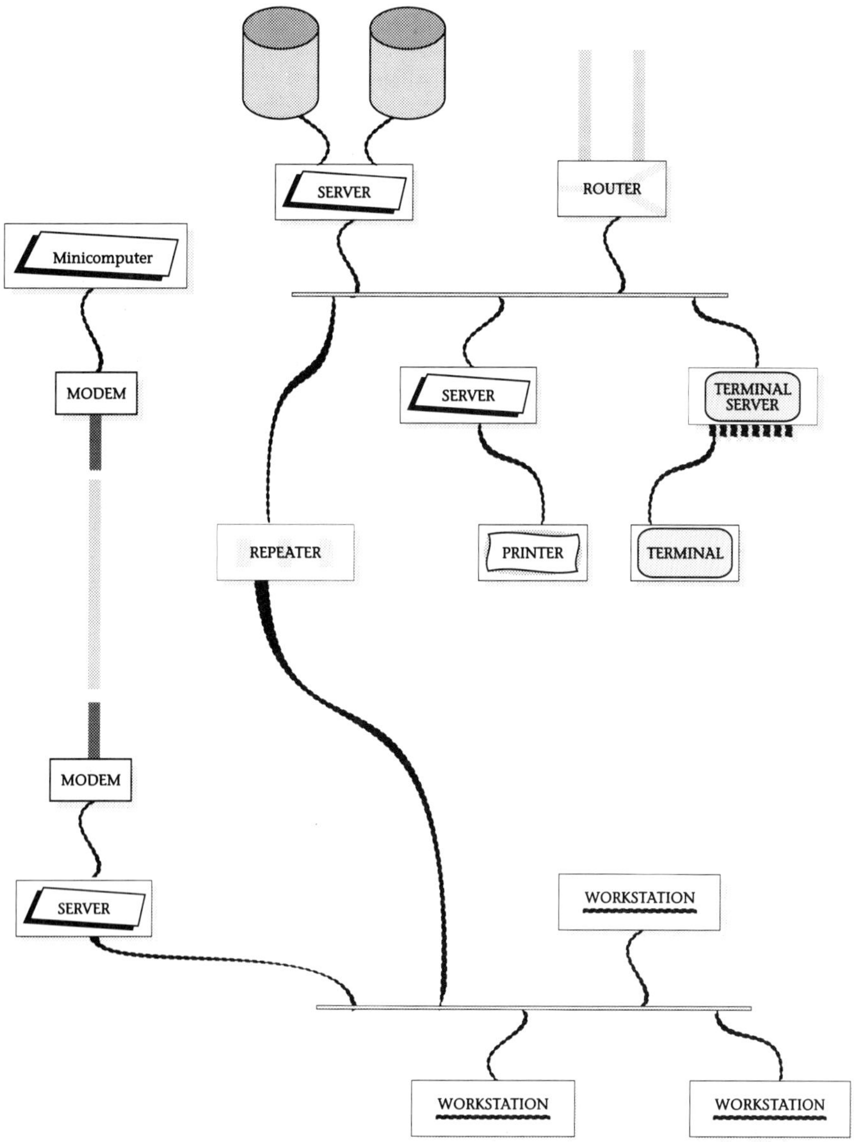

Fig. 2-13 Servers on a Data Link

users (unless, of course, they somehow gained access to a computer with TCP/IP and knew how to use it).

It is possible to connect several different Ethernets together with bridges (see Fig. 2-12). Any two networks can have only one bridge active between them, and the bridges cannot form a loop. Actually, this is not quite true. Physically, some bridges can form a loop. When the bridges initialize, they use a spanning tree algorithm to disable those bridges that would form a loop.

As Figure 2-12 shows, it is possible for a packet to go through several networks, being forwarded each time by a bridge. Each bridge connects two adjacent networks together; there can be several hops between destination nodes. The limitation on the number of hops is the delay added by each successive bridge—it is not uncommon to have four or five networks sucessfully connected this way.

A special type of bridge is the wide area bridge. These bridges (the two half bridges linked with modems in Figure 2-12) can actually forward Ethernet packets over long distances using telephone lines or other wide area transmission facilities such as satellite or microwave. Since Ethernet is a best-effort delivery service, an Ethernet controller doesn't really care how long data takes to get to the destination node. In the case of a wide area network, it obviously takes longer than it does using a 10-Mbps coaxial cable.

The wide area bridge transparently links the two networks together and provides the service of sending data to any nodes on the Ethernets on either side of the bridge. The packet may then go through other bridges before it reaches its eventual destination local area network and finally the destination node. In such a configuration, a packet may take longer than it does on a single network, particularly with the wide area bridge.

Certain protocols (i.e., the LAT protocols from DEC) have been programmed to expect a certain response time; when they send a packet to a peer node they expect to get a response back before a timer expires. In the case of these time-critical protocols, the timers need to be adjusted in an extended Ethernet environment. Usually, however, time-critical applications can be clustered together into a single segment of the Ethernet. The bridge allows connectivity to the rest of the network for noncritical applications.

Novell and Ethernet

The network that we've discussed up to this point, the data link layer, provides a very simple service—transmitting data from one node to another. To the network layer, the Ethernet looks like a single logical wire. With repeaters and bridges, this could be a fairly complex wiring scheme, but it still looks like a single wire to its users.

Merely sending packets of data from one node to another is not a very useful function. Subsequent chapters will show how Novell builds on this basic data link to provide useful network services.

Figure 2-13 shows the type of network one might expect on an Ethernet, which includes a series of workstations and servers. The Novell protocols will use Ethernet to communicate between network nodes.

In Figure 2-13, the basic server is the file server, which allows a workstation to put data on remote disk drives. The concept of the server is more general, however. Other servers might be running specialized programs, such as database management or statistical analysis software.

A router is also a specialized server, dedicated to routing data to other networks. This could be through wide area links such as telephone lines or directly to another local area network.

In addition, the diagram shows a gateway to a minicomputer. The gateway is a server that provides a link to another networking environment. This environment could be very simple, such as the single minicomputer shown in the illustration. The gateway could also link to a large complex network, such as a TCP/IP or SNA environment.

Key Points in This Chapter

- The Logical Link Control is a standard interface to different IEEE Medium Access Control (MAC) standards.
- Ethernet is the MAC standard that uses the CSMA/CD methodology.
- Ethernet supports a variety of physical media including thickwire, thinwire, twisted pair, and fiber.
- A repeater is a device that connects seperate Ethernet segments together into a multisegment Ethernet. All traffic on one segment is repeated on all the others.
- A MAC-layer bridge is a device that connects several Ethernets together into an extended Ethernet. The bridge isolates local traffic on each Ethernet but forwards traffic crossing the boundaries.
- The bridge is transparent to the network layer. All of the users (i.e., IPX) treat the separate Ethernet networks as one integrated data link.

CHAPTER 3

Token Ring and ARCNET

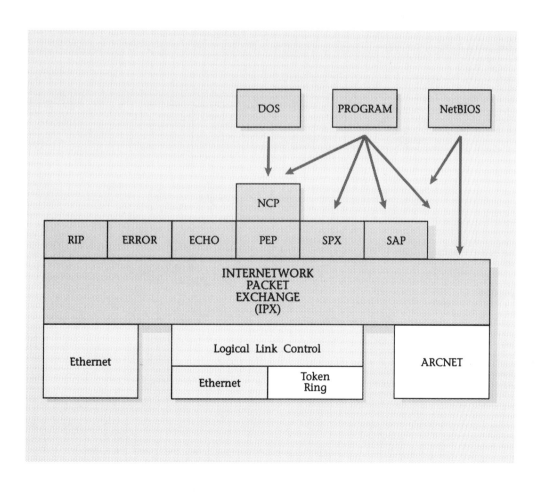

CHAPTER 3

Token Ring and ARCNET

Other Data Links

Chapter 3 examined two different forms of the Ethernet—Ethernet Version 2.0 and the IEEE 802.3 standard. Both standards are quite similar, using the medium access technology and providing the same service to the user: sending a packet of data from one station on the network to another. The service is a best-effort delivery service—a node will not guarantee that the packet will be received at its destination node or that any program at the destination node will know what to do with the packet.

In this chapter we examine two other forms of data links, the token ring and ARCNET. Both provide the same service as Ethernet—sending and receiving data to another node on the network. Since all three of the standards operate at the data link layer, there is no issue of what to do with the packets once they are received at the destination. The packet may be used by a program on the destination node or may be forwarded through another network until it reaches its final destination.

At this point, all the nodes on a single network must share the same data link mechanism. We will see in the next chapter that the network layer builds on that basic service by allowing multiple kinds of networks to be connected together into an internetwork. Many vendors sell interface cards for the various data links that Novell supports. ARCNET, for example, can be purchased from Novell (which markets the product as RX-Net) or from third-party vendors such as Standard Micro Systems, Black Box, and Datapoint Corporation.

In addition to Ethernet, token ring, and ARCNET, Novell supports a few other data link standards. We will see in the last part of the book, for example, that asynchronous telephone lines and X.25 networks can be used to connect several Novell networks together.

Novell supports a particular data link implementation by writing a software program that connects the network interface card with the IPX program that runs at layer 3 of the network. With the advent of STREAMS and other networking support software (see Chapter 10), Novell has published exactly what the interface between the two looks like, allowing third-party vendors to integrate their equipment into a Novell network.

Datapoint's ARCNET

ARCNET is a proprietary network technology based on a token ring methodology developed by Datapoint Corporation. A single ARCNET can have up to 255 nodes. ARCNET is widely used because of the relatively inexpensive cost of the peripherals and wiring as well as the simplicity of the network.

While Ethernet has a bandwidth of 10 Mbps, the speed of an ARCNET is 2.5 Mbps. Reduced bandwidth (at reduced cost) is not necessarily a problem for many environments. In many networks, Ethernet utilization is 10 percent or less of capacity for all periods of activity, meaning that a full 10 Mbps is not necessary.

In addition to the 2.5-Mbps version of ARCNET, an enhanced version, called ARCNET Plus, supports speeds of 20 Mbps. This enhanced version of ARCNET is much newer than regular ARCNET and has not been as widely accepted.

Many user environments have been moving toward standardized data links such as the IEEE 802 series. ARCNET, because of its wide availability, can be considered a de facto standard. User reactions toward ARCNET Plus will determine whether it will retain that de facto standard status.

ARCNET Wiring and Hubs

The Ethernet has a bus topology. Logically, the Ethernet consists of a single wire with many computers attached to it. All packets are broadcast to all nodes,

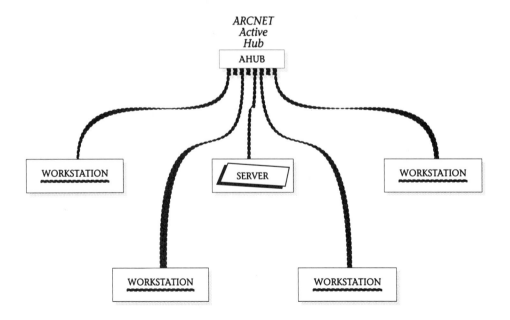

Fig. 3-1 Basic ARCNET Configuration

which then decide if they will accept that particular packet based on the destination address in the header.

ARCNET also broadcasts all packets to all nodes, but it does so using a star topology. Computers are connected together using a hub. In Figure 3-1, we see the nodes connected together using an active hub, which takes signals coming in from one of its eight (or more) ports and sends them out the other seven, ensuring that all ports hear all transmissions. The hub performs a similar function to the Ethernet repeater, broadcasting incoming signals to other cables.

In Novell's version of ARCNET, the workstation is connected to the active hub using RG-62 coaxial cable. The workstation can be up to 2000 feet away from the active hub (although it will often be much closer). Other vendors' implementations of ARCNET allow different kinds of media than RG-62 coaxial cable to be used for the connection.

In Figure 3-2, we see a more complex ARCNET topology; it has multiple types of hubs, including passive, active, and intelligent. The basic rule for this configuration is that there should be only one path for data to flow between any two workstations—there should be no potential loops for the data to travel.

The passive hub, as its name implies, is a passive device that requires no power and therefore does not reamplify the signal. Passive hubs can have one to four connections, with each workstation 100 feet or less away from the hub using coaxial cable.

Passive hubs can only be used near the outer edges of the network. A passive hub cannot be in the path between two active hubs and two passive hubs cannot be in a series. When passive hubs are used, the outer edge of the network is the workstation. The next level in is the passive hub, which is typically attached to an active hub.

Normally, the active hub is used in a wiring closet. From there, cable is run out to the offices. If there are multiple computers in an office, a passive hub is used to further distribute the cables to those computers.

Active hubs can be connected together at a distance of up to 2000 feet, and configurations can be designed that would have up to 10 active hubs in the path between any two workstations. This would be a slightly unusual configuration, however, because of the 255-node limit of a single ARCNET.

A fiber optic hub is used to separate the network by longer distances. Fiber optic cable is used between hubs, allowing separations of up to 15,000 feet between the two hubs. An additional 2000 feet can then separate the intelligent hub from an active one.

The fiber optic cable and hub are typically used in two situations. First, if there is a large distance between two buildings, this may be the only ARCNET-based solution. Second, fiber is a more secure medium than coaxial cable because an intrusion onto the medium can be detected (whereas on the coaxial Ethernet a new node can easily be added while the network is in operation). For this reason, fiber cable is preferred in situations where security is an important consideration.

The last type of hub is the intelligent hub. Two intelligent hubs are connected together using RG-59 or RG-62 cable. The hub has 16 ports and uses a

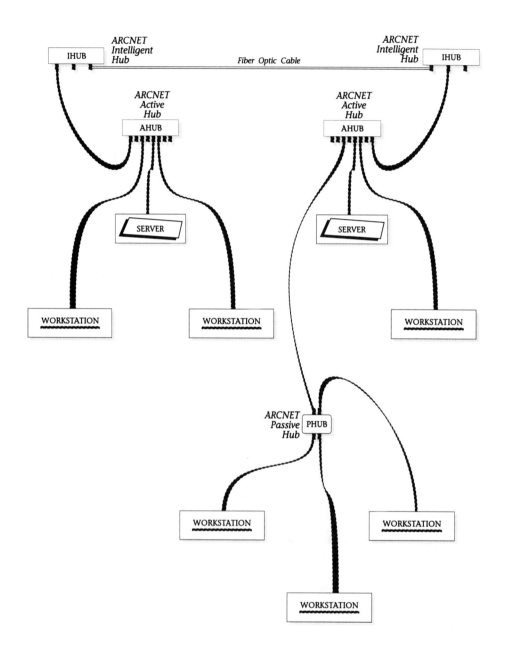

Fig. 3-2 Extended ARCNET Configuration

low frequency of the coaxial cable to continually monitor the integrity of the link.

The maximum separation between devices and in the ARCNET network as a whole is a function of two considerations: the attenuation of the signal and the propagation velocity. The attenuation is the normal dissipation of a signal as it travels on a medium. Different kinds of cables have different attenuation characteristics.

The propagation velocity is how long it takes to send a signal from one end of a wire to the other. Since the network uses a timer to make sure that a response to a packet is received in time, the timer influences the length of a particular piece of wire and the total number of pieces of wire.

Basically, the user can have any kind of cable connecting ARCNET devices (hubs and workstations) together, as long as it meets the basic rule of less than 11 decibels of attenuation at a frequency of 5 MHz over the length of the cable.

Based on this rule, vendors support a variety of different kinds of cables. Figure 3-3 shows the maximum length permissible for different kinds of cabling typically found in an ARCNET environment. Notice that the RG-62 has a longer maximum distance than the RG-59/U which has thinner shielding and a higher impedance.

Cable Type	Maximum Distance (Feet)
RG-62	2000
RG-59/U	1500
RG-11/U	1750
IBM Type 1	660
IBM Type 3	330
3 or 6 shielded twisted pair	330

Fig. 3-3 Maximum ARCNET Cable Lengths

The maximum separation between any two nodes on the ARCNET is calculated by a rule that states that the maximum propagation delay for an ARCNET must be less than 31 microseconds. Delay is caused by the physical wires, as well as by any devices such as hubs. Figure 3-4 shows the amount of delay introduced by various devices and cable types on the ARCNET.

When configuring an ARCNET environment, the installer checks to make sure that both types of limits are observed: first, that the separation between any two devices is the proper length; second, that the total separation leads to a propagation delay of less than 31 microseconds.

As a general rule, the maximum separation between any nodes is limited to 22,000 feet. This would be 11 segments of coaxial cable, each 2000 feet long, plus a series of active hubs connecting them together. Again, this is not normally a problem given the limit on the number of nodes in a single ARCNET.

Delay (Microseconds)	Device
.25	Active Hub
.01	Passive Hub
.12	RG-62 Coax (100 feet)
.13	RG-11 (100 feet)
.14	IBM Type 1 (100 feet)
.15	IBM Type 3 (100 feet)

Fig. 3-4 Delay Caused by ARCNET Devices

Generally, if the node limitation on a single ARCNET is reached, an organization has the option of putting in several small ARCNETs. A NetWare router will connect the ARCNETs together, using the network layer protocol, IPX.

The amount of fiber optic cable used also influences the maximum distance between any two points on the network. If 8000 feet or more of fiber optic is used, the maximum separation between any two nodes is limited to a total of 17,500 feet. If less than 8000 feet of fiber is used, the 20,000-foot maximum separation can be achieved (but through the use of more coaxial cable).

If truly necessary, it is possible to adjust the ARCNET parameters for reconfiguration bursts and response timers. The reconfiguration burst transmits data continuously on the network for a period of time to clear it of any extraneous traffic. A larger network needs a larger reconfiguration burst. The response timer is the amount of time that a node waits to hear a response to a packet it sent out before deciding that the packet was lost and beginning the process of error recovery. An ARCNET board for a computer usually allows the user to adjust both parameters. Figure 3-5 shows the effect of different response timers. Note that for the extreme cases, the user would also have to adjust timers in the upper layers of the network.

Response Time (Microseconds)	Reconfiguration (Seconds)
74.7	0.84
283.4	1.68
561.8	1.68
1118.6	1.68

Fig. 3-5 Maximum Distances in ARCNET

ARCNET Packets

ARCNET, like any data link layer, is not typically used directly by the user. Instead, a network layer program such as IPX uses the services of ARCNET to move data through a particular data link (see Fig. 3-6). There is an intermediate layer, the fragmentation header, which will be discussed in the next section.

The ARCNET header includes an address for the source and destination node. An address of 0 is a broadcast, intended to be received by all nodes on the network. Addresses from 1 to 255 are individual addresses. In addition to the addresses, the ARCNET header includes a 16-bit-long cyclical redundancy check and the address of a higher-level protocol that is using the ARCNET. The CRC is used to make sure that the data was not damaged in transit. The address is used to pass the incoming data packet up to the ARCNET client.

In Ethernet, a node is able to transmit any time the medium is clear of traffic for a period of time. Collisions are handled by backing off for a random period of time. In ARCNET, nodes are required to obtain permission to transmit data. This permission is obtained by passing a token around the network in sequential order by address. When a node receives the token, it may transmit data. It then passes the token to the next node on the network, which in turn can transmit data. If a node doesn't have data to send, it simply sends the token along to the next node.

The token is a special form of data packet. The token doesn't show on the Sniffer Analyzer screen dumps because it is a maintenance activity, used by the ARCNET to manage itself. One can assume that the node transmitting data is in possession of the token.

There are a few other kinds of basic packets that are also used in an ARCNET. Figure 3-7 illustrates how a data packet is sent in this environment. First, the sending node must receive a token (known as an Invitation to Transmit or ITT), indicating permission to send.

Next, the sending node sends a Free Buffer Enquiry to the destination of the data. The destination node will respond that a buffer is free. The Free Buffer Enquiry ensures that the receiving node has room for the data (as opposed to the Ethernet, where a packet may be sent to a "deaf" or overloaded controller).

Next, the sending node sends the actual data packet. This packet must be acknowledged, at which point the token is released. This acknowledged delivery of a packet of data is in sharp contrast to the Ethernet, which is strictly a best-effort service.

A basic ARCNET can handle data packets up to 252 bytes long. An extended mode of ARCNET allows a packet to have up to 508 bytes of user data. The ARCNET header indicates which type of packet this is. Most computers can handle the extended mode of ARCNET. A few peripheral devices, such as printers, might be limited to the smaller packet sizes.

The raw bandwidth of ARCNET, 2.5 Mbps, is not all available to the user. The exchange of Free Buffer Enquiries, acknowledgments, and the token all eat into the available bandwidth. Another reduction in bandwidth is provided by an artifact of the ARCNET data format, which consists of 11 bits to send an 8-bit byte of data. The actual data is preceded by the bit sequence 110, thereby using 30 percent of the available bandwidth.

Error Recovery in ARCNET

An ARCNET, because of the limit on the number of nodes and the maximum propagation velocity of the network, guarantees that each node will receive a

```
DETAIL
DLC: ----- DLC Header -----
DLC:
DLC: Frame 2 arrived at 09:54:19.9862; frame size is 512 (0200 hex) bytes.
DLC: (Only the first 64 of the 512 bytes were captured.)
DLC: Destination: Station FC
DLC: Source      : Station 19
DLC: ARCNET system code = FA
DLC:
NOV: ----- Novell ARCNET fragmentation header -----
NOV:
NOV: Fragment 1 of 2
NOV: Sequence number = 12383
NOV:
XNS: ----- XNS Header -----
XNS:
XNS: Checksum = FFFF
XNS: Length = 552
XNS: *** XNS length is 552, but actual remaining frame length is 504 ***
XNS: Transport = 3
XNS: Packet type = 17 (Novell Netware)
                          Frame 2 of 50
1       2 Set              5         6Display 7 Prev   8 Next            10 New
Help    mark               Menus     options  frame    frame             capture
```

Courtesy of Network General

Fig. 3-6 ARCNET Packet

token within a specific period of time. If a node does not receive a token within that time, something is wrong on the network.

If a node does not receive a token for 840 milliseconds, it initiates a reconfiguration procedure. The reconfiguration burst consists of a set pattern (1111 1111 0) repeated 765 times—long enough to interfere with any node that is about to send a token. After the reconfiguration burst, which clears the network by destroying the token or any other data, the node waits for a quiet period. Then, the token is regenerated. In order for a token to be passed sequentially from node to node, each ARCNET node must know its neighbor. If the node has to know its neighbor for passing a token, there cannot be any duplicate address. Otherwise, to which of the two neighbors would it pass the token?

Regenerating the token involves sending a packet to every one of the possible 255 nodes on the ARCNET and waiting for the response. Based on these packets, nodes are able to determine who their neighbors are, allowing them to pass on a received packet.

Nodes with neighboring ARCNET addresses may not necessarily be next to each other physically. ARCNET uses a star configuration, and every packet is sent to every node because the signal will propagate throughout the wiring. The token protocol allows nodes to ignore those tokens intended for other nodes. We will see that the token ring, discussed later in this chapter, actually passes a token among physical neighbors instead of broadcasting the data.

When testing for the presence of a neighbor, the first node on the network will send out a packet with the address set at 2. It then waits for an acknowledgment. If it receives one, it stores the address in the register containing the

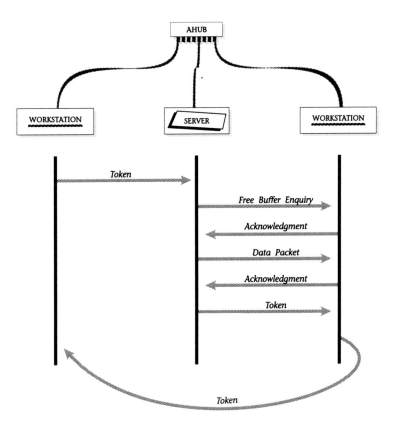

Fig. 3-7 Message Exchange in an ARCNET

upstream neighbor. If no acknowledgment is received, it increments the address by 1 and tries again.

This entire reconfiguration procedure (the reconfiguration burst plus the token loop regeneration) is actually quite quick, lasting from 24 to 61 milliseconds, depending on the number of active nodes and the propagation delay of the cables and hubs. The same reconfiguration procedure also occurs whenever a node joins the ARCNET. The ARCNET board, upon being initialized, sends out the reconfiguration burst, which is followed by regeneration of the token loop. In this way, a new workstation that has just been turned on can force a regeneration, identifying itself to its neighbor, and join the network.

The overall bandwidth of an ARCNET is 2.5 Mbps, equivalent to about 316 kbytes per second. Based on the sequence for sending data and tokens and the propagation delays on the network, Datapoint has calculated some theoretical limits on the throughput of the ARCNET.

Take, for example, a network consisting of 10 nodes, all wishing to send data packets of 100 bytes or less. In such an ARCNET, if no nodes are sending data, a token appears at each node every 282 microseconds. If all 10 nodes are receiving a token and then sending 100 bytes of data before resending the token out, the token loop takes 5,810 microseconds. This is equivalent to a node sending 172 packets per second. The total number of packets on this network is therefore 1,720 packets per second, or a total of 172,000 bytes per second.

With 10 nodes sending short packets, the ARCNET user sees a total network throughput of 172 kbytes per second out of a maximum throughput of 316 kbytes per second. Each user sees a throughput of 17,200 bytes per second.

If only one of the ten nodes is sending, the throughput for that user goes up. Nine of the ten nodes will send the packet to the next node, and the tenth will send data before sending the token along. In this case, the sending node can send one data packet every 833 microseconds, for a throughput of 120 kbytes per second for that user. Note that larger packet sizes increase the throughput on the network, since more data is sent for every round of tokens.

As the network increases in size, the throughput goes down, since the token has to be passed to more nodes. If many nodes have data to send, the throughput for any one user also goes down, because it takes longer to release the token to the next node.

The Ethernet provides higher bandwidth in two ways. First, the overall bandwidth is 10 Mbps (1.25 Mbytes per second). Second, a node can keep on transmitting packets as long as another node isn't using the network, eliminating the token passing overhead.

Note that one thing Ethernet doesn't guarantee is access to the network. A node can try to send, but in a busy Ethernet, the node may never be able to send successfully (such a situation calls for bridges or other solutions to the basic configuration). The indeterministic access method for the Ethernet is in contrast to the deterministic system used in a token ring or ARCNET network.

The Fragmentation Header

The length of an ARCNET packet is limited to 508 bytes in extended mode. This poses a problem with network layers such as IPX, which assume that a data link is capable of carrying 576 bytes of data. To accommodate the requirements of IPX, Novell, in cooperation with a few other companies, has developed a sublayer that sits between IPX and the ARCNET service, known as the ARCNET fragmentation layer. It allows IPX to send 576 bytes of data in a packet. The fragmentation layer breaks this up into two separate packets. At the destination, the fragmentation layer reassembles the data and presents it to IPX.

This approach allows IPX to remain unchanged and to use the services of ARCNET, token ring, or Ethernet. The de facto standard was sponsored by a group including Apple, Novell, and Standard Micro Systems (makers of a variety of ARCNET hardware products).

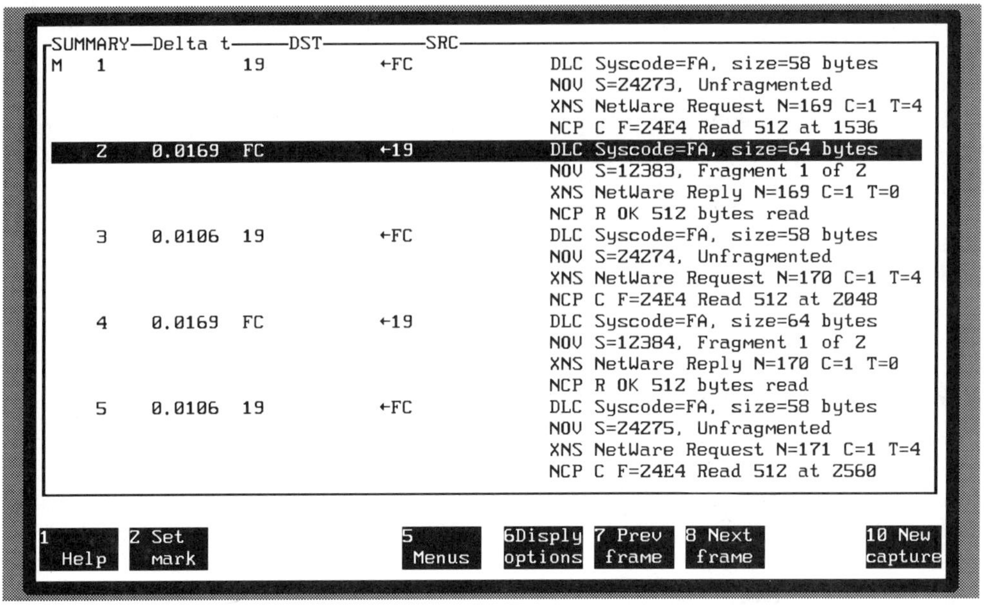

```
 ┌SUMMARY──Delta t──────DST────────SRC──┐
 M  1          19          ←FC           DLC Syscode=FA, size=58 bytes
                                          NOV S=24273, Unfragmented
                                          XNS NetWare Request N=169 C=1 T=4
                                          NCP C F=24E4 Read 512 at 1536
    2       0.0169 FC           ←19      DLC Syscode=FA, size=64 bytes
                                          NOV S=12383, Fragment 1 of 2
                                          XNS NetWare Reply N=169 C=1 T=0
                                          NCP R OK 512 bytes read
    3       0.0106 19           ←FC      DLC Syscode=FA, size=58 bytes
                                          NOV S=24274, Unfragmented
                                          XNS NetWare Request N=170 C=1 T=4
                                          NCP C F=24E4 Read 512 at 2048
    4       0.0169 FC           ←19      DLC Syscode=FA, size=64 bytes
                                          NOV S=12384, Fragment 1 of 2
                                          XNS NetWare Reply N=170 C=1 T=0
                                          NCP R OK 512 bytes read
    5       0.0106 19           ←FC      DLC Syscode=FA, size=58 bytes
                                          NOV S=24275, Unfragmented
                                          XNS NetWare Request N=171 C=1 T=4
                                          NCP C F=24E4 Read 512 at 2560

 1     2 Set              5         6Display 7 Prev  8 Next           10 New
 Help  mark               Menus     options  frame   frame            capture
```

Courtesy of Network General

Fig. 3-8 ARCNET Traffic

Figure 3-8 illustrates some typical data on an ARCNET. Notice that in several cases the fragmentation layer indicates that only a portion of an IPX packet is contained in the ARCNET packet (indicated by the fragmentation number in the *NOV* portion of the packet).

The ability to add a layer in between two others is possible because of the layered network architecture. ARCNET is independent of the upper layer users. It simply delivers data to a user, denoted by the system code byte in the ARC-NET header. Instead of delivering IPX data directly to IPX, it simply delivers it to the ARCNET fragmentation layer, which reassembles packets and delivers them up to IPX.

The fragmentation header in a packet is actually fairly simple. The header has two pieces: a split flag and a sequence number. The split flag indicates which of the several fragments are contained in this particular ARCNET packet.

The sequence number is used when data has been corrupted on the network. Before the fragmentation header can acknowledge a packet, it must make sure that it has all the fragments it needs. The sequence number ensures that fragments that are re-sent don't interfere with a previous partial transmission that was negatively acknowledged.

The split flag is normally used to indicate if this particular packet is fragmented. A flag of 00 indicates that this is the first fragment of a one-fragment transmission. If the packet is the first of two fragments, a 01 is put into the split flag. If it is the second of two fragments, a 02 is put into that field. A special type of flag has a field of FF hexadecimal. This indicates an exception packet and is used to signal a problem in the transmission of a particular sequence number.

Normally, there is a maximum of two fragments per packet. It is possible, using this header, to actually have longer packets sent over the network. This is done using a more general version of the split flag, which is compatible with the values listed above.

The split flag is 1 byte long. The least significant bit is set to 1 to indicate the beginning of a message and to 0 for the continuation of a message. The other 7 bits, for the beginning of a message, contain the total number of fragments to expect.

For message continuation fragments, the other 7 bits are the fragment number of this particular fragment. This method provides a theoretical limit of 120 fragments per frame. With a maximum ARCNET packet size of 504 bytes (the fragmentation header reduces the maximum data size available), it would be theoretically possible for IPX to submit 120 fragments, or 60,480 bytes. Of course, this theoretical limit is not attained, since the current version of IPX uses a maximum packet size of 576 bytes.

ISO/IEEE Token Ring Standard

Another token ring standard is a standard developed by the IEEE. This standard has been adopted as an official national standard by ANSI and as an international standard by the ISO. This standard operates at 4 million bits per second,

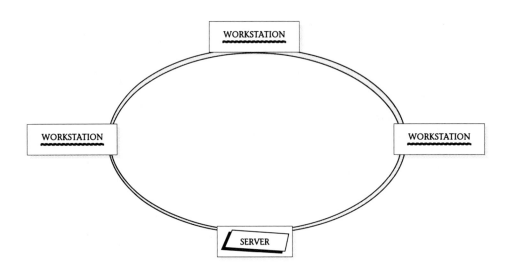

Fig. 3-9 Basic Token Ring Configuration

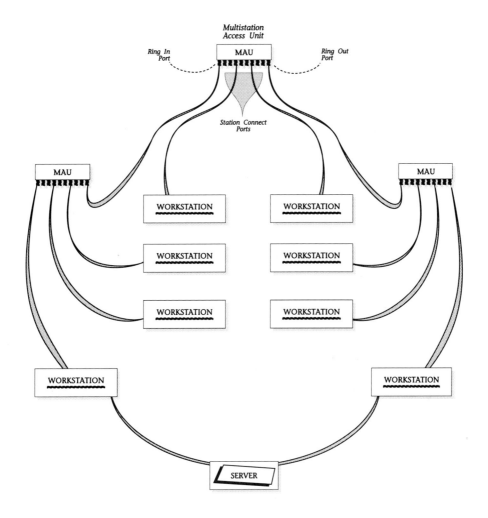

Fig. 3-10 Extended Token Ring Configuration

in contrast to the 2.5 Mbps of the ARCNET token ring. An extended version of the token ring standard operates at 16 Mbps.

A basic token ring configuration is shown in Figure 3-9. Each computer has a wire run to its neighbor. The ring is closed by connecting a wire from the last computer to the first one. The basic function of the token ring controller card is to take all data received in one side and copy it back to the other side.

Figure 3-10 shows a more complex token ring configuration that uses the ring and a special type of node called a multistation access unit (MAU). Many MAU products, including the basic IBM product, have 10 ports. In a stand-alone configuration, eight computers can be connected to it to form a "canned" ring. The MAU senses which of the eight ports has computers attached to it and takes any data received on one port and copies it out to the next connected port.

The other two ports are the ring-in and ring-out ports. They are connected to the next station or MAU on the network. A MAU is often used for token ring implementations because it allows the ring to keep on functioning if a computer goes down. If a computer is directly connected to the ring, when it ceases to operate, it will be unable to copy incoming data out, thereby breaking the ring. With a MAU, the port containing the defective (or powered-off) computer is automatically bypassed, preserving the integrity of the ring.

There are a variety of vendors that manufacture equipment for a token ring. Usually, a vendor provides cable, MAUs, and adapter cards for the PC. For example, the IBM Token-Ring product is a collection of this equipment.

Rules for configurations vary based on the vendor. The basic limitation is the ability to propagate signals around the ring within a period of time. The propagation delay then gets translated into the number of stations, cable lengths, and other physical parameters set by a vendor.

The IBM Token-Ring product set includes the IBM 8228 Multistation Access Unit. All workstations connect to the ring using the MAU. The computers can be configured using the standard cabling system provided by IBM, known as the "small moveable" cabling system, which allows up to 96 stations to be configured in a token ring. The network can have up to 12 IBM 8228 MAUs in it. The distance between two MAUs or between a station and a MAU can be up to 45 meters.

For larger token rings, users can install the "large nonmoveable cabling system." When a company like IBM, not noted for its clarity and simplicity, uses terms like *large* and *nonmoveable* to describe a product it wishes to sell, the user can imagine that installation is not necessarily easy. An alternative to the extremely large token ring is to use a MAC-layer bridge, as in the Ethernet example, to connect multiple token rings together. Another alternative is to use a higher layer, the network layer, to connect multiple systems together into an internetwork.

Basic Token Ring Operation

Figure 3-11 shows the token ring medium access layer carrying data for the Logical Link Control. LLC, in turn, may provide services to its clients, such as Novell's IPX. As in other networks, there can be several different users of the LLC service—Novell's IPX and another vendor's TCP/IP, for example.

The source and destination addresses on a token ring can be either 2 or 6 bytes long. The 6-byte address is compatible with the Ethernet address size. The addresses can be locally administered or assigned by the manufacturer.

Notice that the token ring header is significantly more complicated than either the ARCNET or Ethernet headers. Each packet contains a variety of indicators of the present status of this packet. The token ring has many different

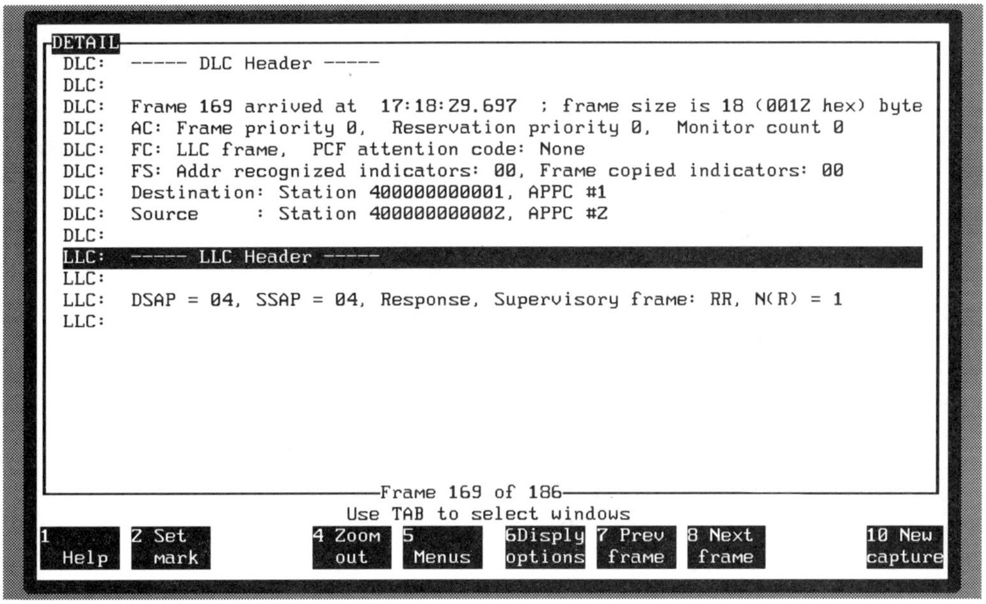

```
┌─DETAIL──────────────────────────────────────────────────────────┐
│ DLC:  ----- DLC Header -----                                    │
│ DLC:                                                            │
│ DLC:  Frame 169 arrived at  17:18:29.697  ; frame size is 18 (0012 hex) byte │
│ DLC:  AC: Frame priority 0,  Reservation priority 0,  Monitor count 0 │
│ DLC:  FC: LLC frame,  PCF attention code: None                  │
│ DLC:  FS: Addr recognized indicators: 00, Frame copied indicators: 00 │
│ DLC:  Destination: Station 400000000001, APPC #1                │
│ DLC:  Source      : Station 400000000002, APPC #2               │
│ DLC:                                                            │
│ LLC:  ----- LLC Header -----                                    │
│ LLC:                                                            │
│ LLC:  DSAP = 04, SSAP = 04, Response, Supervisory frame: RR, N(R) = 1 │
│ LLC:                                                            │
│                                                                 │
│                      ─Frame 169 of 186─                         │
│                    Use TAB to select windows                    │
│ ┌─┐ ┌2 Set─┐    ┌4 Zoom┐ ┌5────┐ ┌6Disply┐ ┌7 Prev┐ ┌8 Next┐  ┌10 New──┐ │
│ │1│ │ mark │    │ out  │ │Menus│ │options│ │ frame│ │frame │  │capture │ │
│ │Help│                                                          │
└─────────────────────────────────────────────────────────────────┘
```

Courtesy of Network General

Fig. 3-11 Token Ring and LLC Data

packets on the network. In the Ethernet environment, there is only one kind of packet. For ARCNET, there are several kinds of packets, including the token, the data packet, and a few miscellaneous packets.

We will see that the token ring uses special packets for maintenance of the ring. This allows one of the nodes to be chosen as the ring controller, known as the active monitor. Other computers periodically verify the presence of that active monitor and make sure it is functioning properly.

As in ARCNET, a token is sent around the ring. The token gives the receiving node permission to send data. In ARCNET, the token is passed from one node to another based on the address of the ARCNET node. In a token ring, the token is simply passed from one physical neighbor to another. The token has a priority associated with it. Each data packet also has a priority associated with it, based on the type of data to be transmitted. Error recovery packets, for example, have a higher priority than an ordinary data packet. Any node that receives a token may send a packet of equal or higher priority. Note that priority tokens are not usually seen by the user (i.e., IPX) and are usually only used by the token ring for error recovery and other maintenance tasks.

Before the packet can be sent, the computer must "capture" the token. Instead of copying the token out the other end of the adaptor, it sends the data packet. Since the packet is not a token, every computer on the network takes the data and copies it back out to its neighbor, without attempting to send its own data.

When the destination node indicated in the token ring header sees this packet coming from its upstream neighbor, it copies the packet into its buffer, and sends it on through to the other side.

The destination node does make a slight change in the packet. It changes 2 bits to indicate that it recognized its address and that it copied the data successfully into its buffers. If the computer doesn't have room in its buffers for the incoming data, it will at least change the address-recognized bit.

There are now two copies of the packet. The first copy is in the destination node's memory buffers. That computer will initiate appropriate action for the packet, probably sending it up to the Logical Link Control, which in turn will send it up to the network layer.

The second copy is still circulating the ring. Eventually, the packet will make it back to the original sender. The original sender will see that the address-recognized and frame-copied bits are turned on, indicating that the destination node successfully received the packet.

The original sender is allowed to capture the token for a certain period of time. When it first receives the token, it starts the token holding timer. It is possible that several packets can be sent out during the duration of this timer. If the timer expires, or there is no more data to send, the computer will release the token. The token will be sent back out and forwarded to the next computer. That computer, if it has data to send, will capture the token.

Every node on a token ring is thus assured of seeing a token at some point. The period of time that elapses is a function of the number of nodes on the network that have to copy the token and how many of those nodes send data when they get the token.

In addition to the frame-copied and address-recognized bits, there are several other bits in the header including priority indications and a reservation field. A computer may change these bits even if the frame is not destined for its particular address.

In order to send data, the token received has to have a priority indication that is less than or equal to the data that is to be sent. Both the token and the data packet thus have priority fields and also have a reservation field. If a computer has data to send that is of lower priority than the token, it indicates the desired priority it would like in the reservation field.

The active monitor, which controls the issuance of tokens, will notice the reservation request and store that information. Whenever a token is received, the active monitor checks the reservation requests. If there is a request for a higher priority than the current token, it raises the priority. If there are no higher-priority reservations but there are lower-priority ones, it will lower the priority of the token to allow those nodes to send data.

Eventually, all reservations are satisfied and the token is lowered to a priority of 0. A zero priority token allows any computer to send any packet once it gets the token. Once all nodes have sent their data, the zero priority token continues to circulate around the ring.

A zero priority token is the only type of frame that is allowed to continuously circulate the ring. If a data frame continuously circulates, the original sender has failed to change the frame back into a token. If a high-priority token continues to circle, it probably means that the active monitor is failing to lower the priority level back to zero.

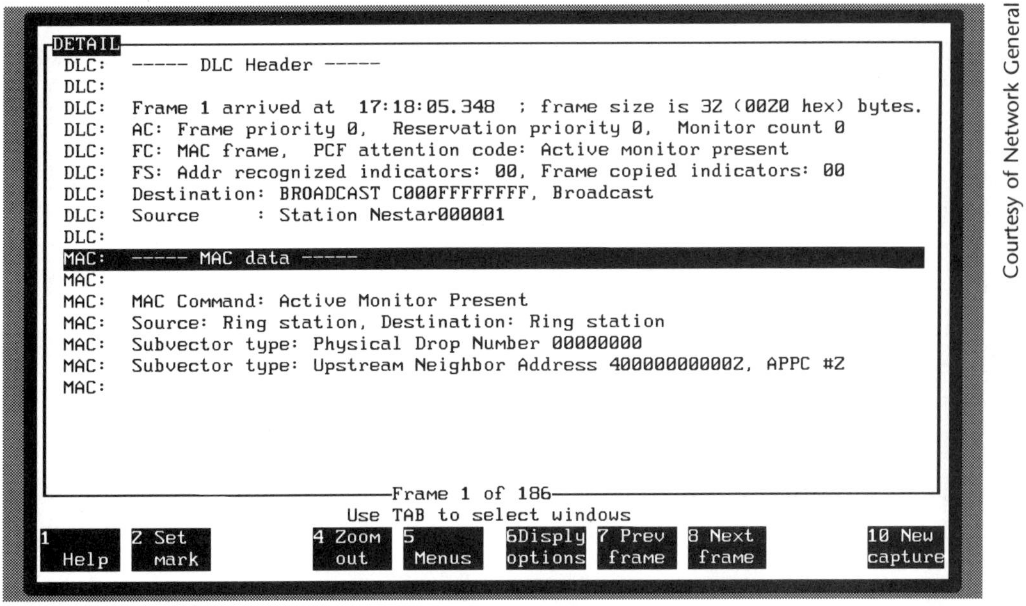

```
 DETAIL
 DLC:  ----- DLC Header -----
 DLC:
 DLC:  Frame 1 arrived at  17:18:05.348  ; frame size is 32 (0020 hex) bytes.
 DLC:  AC: Frame priority 0,  Reservation priority 0,  Monitor count 0
 DLC:  FC: MAC frame,  PCF attention code: Active monitor present
 DLC:  FS: Addr recognized indicators: 00, Frame copied indicators: 00
 DLC:  Destination: BROADCAST C000FFFFFFFF, Broadcast
 DLC:  Source     : Station Nestar000001
 DLC:
 MAC:  ----- MAC data -----
 MAC:
 MAC:  MAC Command: Active Monitor Present
 MAC:  Source: Ring station, Destination: Ring station
 MAC:  Subvector type: Physical Drop Number 00000000
 MAC:  Subvector type: Upstream Neighbor Address 400000000002, APPC #2
 MAC:


                         -Frame 1 of 186-
                      Use TAB to select windows
 1       2 Set         4 Zoom  5        6Disply  7 Prev  8 Next        10 New
 Help    mark          out     Menus    options  frame   frame         capture
```

Fig. 3-12 Active Monitor Present Message

```
 DETAIL
 DLC:  ----- DLC Header -----
 DLC:
 DLC:  Frame 2 arrived at  17:18:05.369  ; frame size is 32 (0020 hex) bytes.
 DLC:  AC: Frame priority 0,  Reservation priority 0,  Monitor count 0
 DLC:  FC: MAC frame,  PCF attention code: Standby monitor present
 DLC:  FS: Addr recognized indicators: 00, Frame copied indicators: 00
 DLC:  Destination: BROADCAST C000FFFFFFFF, Broadcast
 DLC:  Source     : Station 400000000002, APPC #2
 DLC:
 MAC:  ----- MAC data -----
 MAC:
 MAC:  MAC Command: Standby Monitor Present
 MAC:  Source: Ring station, Destination: Ring station
 MAC:  Subvector type: Physical Drop Number 00000000
 MAC:  Subvector type: Upstream Neighbor Address Nestar000001
 MAC:


                         -Frame 2 of 186-
                      Use TAB to select windows
 1       2 Set         4 Zoom  5        6Disply  7 Prev  8 Next        10 New
 Help    mark          out     Menus    options  frame   frame         capture
```

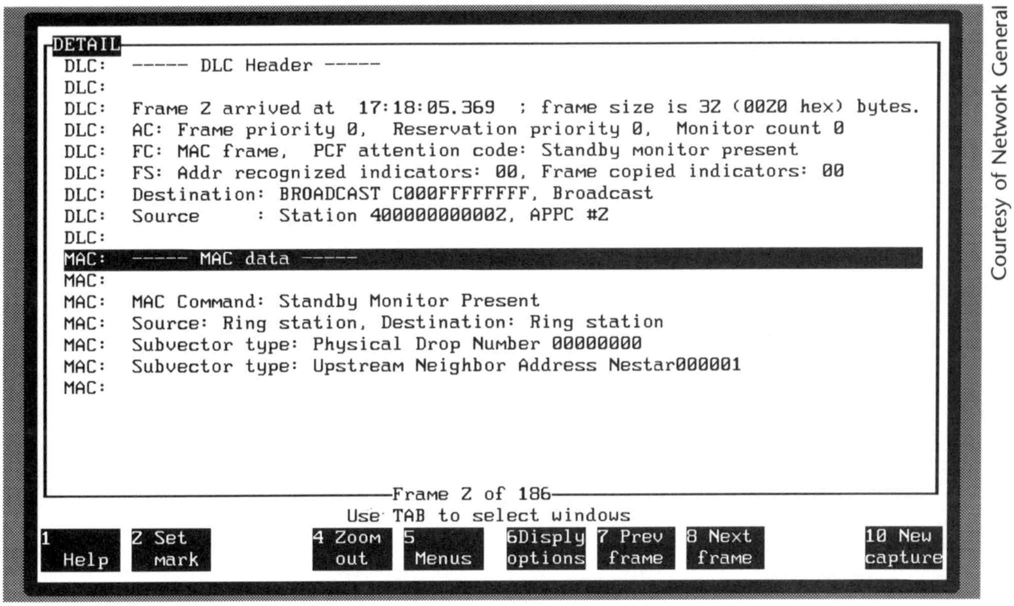

Fig. 3-13 Standby Monitor Present Message

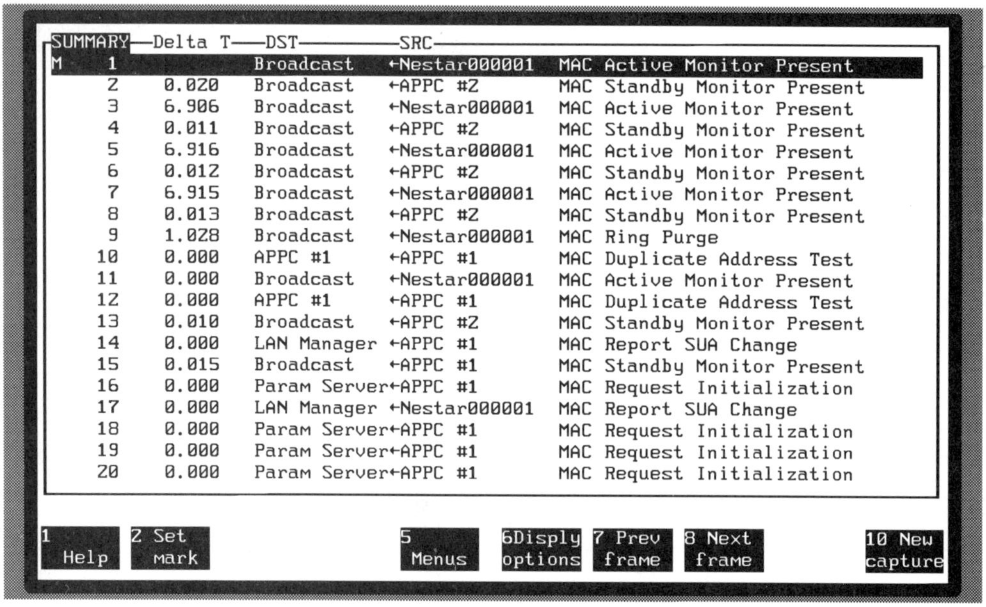

```
SUMMARY —Delta T— —DST—        —SRC—
M    1             Broadcast    ←Nestar000001  MAC Active Monitor Present
     2   0.020     Broadcast    ←APPC #2       MAC Standby Monitor Present
     3   6.906     Broadcast    ←Nestar000001  MAC Active Monitor Present
     4   0.011     Broadcast    ←APPC #2       MAC Standby Monitor Present
     5   6.916     Broadcast    ←Nestar000001  MAC Active Monitor Present
     6   0.012     Broadcast    ←APPC #2       MAC Standby Monitor Present
     7   6.915     Broadcast    ←Nestar000001  MAC Active Monitor Present
     8   0.013     Broadcast    ←APPC #2       MAC Standby Monitor Present
     9   1.028     Broadcast    ←Nestar000001  MAC Ring Purge
    10   0.000     APPC #1      ←APPC #1       MAC Duplicate Address Test
    11   0.000     Broadcast    ←Nestar000001  MAC Active Monitor Present
    12   0.000     APPC #1      ←APPC #1       MAC Duplicate Address Test
    13   0.010     Broadcast    ←APPC #2       MAC Standby Monitor Present
    14   0.000     LAN Manager  ←APPC #1       MAC Report SUA Change
    15   0.015     Broadcast    ←APPC #1       MAC Standby Monitor Present
    16   0.000     Param Server ←APPC #1       MAC Request Initialization
    17   0.000     LAN Manager  ←Nestar000001  MAC Report SUA Change
    18   0.000     Param Server ←APPC #1       MAC Request Initialization
    19   0.000     Param Server ←APPC #1       MAC Request Initialization
    20   0.000     Param Server ←APPC #1       MAC Request Initialization
```

Courtesy of Network General

Fig. 3-14 AMP and SMP Data

To ensure that a packet does not continue to circulate, the active monitor flips the monitor bit to 1 on all packets it sees. A packet coming in with the monitor bit already set to 1 has circulated the ring completely and should be taken off the ring.

Active and Standby Monitors

The active monitor is a crucial part of the ring. In addition to controlling token priorities, it provides a latency buffer that synchronizes the rate of flow on the ring. Since each computer may transmit slightly faster or slightly slower than the standard transmission rate, the bits on the ring may get slightly out of phase. The latency buffer is used to adjust for data coming in too slowly or too quickly.

To advertise its presence, the active monitor periodically sends out an active monitor present (AMP) frame (see Fig. 3-12). All other nodes maintain a timer. If a computer does not receive an AMP frame before the timer expires (usually every 3 seconds), that computer will initiate action to become the active monitor.

Computers that are ready to become the active monitor are called standby monitors. Like the active monitor, standby monitors also periodically advertise their presence (see Fig. 3-13). The standby monitor sends out a frame every 7 seconds, as opposed to the 3-second interval used for active monitor present frames.

We can see that in addition to data traffic, a typical token ring includes a variety of these AMP and SMP frames (see Fig. 3-14). The AMP and SMP frames also serve the important purpose of making sure that every computer knows the address of its upstream neighbor.

An AMP or SMP frame has a broadcast address, meaning every node will recognize its address and flip the address-recognized bit to 1. When the active monitor sends the AMP frame, it is sent with a 0 for the address-recognized bit. The immediate upstream neighbor sees that and therefore knows that the active monitor is its immediate neighbor.

The station stores the address of the upstream neighbor and then sends the AMP frame back out with the address-recognized bit flipped to 1. Later, that station, being a standby monitor, will send out its own broadcast SMP frame. This procedure allows a node's neighbor to learn its address, and is repeated until every node knows its neighbor.

If a standby monitor does not see an AMP frame periodically, it will suspect that the active monitor is no longer functioning properly. In this case, the standby monitor will send out a claim token frame. When the claim token is received through the ring, the sending station examines the source address on that frame. If the source address is its own, it has successfully claimed the token. The node then becomes the active monitor on the network and takes control of the token.

If the returned address in the packet is not its own, the station has lost the bid to become the active monitor. In this case, the node that has put its address into the claim token packet becomes the new bidder for active monitor status.

Error Recovery and Initialization

Figures 3-15 through 3-18 show a variety of special-purpose frames that can be found on a token ring. Figure 3-15, for example, is a ring purge. The purge is intended to clean the ring of any remaining data that is circulating. A purge is performed when an active monitor first takes over. After the purge, the active monitor issues a new token.

When a node joins the network, it sends out an initialization packet (see Fig. 3-16). This is used to check that compatible versions of hardware and software are being used and informs the upstream neighbor of its new address. That neighbor in turn reports a change in the stored upstream address (see Fig. 3-17).

Occasionally, a duplicate address may be present. This can be easily detected by a node sending out a frame with its own destination address (see Fig. 3-18). If the address-recognized bit is flipped when the frame comes back, another node must have the same address.

A common cause of a duplicate address is when, for some reason, the network manager uses locally assigned addresses instead of the unique address burned into the card. Figure 3-18 illustrates the resulting packet when this situation occurs. The solution to this problem is simple—use the unique addresses assigned with the controller.

A last type of frame that is occasionally seen is the beacon, which is sent out as the result of a serious failure, such as a jabbering station or a broken cable.

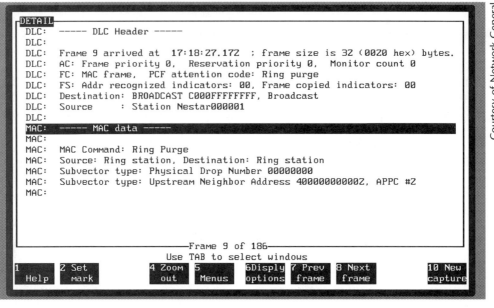

Fig. 3-15 Ring Purge Message

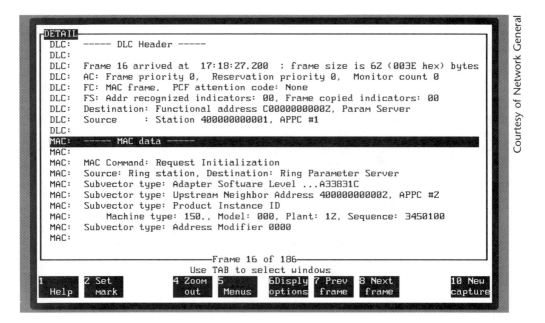

Fig. 3-16 Initialization Request

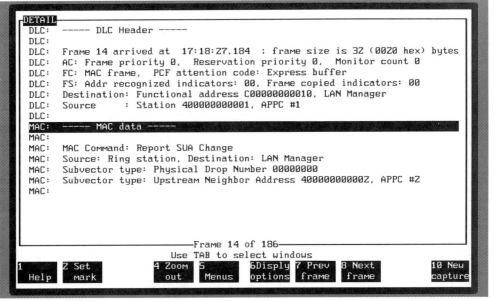

Fig. 3-17 Change of Address Message

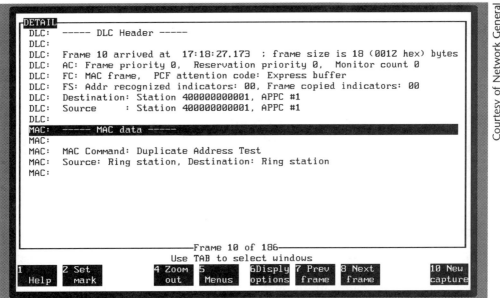

Fig. 3-18 Duplicate Address Test

For example, if a timer expires after a claim token frame is sent out, a station may suspect that there is a serious problem on the ring.

The beacon frame helps isolate the failure domain in the ring. If a node doesn't receive a claim token back, for example, it will start sending out beacons, one after another. If the ring is broken, the beacon will not be received back through the ring.

If a node gets a beacon, it examines the source address field and determines whether it is the sender or not. If it is not the sender, the beacon must have come upstream from another node closer to the failure. The original beaconing station will then stop issuing beacons and simply copy through the beacons received from its upstream neighbor.

This process continues until the node sending the beacon is the one closest to the failed station. This node will then continue sending beacons until the ring is fixed. Eventually, the ring will get fixed and the node will receive the beacon that it sent. At this point, the node closest to the failed station will try to claim the token and become the active monitor. Next, it will purge the ring and issue a new token. At this point the ring is back in operation.

Token Ring Extensions: 16 Mbps and FDDI

Two extensions of the token ring that offer increased performance are becoming available. IBM has issued a 16-Mbps version of the token ring. In addition to increased bandwidth, this version allows the token to be immediately put back on the ring after the data is sent. This means that the data doesn't have to circulate the whole ring before another packet of data can be sent.

The 16-Mbps version of the token ring can be used to upgrade an existing token ring installation. Or, it can be used to form a backbone network. Bridges or routers are used to connect the backbone network to each of the 4-Mbps workgroup networks.

The other token ring implementation is the Fiber Distributed Data Interface, which operates at 100 Mbps. FDDI's increased bandwidth is useful as a local area network for data-intensive operations, such as graphics. FDDI is especially useful as a corporate backbone. Local area networks, such as a 4- or 16-Mbps token ring or an Ethernet, would be connected to the FDDI backbone, which would be used to move data among networks.

Integrating Different Subnetworks

Figure 3-19 shows a configuration that has several different networks connected together. Notice that several computers are connected to two different networks. These communications servers, or routers, are used to move data between the different networks.

As far as the data link layer is concerned, this wider network is not apparent. The data link simply offers the service of sending the packet to another node on that network. If that node is a router, it may take the packet and retransmit it out another data link.

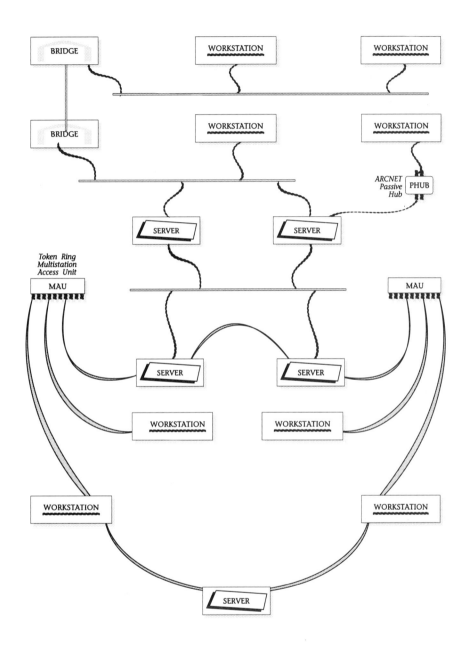

Fig. 3-19 Extended Series of Data Links

We will see in the next chapter that this routing of packets is the responsibility of the network layer. Programs on the network rarely interact directly with the data link layer. Instead, a message is sent to the network layer that has an internetwork address.

The network layer is responsible for deciding which router will handle this packet. It takes the packet with the internetwork address of the eventual destination and sends it over the data link to the router.

The router sees that the packet has not reached its final destination and again encapsulates the packet (puts an IPX envelope around it) and sends it over the next data link and so on until it reaches its eventual destination.

Key Points in This Chapter

- ARCNET is a proprietary data link standard developed by Datapoint. It uses a star topology and a token passing algorithm.
- An ARCNET can have up to 255 nodes and operates at 2.5 Mbps. ARCNET Plus operates at 20 Mbps.
- ARCNET nodes are connected together with passive, active, intelligent, or fiber hubs.
- ARCNET gaurantees the delivery of data at the data link level by making a Free Buffer Enquiry before sending the data. The data is then acknowledged.
- The ARCNET fragmentation layer allows the network layer to send packets longer than the 508-byte ARCNET maximum.
- Token ring is an IEEE standard operating at 4 Mbps. IBM has developed a 16-Mbps version of token ring.
- Token ring stations can be connected to each other or use a multistation access unit (MAU) as a concentrator.
- There is a wide variety of packets in a token ring network that regulate the operation of the ring and who can send.

CHAPTER 4

IPX and SPX

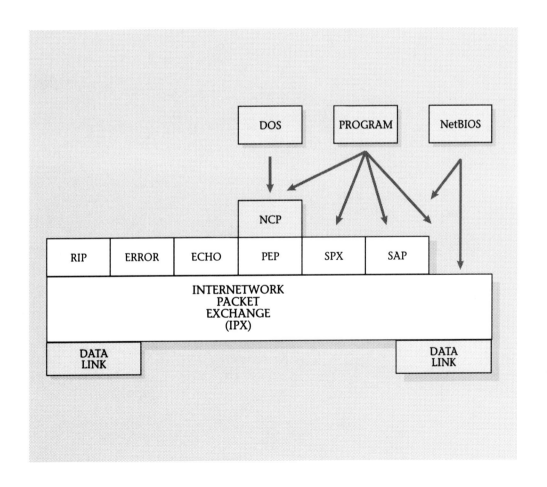

CHAPTER 4

IPX and SPX

The Network and Transport Layers

The previous two chapters described different methods of allowing computers to exchange data with one another. Both of these computers shared a common data link—Ethernet, ARCNET, or token ring. Using techniques like MAC-layer bridges, it is possible to have a single data link with many nodes. For a variety of reasons, however, a particular network—the computers maintained by one group of people—may outgrow the capacity of a single LAN. First, there may be too many computers to fit into a single LAN. For example, a single ARCNET is limited to 255 nodes.

Second, the complexity of the network may make a single LAN unworkable. For example, an organization may have sites in many different places in the city. Wide area bridges might allow the connection of all these LANs together, but the number of bridges involved could quickly become a confusing tangle of connections. As we will see, we can connect several different LANs together into a simple group called an internetwork.

Third, the broadcast nature of a LAN may make performance an issue as the number of nodes and the complexity of the applications that those nodes use grows. In a single network, the bandwidth available is limited. If nodes are performing tasks such as booting off the network, exchanging graphics images, or doing large file transfers (e.g., backing up over the network), that bandwidth can be used up long before the theoretical limit on the number of nodes has been reached.

Segmenting networks based on their physical proximity and the locality of reference (who they communicate with) is one way to allow increasingly complex configurations to be reached. If two nodes are typically communicating with each other, as in the case of a computer that prints over the network to the laser printer in the next office, it makes sense to isolate those nodes into a single data link.

The network layer of the architecture is where different LANs or stand-alone computers are connected together. The network layer is a software module that uses the services of the data link layer to send data over a particular LAN. Each of the three LANs discussed in the previous chapters basically offers the same service—sending and receiving data to another node specified by their address on that network.

The goal of the network layer is to provide a more sophisticated service to its users. The network layer provides the service of sending a packet of data to any computer in a collection of networks, or an internetwork.

The data link frees its users of having to know about how to use a particular kind of network. The network layer frees its users of a more complex problem, knowing the different routes needed to get from one network to another. To accomplish its tasks, the network layer has to concern itself with two issues. First, there has to be a different kind of address to differentiate nodes that reside on different data links. Knowing which network a node resides on lets the network layer distinguish between two instances of the same local address (i.e., two ARCNET nodes with an address of 254). It also gives the network layer a way to make a routing decision, the process by which the packet will be delivered.

The network layer preserves the local address of each node so that nodes will not have to look up the address before submitting a packet to the data link. The network layer then adds another address—the network address. The full address of a node is now the network address plus the local address on that network.

The second thing the network layer does is to keep itself apprised of the different routes available to reach a particular network in the internetwork. Nodes that know about the topology of the network are known as routers. Not every node on a network is a router.

When a nonrouter wants to send data to a node on another network, it sends the packet to a local router. That router will consult its routing tables and forward the packet to another computer. The packet will continue to be forwarded until it reaches the destination network. At that point, the router on the destination network will forward the packet to the destination node.

Now we have the capability to send a packet to any other node on the network, but two important things have not yet been provided. First, there is no way to identify a particular software program that is on the destination node. Second, there is no guarantee that the packet has reached its destination.

Both of these issues are the concern of the transport layer of the network. The transport layer is responsible for the maintenance of logical connections on the network—communications between two entities on two different computers. The transport layer is also responsible, to varying degrees, for the orderly, guaranteed transmission of data over the network.

This chapter looks at how a Novell-based network performs these tasks. At the network layer, Novell provides the IPX protocols. At the transport layer, Novell uses two different types of protocols, each offering a different level of service to its clients.

We will also examine a variety of other protocols that are used for maintenance of the internetwork. The Routing Information Protocol (RIP), for example, is used for the maintenance of routing tables. The Service Advertisement Protocol is used to advertise the presence of network resources, such as printers, database management systems, communications servers, and any other resource that an organization chooses to make available.

XNS and Novell

The Novell networking protocols are derived from the Xerox Network System (XNS), devised at the Xerox Palo Alto Research Center (PARC). XNS forms the basis for several popular networks, including Banyan's VINES, 3Com's 3+, and several specialized environments, such as Metaphor's products, which combine workstations and file servers into an integrated network.

XNS defines a series of protocols that cover the network through the application layers. Like many network architectures, the data links are incorporated by reference—vendors have supported a wide variety of data links including Ethernet, ARCNET, token ring, X.25 wide area networks, and asynchronous links (such as modems over telephone lines).

Novell has taken the bottom portion of this network architecture and incorporated it into their own. The network layer of XNS, the Internetwork Datagram Protocol (IDP), has been adopted by Novell and renamed the Internetwork Packet Exchange (IPX). As we will see, it is virtually identical to the Xerox protocol.

Novell also uses variants of the two transport layer protocols supported in XNS, the Sequenced Packet Protocol and the Packet Exchange Protocol. As we will see, PEP offers a lower degree of service than SPP (or Novell's version, which is the Sequenced Packet Exchange, or SPX).

Several upper-layer protocols in XNS have not been adopted by Novell. For example, XNS defines a Clearinghouse protocol, which is used for finding names of servers on the network. Novell has instead developed their own Service Advertisement Protocol, which is closely tied in with the Novell file servers.

There are many document exchange and printing capabilities in XNS that have not been implemented in Novell networks. In some cases, equivalent protocols have been adopted by users. For example, PostScript is often used as a printing protocol in a Novell network instead of the Interpress standard used in a complete implementation of XNS.

Novell has also not adopted the XNS Mail Transport Protocol, instead having used the Message Handling Service from Action Technologies. For remote procedure calls, Novell has adopted Netwise's Remote Procedure Call instead of Xerox's Courier protocols.

This is not to say that it was not good for Novell to adopt only a portion of the XNS protocol stack. Very few vendors have implemented true versions of XNS for their systems. Instead, XNS forms the foundation layer—the topics discussed in this chapter—for building network-based services, such as access to data, printers, or communications resources.

One of the primary reasons that the upper-layer services from XNS were not implemented more widely is that advanced services like Clearinghouse and Interpress were not published until several years after the basic services were defined.

IPX

Novell's Internetwork Packet Exchange (IPX) is a derivative of Xerox's Internetwork Datagram Protocol (IDP). In fact, at the network layer, IPX is almost identical with IDP. The basic service provided by this layer is the forwarding of packets.

A Novell node can be a router or a nonrouter (known sometimes as an endnode). Nonrouters are usually workstations. Some servers are routers. If a network has only one server, and it is connected to another networks, the server will double as a router.

A router is a computer that provides routing services. When a node routes packets among different network, Novell calls it a bridge. Care should be taken in distinguishing the Novell meaning of a bridge from the more widely adopted term that refers to a MAC-layer bridge, discussed in Chapter 2.

Why worry about the distinction? After all, both the MAC-layer bridge and the router perform the service of forwarding a packet from one network to the next. The difference, as we shall see, is that a router is able to make more intelligent routing decisions than the MAC-layer bridge, which is simply a store-and-forward device. The router does so, of course, at the expense of the performance that the MAC-layer bridge can provide. Many networks have both types of devices installed.

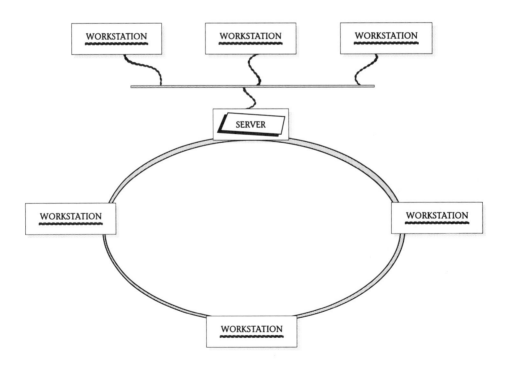

Fig. 4-1 A Small Internetwork

Figure 4-1 illustrates a small internetwork. Notice that the network has both a token ring and an Ethernet. A server is connected to both computers. If this router sees a packet meant for the other network, it will gather the message from the original network and send it to the next.

Each computer on this internetwork has an internetwork address, composed of a network number and a local address on that network. The router actually has two addresses, one for each network on which it resides.

The local address is whichever address the node had before it joined the internetwork. In the case of an Ethernet node, the local portion of the address is the 48-bit address assigned when the card was manufactured. In the case of an ARCNET, the local address is somewhere between 1 and 255.

Keeping the local address the same makes it easy to switch networks. The network address is easily configurable in software, allowing a node to join a new network quickly.

A workstation, a nonrouter, has a simple version of IPX. When IPX sees an address that is not on the local network, it sends the packet to a designated router. In Figure 4-1, this would be the server. The workstation has no knowledge of how to get to any nodes on another network.

The server version of IPX accepts the incoming packet from the data link layer (Ethernet) and examines the IPX header. It sees that the address in the IPX header is different from the address in the data link layer header, meaning that the packet must be forwarded.

The server checks its routing directory and sees that the destination network is the token ring. Since the token ring is local to the server, it sends the packet directly to the destination node.

In some networks, the destination address could be several networks, or hops, away. If this were the case, the server would check the routing directory and find out which router was handling services for that destination network. Eventually, the packet would reach the destination network and be delivered to the host.

Sockets

IPX provides its services to programs at a higher layer through the use of a socket (see Fig. 4-2). A socket is just the address of a higher-level program that is using the services of IPX. This is similar to the local service address that a data link service uses to distinguish among its users.

In order for a client of IPX to communicate with its peer, it needs to know three things. First, it needs to know the network number of the remote host. Next, it needs the local address on that remote network. Third, it needs to know the socket number of the remote program with which it is communicating.

Let us assume for the time being that we know the address of a remote program with which we wish to communicate. We will see later that the Service Advertisement Protocol is used to find out what that address is.

Figure 4-3 shows an IPX packet on a network. Notice that both the source and destination addresses in the IPX portion of the packet include a network

84 Analyzing Novell Networks

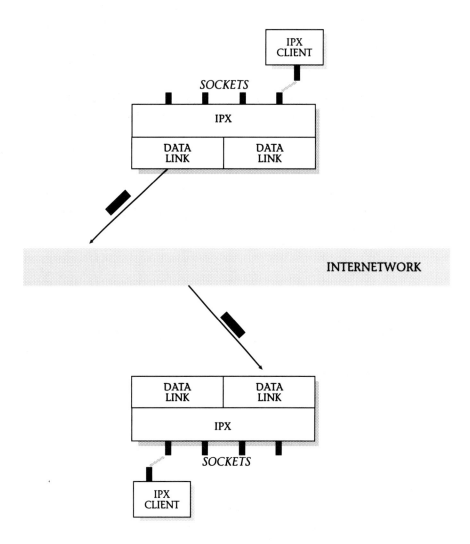

Fig. 4-2 IPX Sockets

number, host number, and socket number and that the IPX header (denoted as *XNS* on the screen) comes after the Ethernet header. A node has two different addresses: a network layer address plus an address on the data link. In almost all cases, the local address of the host on a data link corresponds to the local host portion of the internetwork address.

Incidentally, the data link layer (labeled *DLC* on the screen) is the 802.3 version of Ethernet. Normally, the packet would have a Logical Link Control header after the Medium Access Control layer. Instead, the IPX packet comes directly after the MAC layer. This is an artifact of the way Novell has chosen to use Ethernet. This nonstandard use of the Ethernet can be changed by using

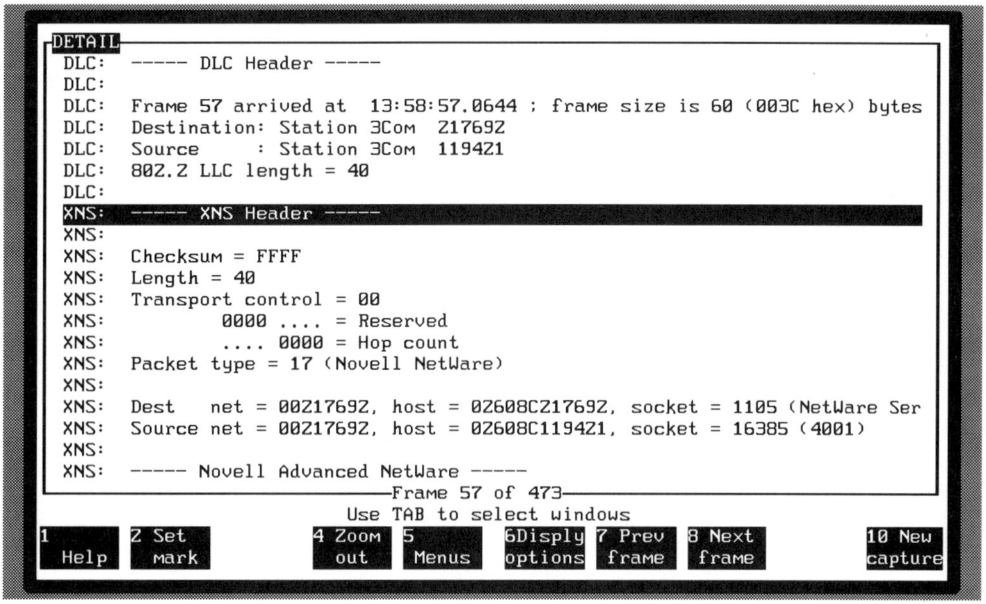

```
┌DETAIL─────────────────────────────────────────────────────────────────┐
│  DLC:  ----- DLC Header -----                                         │
│  DLC:                                                                 │
│  DLC:  Frame 57 arrived at  13:58:57.0644 ; frame size is 60 (003C hex) bytes │
│  DLC:  Destination: Station 3Com   217692                             │
│  DLC:  Source     : Station 3Com   119421                             │
│  DLC:  802.2 LLC length = 40                                          │
│  DLC:                                                                 │
│  XNS:  ----- XNS Header -----                                         │
│  XNS:                                                                 │
│  XNS:  Checksum = FFFF                                                │
│  XNS:  Length = 40                                                    │
│  XNS:  Transport control = 00                                         │
│  XNS:         0000 .... = Reserved                                    │
│  XNS:         .... 0000 = Hop count                                   │
│  XNS:  Packet type = 17 (Novell NetWare)                              │
│  XNS:                                                                 │
│  XNS:  Dest   net = 00217692, host = 02608C217692, socket = 1105 (NetWare Ser │
│  XNS:  Source net = 00217692, host = 02608C119421, socket = 16385 (4001)      │
│  XNS:                                                                 │
│  XNS:  ----- Novell Advanced NetWare -----                            │
│                            ─Frame 57 of 473─                          │
│                      Use TAB to select windows                        │
│  ┌─┐ ┌─────┐       ┌─────┐ ┌─────┐ ┌────────┐ ┌──────┐ ┌──────┐ ┌───────┐ │
│  │1│ │2 Set│       │4 Zoom│ │5    │ │6Disply │ │7 Prev│ │8 Next│ │10 New │ │
│  │Help│ │mark │    │ out │ │Menus│ │options│ │frame │ │frame │ │capture│ │
│  └─┘ └─────┘       └─────┘ └─────┘ └────────┘ └──────┘ └──────┘ └───────┘ │
└───────────────────────────────────────────────────────────────────────┘
```

Fig. 4-3 An IPX Header

the Novell ECONFIG utility to force the standard use of the protocols. This step would only be necessary if this network were being shared with other Ethernet users—LAN Manager, 3Com, DECnet, or TCP/IP, for example.

In addition to the source and destination addresses, Figure 4-3 shows that the IPX header also includes four other fields. First, there is a checksum field, which is used to make sure that there were no transmission errors in the packet. IPX regenerates the checksum from the data received and compares it to the checksum in the packet.

The checksum only catches certain kinds of errors, like a packet that was not properly constructed by the sending IPX process. Lost packets, out-of-sequence packets, bad addresses, and other errors must be detected by higher layers of the network.

One interesting note on the checksum in Figure 4-3 is that, in this particular example, the checksum has been disabled. A checksum of FFFF is how the protocol indicates that a checksum is not being performed. Since this packet is staying on a single Ethernet, which is relatively error-free, packets don't necessarily need the checksum.

The length field tells IPX how long the data in this packet is. The length field is for the IPX data—the data link control fields, such as a pad or header, are not included in this calculation. In theory, an IPX packet can be only 576 bytes, but in reality a packet is only limited by the size of the data link packet.

When sending data on an Ethernet, for example, it is not uncommon to see packets of 1024 bytes carrying IPX data. However, when a router accepts a packet for forwarding, it does enforce the limit. Within a network, the limit is

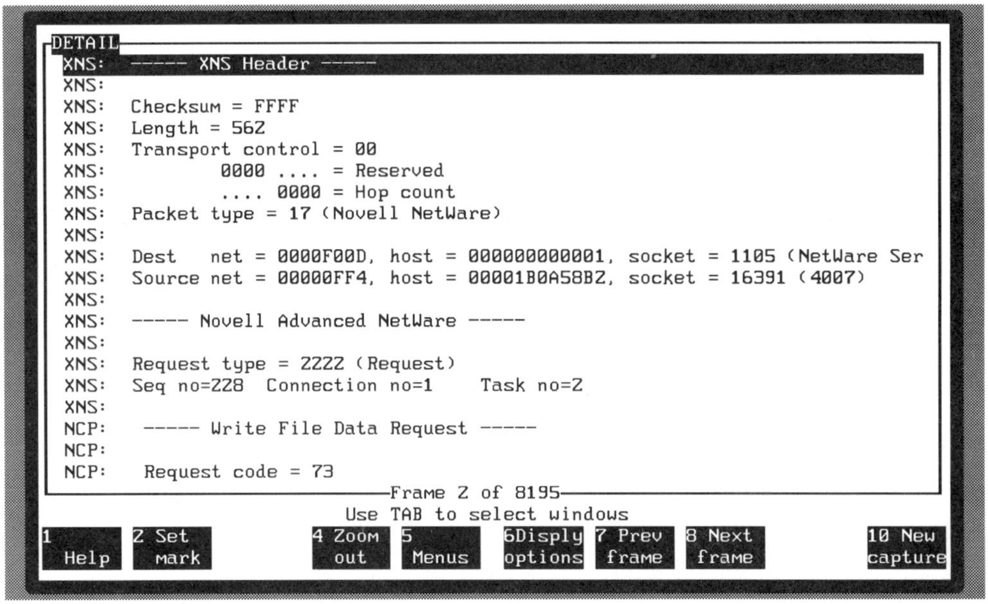

86   Analyzing Novell Networks

```
DETAIL
   XNS:  ----- XNS Header -----
   XNS:
   XNS:  Checksum = FFFF
   XNS:  Length = 562
   XNS:  Transport control = 00
   XNS:        0000 .... = Reserved
   XNS:        .... 0000 = Hop count
   XNS:  Packet type = 17 (Novell NetWare)
   XNS:
   XNS:  Dest  net = 0000F00D, host = 000000000001, socket = 1105 (NetWare Ser
   XNS:  Source net = 00000FF4, host = 00001B0A58B2, socket = 16391 (4007)
   XNS:
   XNS:  ----- Novell Advanced NetWare -----
   XNS:
   XNS:  Request type = 2222 (Request)
   XNS:  Seq no=228   Connection no=1     Task no=2
   XNS:
   NCP:  ----- Write File Data Request -----
   NCP:
   NCP:  Request code = 73
                               ─Frame 2 of 8195─
                        Use TAB to select windows
 1       2 Set           4 Zoom  5        6Disply  7 Prev  8 Next         10 New
 Help    mark            out     Menus    options  frame   frame          capture
```
Courtesy of Network General

Fig. 4-4 Data Carried by the IPX Packet

unenforced. Over the internetwork, it is enforced, meaning that the packet would be truncated before forwarding.

The transport control field is used to indicate how many hops a packet has gone through. Each time a packet gets forwarded by a router, that is a hop. The packet in Figure 4-3 has not been forwarded, thus the hop count of 0.

The last field before the address is the packet type. Xerox has assigned a variety of different predefined packet types. When an IDP implementation in XNS receives a packet, it looks at the packet type to decide what type of packet this is. For example, a routing error would be signaled by sending a packet of type error to the well-known socket used by RIP.

Figure 4-3 showed that this particular IPX user is Novell's NetWare. Figure 4-4 shows how IPX is carrying data for the NetWare Core Protocols (NCP), which in turn is transmitting a write file data request. We will see later in this chapter there are other users of the IPX services, such as the RIP, Error, SPX, and Echo protocols.

Usually, most of the traffic on a Novell network will be just the NetWare Core Protocols. Figure 4-5 shows some typical traffic on such a network. Notice that all the traffic is Ethernet, followed by the XNS portion of the packet. Since IPX and IDP are identical, the Sniffer Network Analyzer is pooling those together as one type of header. Next, there are a variety of NetWare Core Protocol messages carried in these packets. The traffic is in the nature of a request followed by a reply. In this example, the workstation is attempting to verify a user's password.

Figure 4-6 shows a more complex network topology. Let's say that a workstation on the Ethernet wants to communicate with a workstation on the ARCNET.

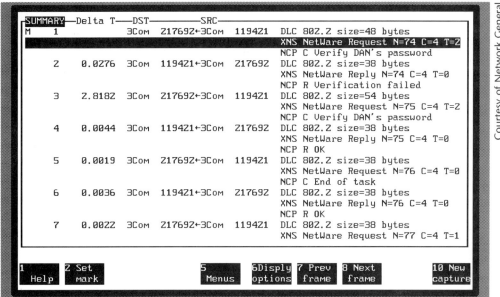

Fig. 4-5 Typical IPX Traffic

In order to do so, the workstation must know two things: the network address of the ARCNET node and the local token ring address of the router.

The router will examine the incoming packet and see that to reach the destination network it must send it to the second server on the token ring, which in turn must send the packet across the second Ethernet to another server. Finally, the packet is sent through the ARCNET to the destination workstation.

IPX provides a best-effort delivery of a packet of data across an internetwork, which means that the packet may or may not get there—there is a possibility that the packet will be lost. It is possible that the packet will be duplicated while traveling through the network, and the receiving user will get the packet twice.

For example, let's say that the packet made it through the token ring. The server there sees that the packet must make it through the Ethernet. It therefore broadcasts the packet with the address of the second server on the Ethernet. If that server has just received many different packets, its Ethernet controller could be "deaf" because all the receive buffers are full.

At this point the packet is lost. The first server on the Ethernet thought the packet went out successfully because it did not see a collision. The second server doesn't know it didn't receive the packet, so the packet is now lost. This type of situation will not happen very often, but it is certainly possible.

If a receiver becomes "deaf" on an Ethernet, neither the data link nor the network layers will detect the problem. The transport layer, before sending data on down the protocol stack, assigns each packet a sequence number. At the

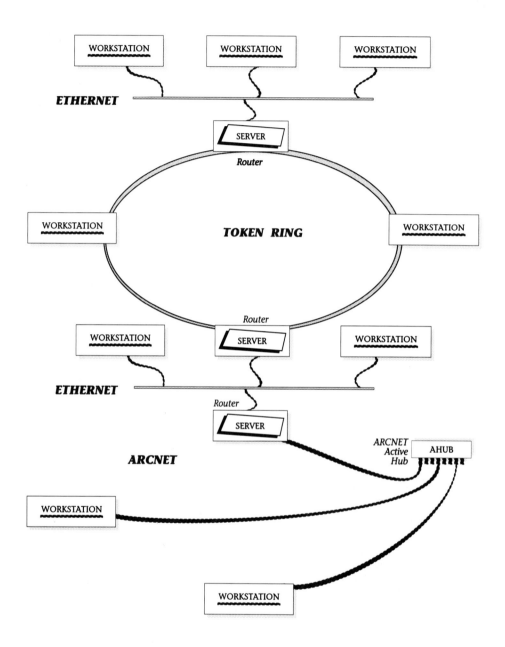

Fig. 4-6 Three Data Links in an Internetwork

Fig. 4-7 Routing Information Protocol

receiving end, the transport module will notice that one or more sequence numbers are missing and request retransmission.

Now, take a more extreme example. What if the Ethernet cable is cut? Not only will the current packet not be deliverable, but neither will future packets. This problem raises the question of an alternate route to deliver the packet. If there is an alternate route, the routers will update their routing directories so that future packets will use the alternate route.

If there is no alternate route available, the ARCNET has in effect become unreachable—it is no longer part of the internetwork. The routers will update their routing directories to show that the destination network is an infinite number of hops away.

RIP and the Internet

The Routing Information Protocol (RIP) uses the services of IPX to allow routing nodes to exchange information and update their routing directories (see Fig. 4-7). RIP is an example of a mainenance protocol, which is a service hidden from users (such as database or messaging systems) of the network.

Other services, such as SPX, SAP, and the NetWare Core Protocols, are also users of IPX and in turn offer services to other users. These support protocols will often be visible to the program using the network, if not directly to the end user.

RIP is used to maintain the routing table for a router. The routing table has four entries:

- Destination network
- Router port
- Intermediate node
- Hop count

Each remote network that a router knows about has an entry in this table. The router port indicates which data link on this router is to be used to reach that destination network. The intermediate node is the local address on the data link indicated by the router port. The local address is the router that will in turn forward the packet on through the internetwork.

The hop count indicates how many networks away the destination network is. A hop count of 16 indicates that the destination network is unreachable; the maximum hop limit of 15 for an active network is not really a limitation. Fifteen hops away would mean going through 15 different LAN or wide area links, which is more than enough for almost any network configuration.

The hop count is a crude indicator of how long it will take to route a packet to the destination network. Based on information coming in from the RIP protocols, the hop count indicates the best available current path to the destination network.

Figures 4-8 and 4-9 show an exchange of RIP packets on a network being used to update the routing table of a router. Figure 4-8 is the RIP request that is being sent to find the location of network 5. Notice that the destination and source networks in the XNS header are set to 0, indicating that the packet is only being circulated on the current network (data link).

The destination host for this packet is an address consisting of all Fs, which means a broadcast. The destination socket is 1107, which is the socket always used by the Novell version of RIP. Thus, any host that has a RIP socket active on this particular network will accept the RIP request.

The reply, shown in Figure 4-9, has the source and destination networks filled out in the XNS header (which is IPX). In this case, the source and destination addresses for the packet are filled out to 5. This indicates that both hosts are on network 5, which also happens to be the network requested. What happened here is that a host did not know what network number it was on. If a host is only communicating across one data link and not over the internetwork, it doesn't need to know what network it is on.

The hop count for the object network in Figure 4-9 is set to 1. In other words, for a computer on network 5 to communicate with another computer on network 5, it will take one hop for the message to go through. If there had been one intervening router, the hop count would be set to 2 and so on up to the maximum of 15.

The RIP reply in Figure 4-9 is a directed RIP reply—it is destined for a specific destination host. In addition, if a node is maintaining a routing table, it will periodically broadcast that information. The RIP broadcast includes the network number of any hosts that this router can reach and the hop count. The hop count in the routing directory is incremented by 1 for this broadcast. A node that receives this RIP broadcast will first have to send it to the router, then on through the internetwork for the indicated number of hops.

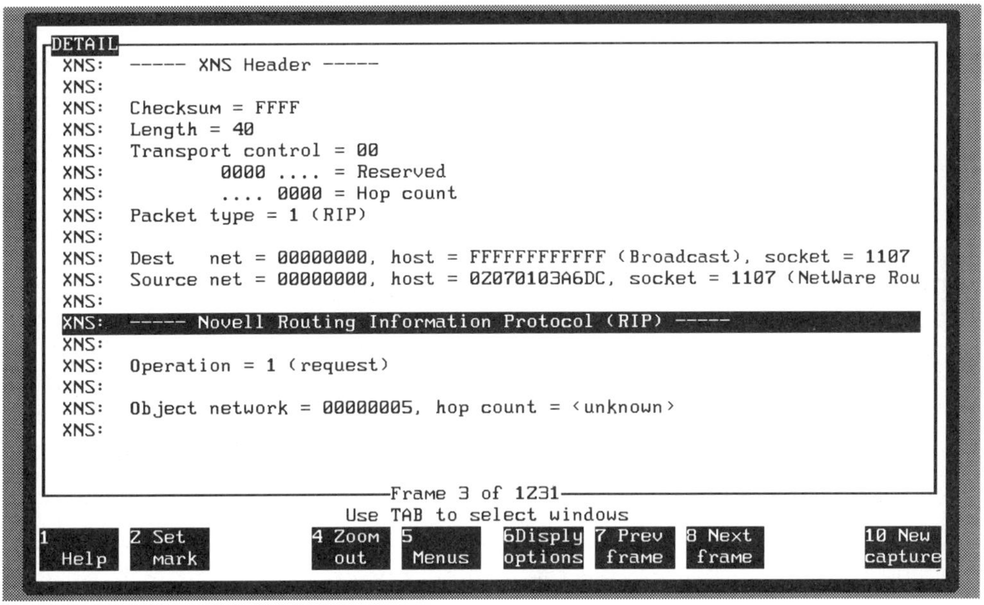

```
 DETAIL
  XNS:  ----- XNS Header -----
  XNS:
  XNS:  Checksum = FFFF
  XNS:  Length = 40
  XNS:  Transport control = 00
  XNS:          0000 .... = Reserved
  XNS:          .... 0000 = Hop count
  XNS:  Packet type = 1 (RIP)
  XNS:
  XNS:  Dest   net = 00000000, host = FFFFFFFFFFFF (Broadcast), socket = 1107
  XNS:  Source net = 00000000, host = 02070103A6DC, socket = 1107 (NetWare Rou
  XNS:
  XNS:  ----- Novell Routing Information Protocol (RIP) -----
  XNS:
  XNS:  Operation = 1 (request)
  XNS:
  XNS:  Object network = 00000005, hop count = <unknown>
  XNS:

                          Frame 3 of 1231
                       Use TAB to select windows
  1       2 Set          4 Zoom  5       6Disply  7 Prev  8 Next         10 New
  Help    mark           out     Menus   options  frame   frame          capture
```

Fig. 4-8 RIP Request

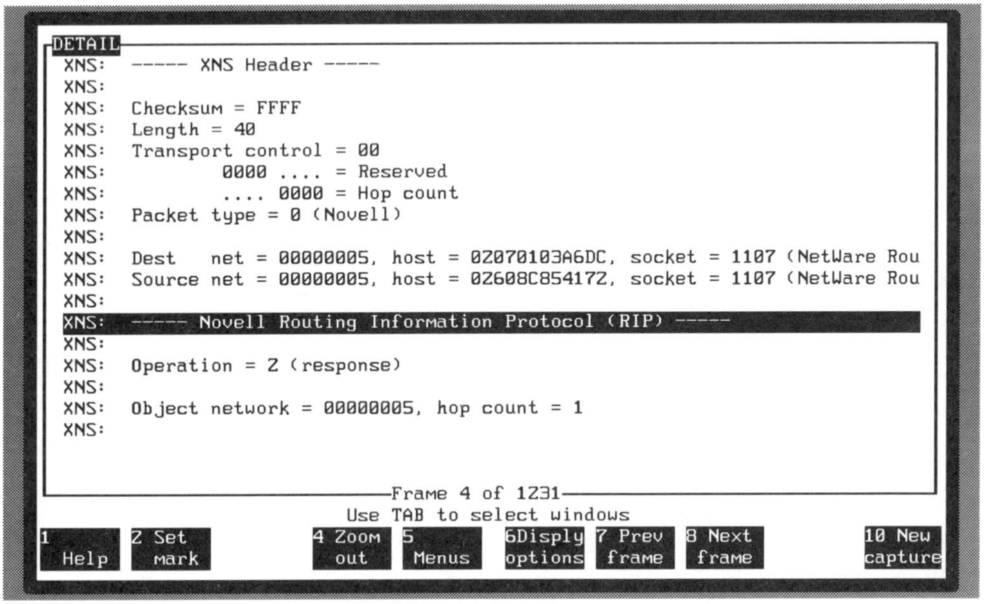

```
 DETAIL
  XNS:  ----- XNS Header -----
  XNS:
  XNS:  Checksum = FFFF
  XNS:  Length = 40
  XNS:  Transport control = 00
  XNS:          0000 .... = Reserved
  XNS:          .... 0000 = Hop count
  XNS:  Packet type = 0 (Novell)
  XNS:
  XNS:  Dest   net = 00000005, host = 02070103A6DC, socket = 1107 (NetWare Rou
  XNS:  Source net = 00000005, host = 02608C854172, socket = 1107 (NetWare Rou
  XNS:
  XNS:  ----- Novell Routing Information Protocol (RIP) -----
  XNS:
  XNS:  Operation = 2 (response)
  XNS:
  XNS:  Object network = 00000005, hop count = 1
  XNS:

                          Frame 4 of 1231
                       Use TAB to select windows
  1       2 Set          4 Zoom  5       6Disply  7 Prev  8 Next         10 New
  Help    mark           out     Menus   options  frame   frame          capture
```

Fig. 4-9 RIP Reply

When a router receives a RIP packet, it examines the object network portion of the packet (there may be several listed). If it sees an object network already in its routing table, it compares the information. If the host sending the RIP packet is the same as the intermediate host indicated in the routing table, this is an update of the old routing information.

For an update, the router looks at the hop count to see if it has changed. For example, the hop count may be 16, indicating that the router that sent the RIP broadcast can no longer reach the destination network.

If the RIP broadcast contains a new network, that information will be added to the routing table, allowing this router to now forward packets to that destination network.

The last possibility is that there is a network already listed in the table, but the node that sent the RIP broadcast is different from the one listed as the intermediate node in the routing table. This indicates that there is an alternate path to the destination network. The router will check the hop count and see if this alternate path is quicker than the one listed. If so, it will update the routing table to indicate that another router should be used to reach the destination network.

A node sends a RIP broadcast every 60 seconds in a Novell network. In an XNS network, this broadcast is sent every 30 seconds. Thus, in a Novell network, every router that is one hop away from the sender of the RIP broadcast will know the state of the sender's routing table. This enables the recipients to update their routing tables, which they in turn will broadcast periodically. In this way, any changes in the network topology are gradually propagated throughout the network.

What happens, however, when a router ceases to operate? Each entry in the routing table has a timer associated with it, indicating when it was last updated. If a node sees that a particular entry has not been updated (typically for 90 seconds), the router that is providing this service is out of operation.

When the timer expires, the hop count is changed to 16 for the destination network. Just in case the service failure was temporary, the entry will still be kept in the routing table for another 90 seconds (these numbers vary among different RIP implementations). This ensures that the information that the destination network is unreachable will be broadcast to neighboring routers. After the second 90 seconds expire, the destination network is deleted from the routing table.

RIP uses what is known as a flat network topology. Every router must know how to get to every other network on the internetwork. Just as knowing how to get to every node is no longer feasible as the number of nodes grows, so is knowing every network as the internetwork grows. For this reason, Xerox stipulated in the XNS architecture that this routing methodology is unsuitable for complex network topologies.

Networks such as DECnet use a hierarchical routing system in which collections of networks are grouped together into domains. A local router knows how to get to all networks within a domain. If a packet is destined for another domain, a second level of router is given the packet. That router will send it to the destination domain, where it will be routed to the destination network and finally to the destination node.

It is important to note that a complex topology will not be necessary, or desirable, in some environments. For local computing, such as accessing disk drives or databases, IPX is essentially a null layer, since all hosts are one hop away. For most computing, the user will use local resources.

The more complex topology becomes necessary to connect the environments together. Most traffic is localized, but occasionally messages need to traverse the boundaries of the internetwork. Sending electronic mail, accessing a remote database, or logging on to a remote computer are all examples of this occasional need.

The Error and Echo Protocols

Error and Echo are two additional protocols that make use of the services of IPX (see Fig. 4-10). The protocols are used by other programs for internal maintenance. The error protocol is used to tell a destination socket that there has been an error in a particular operation. Echo is used to test that the path to a given destination is working properly.

We saw that the IPX header included two types of destination information. First, there was a packet type. Second, there was a destination socket. This information may seem somewhat redundant, since the destination socket is the one that always receives the incoming packet.

When IPX receives an incoming packet, it sends it up to the destination socket, along with the packet type. For normal operations, the RIP socket always expects to get a packet of type 1: a RIP packet. The NetWare Core Proto-

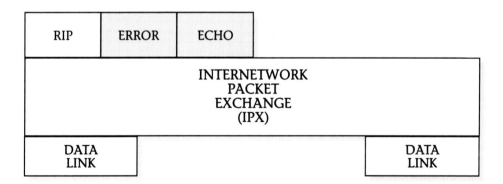

Fig. 4-10 Error and Echo Protocols

cols, which operate on socket 1105, normally expect to get a packet type of 17, which is the NetWare Core Protocols packet type.

If the client sees another packet type, it knows that this is an unusual condition and should be handled differently. If the packet type is 2, it is an echo packet. A packet type of 3 is an error packet.

For example, the NetWare Core Protocols may wish to communicate with a foreign node. It will send a request down to IPX, indicating the destination address and the remote node. Normally, it expects to get a packet back from its peer, the NetWare Core Protocols on the destination node. When this packet is received at the router, it will check its routing directory. If the destination network is unreachable or nonexistent, it will be unable to send the packet. It will then send an error packet back to the sending node, indicating that the destination network is unreachable. The NCP module can then handle the situation as it wishes. One strategy would be to immediately tell its client that the destination network is unreachable. Another strategy would be to try sending the packet several more times before notifying the user.

Note that there is no guarantee that NCP will receive this error message. The fact that the destination network is unreachable may not yet be reflected in the router's directory. The router would then send the packet out anyway. Even if an error message is sent, there is no guarantee that it will reach its destination—the receiving Ethernet controller may be deaf, for example.

Both Error and Echo are very general protocols, with most of the interpretation of the contents left up to the programs that are receiving the packets. To generate an echo packet, for example, the user program simply submits any normal packet to IPX but sets the type flag to "echo." The remote node, on receiving the packet, will simply echo it back instead of processing it.

An error packet is equally simple, allowing it to be used for a wide variety of situations. The error packet consists of the IPX header plus an error number, an error parameter, and a portion of the offending packet. Although a few error numbers (such as *packet too large*) are defined, most are left up to the interpretation of the sending and receiving programs. If RIP sees an incoming error packet, it may interpret it differently than NCP does.

It is customary to include at least 42 bytes of the offending data. This allows the 30-byte IPX header plus 12 bytes of the next layer's header to be included in the error message, allowing the receiving program to determine which of its packets caused the problem.

NetWare Core Protocols

The prime user of IPX in a Novell network is the NetWare Core Protocols. NCP allows the user to access remote data, print files, and perform other basic operations. NCP uses a primitive form of transport protocol based on the Packet Exchange Protocol (PEP) in XNS (see Fig. 4-11). The reader will not see PEP referred to in Novell literature. The protocol is there, but is considered to be a part of NCP. This is contrast to SPX, another transport layer protocol, which provides a general-purpose interface to a wide variety of clients.

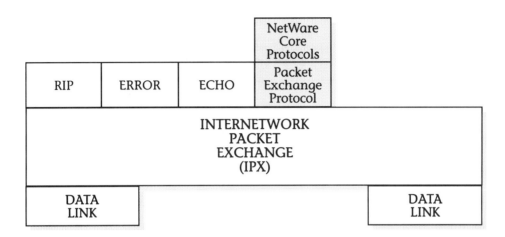

Fig. 4-11 Novell Core Protocols

NCP allows a user to create a connection to a server. Figures 4-12 and 4-13 show the establishment of such a connection. In this exchange of traffic, the workstation first looked for its address using RIP. Once it had its local address, it sent out a message to create a connection to a server. This connection request includes a buffer negotiation period. Notice that the two nodes have agreed on a buffer size of 1024, meaning that they are directly connected on the same network.

We don't know with which node the workstation is communicating from these two illustrations. The packets are being exchanged by two computers with Ethernet cards manufactured by 3Com and Interlan. It could be that the 3Com node is a router and is forwarding the packets on to another network. We would have to examine the IPX portion of the header to determine which nodes are communicating at this upper layer.

The server NCP program may have several connections active, one to each workstation. In addition, the workstation may have several active connections. NCP assigns a connection identification to each connection it is maintaining. The connection ID may be different on each side of the connection.

Figures 4-14 and 4-15 illustrate the basic operation of NCP. Each packet coming into the NCP socket contains four pieces of information that help identify the operation. The connection number indicates which of the connections that NCP is maintaining should work with this packet.

The request type indicates whether this packet is a request or a response. NCP operates on a ping-pong principle. A node sends a request, which is an-

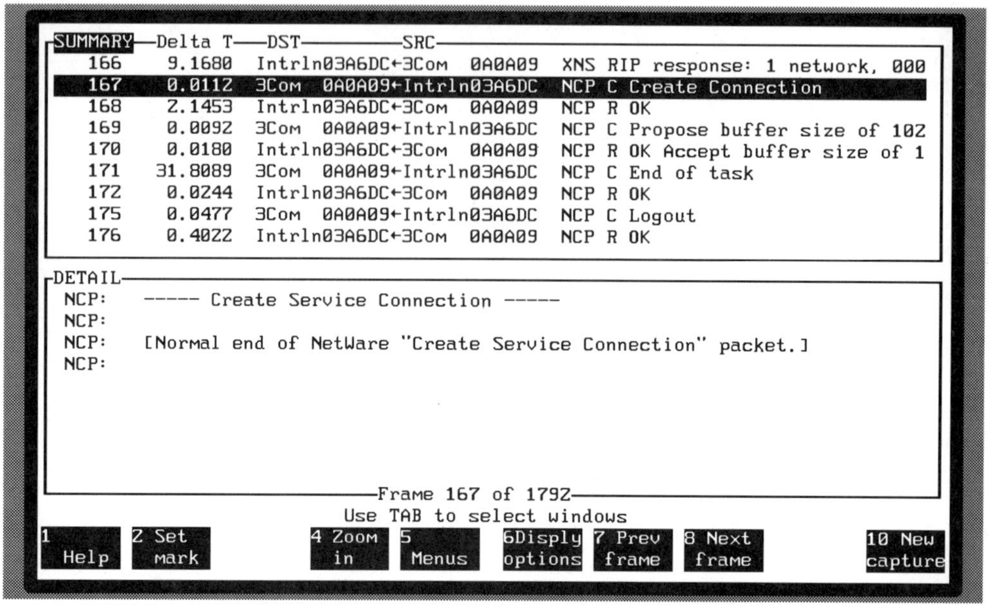

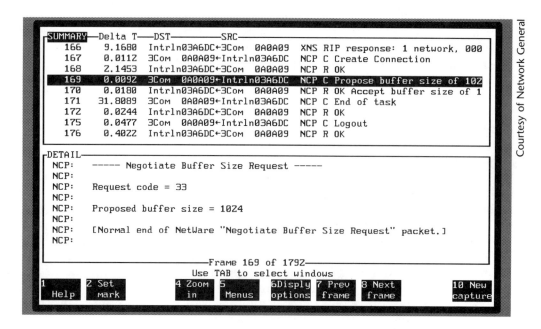

Fig. 4-12 Create Connection Request

Fig. 4-13 Buffer Size Negotiation

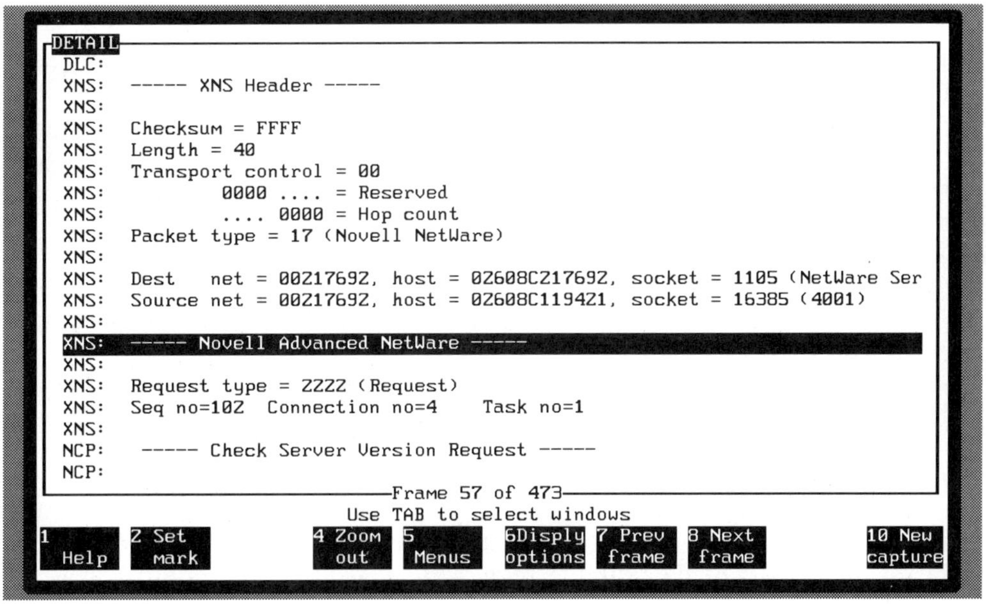

```
DETAIL
 DLC:
 XNS:  ----- XNS Header -----
 XNS:
 XNS:  Checksum = FFFF
 XNS:  Length = 40
 XNS:  Transport control = 00
 XNS:        0000 .... = Reserved
 XNS:        .... 0000 = Hop count
 XNS:  Packet type = 17 (Novell NetWare)
 XNS:
 XNS:  Dest   net = 0021769Z, host = 02608C21769Z, socket = 1105 (NetWare Ser
 XNS:  Source net = 0021769Z, host = 02608C1194Z1, socket = 16385 (4001)
 XNS:
 XNS:  ----- Novell Advanced NetWare -----
 XNS:
 XNS:  Request type = 2222 (Request)
 XNS:  Seq no=102  Connection no=4    Task no=1
 XNS:
 NCP:  ----- Check Server Version Request -----
 NCP:
                        Frame 57 of 473
                 Use TAB to select windows
 1       2 Set          4 Zoom  5        6Display 7 Prev  8 Next         10 New
 Help    mark           out     Menus    options  frame   frame          capture
```

Fig. 4-14 NCP Request

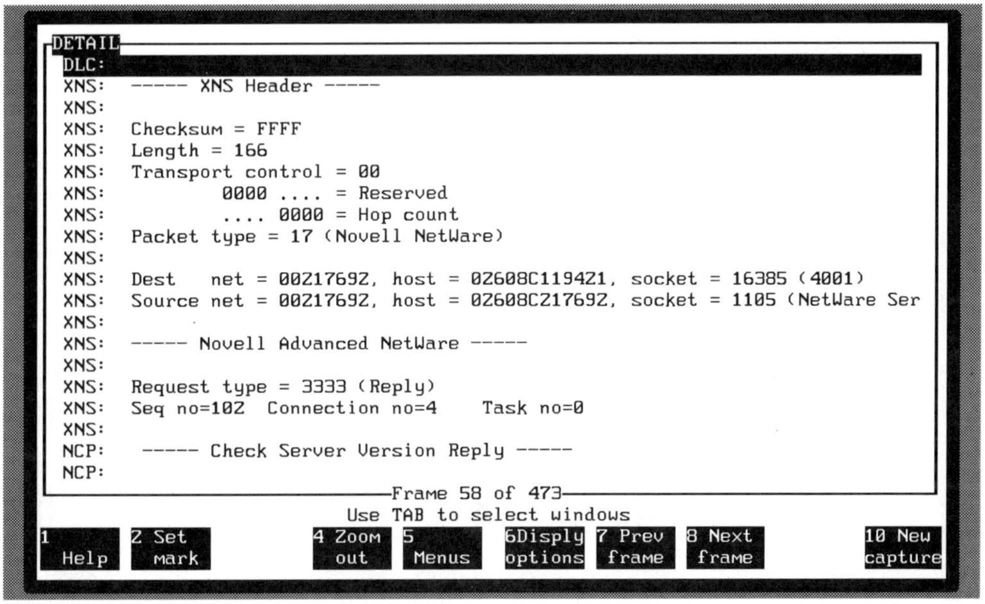

```
DETAIL
 DLC:
 XNS:  ----- XNS Header -----
 XNS:
 XNS:  Checksum = FFFF
 XNS:  Length = 166
 XNS:  Transport control = 00
 XNS:        0000 .... = Reserved
 XNS:        .... 0000 = Hop count
 XNS:  Packet type = 17 (Novell NetWare)
 XNS:
 XNS:  Dest   net = 0021769Z, host = 02608C1194Z1, socket = 16385 (4001)
 XNS:  Source net = 0021769Z, host = 02608C21769Z, socket = 1105 (NetWare Ser
 XNS:
 XNS:  ----- Novell Advanced NetWare -----
 XNS:
 XNS:  Request type = 3333 (Reply)
 XNS:  Seq no=102  Connection no=4    Task no=0
 XNS:
 NCP:  ----- Check Server Version Reply -----
 NCP:
                        Frame 58 of 473
                 Use TAB to select windows
 1       2 Set          4 Zoom  5        6Display 7 Prev  8 Next         10 New
 Help    mark           out     Menus    options  frame   frame          capture
```

Fig. 4-15 NCP Reply

swered with a reply. The next request cannot go until the first one is answered (or presumed lost because of the expiration of a timer).

The sequence number ensures that the reply is matched up to the request. For example, a node may send a request with a sequence number of 101 and then wait. When the timer expires, the node will send the same request again, this time with a sequence number of 102.

The delay in replying could have been caused by a temporary slowdown at the destination node. In fact, the destination node may already have sent the reply, but it had not yet been received at the source before the timer expired and it resent the packet.

The destination node will simply reply to request number 102, just as it did to request 101. The requesting node will see the duplicate reply and make sure that the client only sees one of them.

In a typical Novell environment, most packets are a series of NCP request and reply packets (see Fig. 4-16). Notice that the task number changes periodically as the exchange of data progresses. NCP divides up a connection into a series of tasks. A task might be a simple request/reply sequence or might consist of several request/reply operations.

NCP uses tasks to make sure that all parts of a transaction are successfully accomplished. For example, creating a connection and setting up a new connection are typically parts of the same task. At the end of each task, NCP will send an end of task request. For example, in Figure 4-17, we see that a node attempted to verify a password. This exchange took a series of four packets, at the end of which an end of task request was sent.

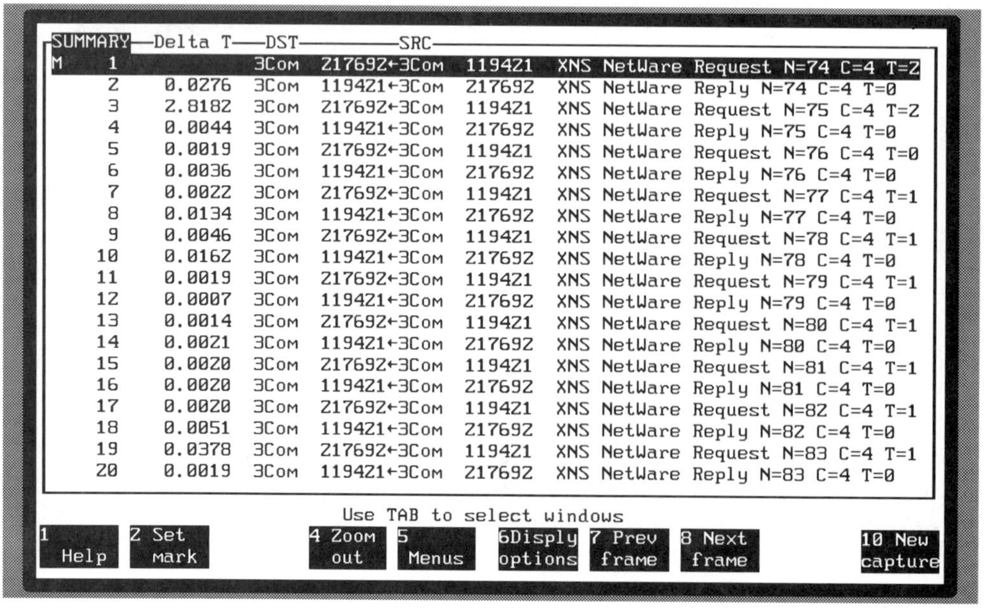

Fig. 4-16 NCP Request/Reply Traffic

```
┌SUMMARY──Delta T──DST──────SRC──────
M    1                 3Com   21769Z←3Com  11942Z  NCP C Verify DAN's password
     2      0.0276     3Com   11942Z←3Com  21769Z  NCP R Verification failed
     3      2.8182     3Com   21769Z←3Com  11942Z  NCP C Verify DAN's password
     4      0.0044     3Com   11942Z←3Com  21769Z  NCP R OK
     5      0.0019     3Com   21769Z←3Com  11942Z  NCP C End of task
     6      0.0036     3Com   11942Z←3Com  21769Z  NCP R OK
     7      0.0022     3Com   21769Z←3Com  11942Z  NCP C Logout
     8      0.0134     3Com   11942Z←3Com  21769Z  NCP R OK
     9      0.0046     3Com   21769Z←3Com  11942Z  NCP C Login DAN
```

```
┌DETAIL─
 NCP:    ───── End of Task Request ─────
 NCP:
 NCP:    Request code = 24
 NCP:
 NCP:    (No parameters)
 NCP:
 NCP:    Padded with 1 byte(s) of additional data.
 NCP:
 NCP:    [Normal end of NetWare "End of Task Request" packet.]
```

Fig. 4-17 End of Task Request

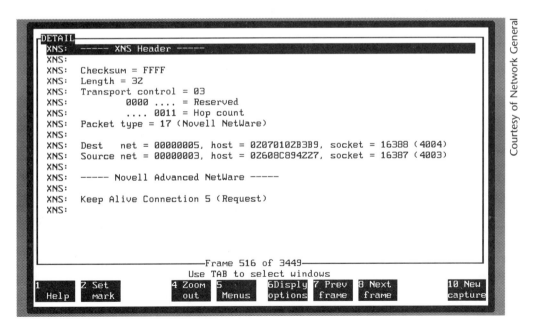

```
┌DETAIL─
 XNS:    ───── XNS Header ─────
 XNS:
 XNS:    Checksum = FFFF
 XNS:    Length = 32
 XNS:    Transport control = 03
 XNS:            0000 .... = Reserved
 XNS:            .... 0011 = Hop count
 XNS:    Packet type = 17 (Novell NetWare)
 XNS:
 XNS:    Dest   net = 00000005, host = 0207010ZB3B9, socket = 16388 (4004)
 XNS:    Source net = 00000003, host = 02608C894227, socket = 16387 (4003)
 XNS:
 XNS:    ───── Novell Advanced NetWare ─────
 XNS:
 XNS:    Keep Alive Connection 5 (Request)
 XNS:
```

Fig. 4-18 Keep Alive Request

Remember that IPX did not guarantee that it would deliver the data. NCP maintains a timer. Every time a packet of data is sent, it sets the timer. It expects to get the reply from the destination node before the timer expires. If the timer expires, it will try sending the packet again, each time resetting the timer. After it reaches a retry limit, it assumes that the remote host is unreachable and informs the user.

When there is no traffic between the two users—that is, the user on a workstation is examining data and is not communicating with the file server—a timer also operates to make sure that the connection is still good. If no packets are received and the timer expires, NCP will assume that the node has become unreachable and inform its user.

A keep alive message is exchanged during periods when the two users are not communicating (see Fig. 4-18). In this case, the packet requests that connection number 5 be kept alive. If the destination host is still in operation, the workstation expects to see a reply packet soon after sending the keep alive request.

The keep alive operation serves the same purpose as periodic RIP packets—to ensure that resources on the network are in fact available. RIP packets are used for destination nodes. Keep alive connection requests are used to ensure that remote NCP processes do in fact exist.

SPX

A more general type of service is the Sequenced Packet Exchange. SPX is a general programming interface available to developers of third-party software. SPX provides a virtual connection between the two SPX clients (see Fig. 4-19). SPX builds on IPX by guaranteeing the delivery of data between two programs.

Like the NetWare Core Protocols, the clients begin by asking SPX to establish a connection with the remote program. The program must have already posted a "listen for connection" request with SPX. We will see in the next section that the destination program will also have advertised its availability (and the socket number that it is using) with the Service Advertisement Protocol.

Rather than use a request/response protocol, SPX allows several requests to be outstanding at once. This window of unacknowledged requests is more efficient for operations like file transfers. Instead of acknowledging every single packet, it waits until the "window"—the allowable number of outstanding packets—is reached. Then, it sends a single acknowledgment for all of the packets received.

One of the functions of SPX is to recover from duplicate data and lost data errors. This is closely tied into the windows for packet acknowledgment. Each side of an SPX connection maintains a sequence number for each packet it sends out. Along with the sequence number of the current packet, SPX will send two other sequence numbers. The first number indicates the sequence number of the last packet that it has received. The acknowledgment of a packet from the other side can be "piggybacked" into data going in the other direction, preventing the need for a separate acknowledgment packet.

In addition to the acknowledgment, it also sends out an allocation number. This allocation number is the highest sequence number the remote node is able to send. The remote node will send packets up to and including this allocation

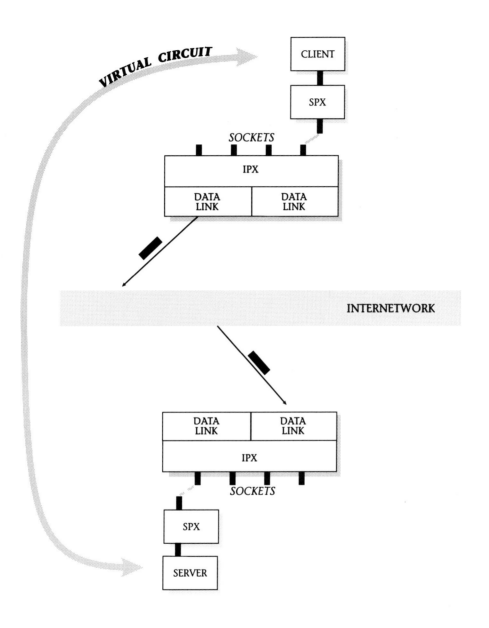

Fig. 4-19 SPX Virtual Connections

number and then wait until it gets a new allocation. If a node sees that its buffers are getting full, it can thus reduce the allocation window allowed to the remote node. The remote node will then wait until it is allowed to send again.

It is possible for a node to send a negative acknowledgment with a sequence number. The negative acknowledgment (NAK) indicates that an expected packet has not been received. The node that receives a NAK will look for the sequence number of the last packet that has been acknowledged. It will then resend all packets up to and including the sequence number in the NAK packet.

Setting up a large window allows many packets to be outstanding, allowing data to be immediately sent instead of queued up at the sending node. The receiving node can send fewer acknowledgments, freeing it to handle the incoming data. However, when there is an error, a large window may cause many packets to be resent. If there is a large window, SPX must keep copies of all sent but unacknowledged packets, consuming buffer space.

SPX provides a higher-level service than the Packet Exchange Protocol employed in the NetWare Core Protocols. SPX frees the user from the request/response model, allowing either side to send messages at any time. The client, of course, must be able to interpret the incoming packet and decide if it is in fact the reply to the request it is expecting.

Clients communicate with SPX by first opening a connection. Then, a client posts a series of SPX listen commands, telling its SPX module that it has reserved memory space for incoming packets. When SPX receives a packet for that connection ID, it moves it into the indicated buffer space and notifies the client.

A client may send data packets by submitting them to SPX. SPX guarantees that all data will be delivered across the network in the order that it was received. It is also possible for a client to use the services of IPX at the same time. SPX might be used for a workstation and a server to communicate with each other. Servers might communicate among each other by sending out IPX broadcasts. Since the broadcasts are repeated periodically, there is no need for guaranteed delivery of data.

The Service Advertisement Protocol

Strictly speaking, the concept of advertising services is an issue for the application layer of the network. However, two considerations make discussing the Service Advertisement Protocol at this point worthwhile.

First, this program makes direct use of the services of IPX (see Fig. 4-20). The services we will examine in subsequent sections are normally built on top of the services of the transport layer. Since SAP is the last program that makes direct use of IPX, it makes sense to discuss it here.

Second, SAP is used extensively by a variety of other network services. The NetWare Core Protocols, for example, use SAP to find file servers or print servers in the network. Application programs written by third-party developers or users also use SAP to advertise the presence of custom services on the network.

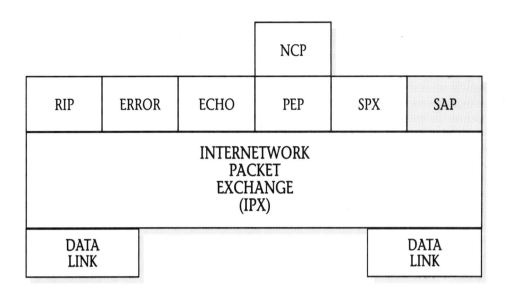

Fig. 4-20 Service Advertisement Protocol

SAP advertises the presence of a server—a computer that is making resources available over the network. That server can be anything, but several types have been defined, including file servers, routers, and print servers.

Note that the words *client* and *server* take on different meanings at different layers of the network. SPX, for example, is a client of IPX. SPX, in turn, provides services to its clients. In the context of SAP, we are usually referring to the top layer of a network. Thus, a file server (which is a client of IPX) advertises its presence to clients—users on a workstation wishing to access data.

The service advertisement protocol allows a program to register its name on the network. A SAP request will then ask for the translation of that name to a socket on a particular node of a network. A user might send out a SAP request for all file servers (see Fig. 4-21). The request is broadcast to all nodes on the network (and possibly other networks).

SAP requests are received by NetWare file servers, which maintain a socket to listen for these requests. The file server then searches its database and looks to see if the specified service is present. In Figure 4-21, the request was heard by a NetWare server, which responded with an internetwork address for the server (see the packet labeled "NCP R TCP_GATE" in the summary section).

In the illustration, the workstation then goes on to send out a RIP request for a network number. What happened in this case is that a workstation, when it initialized on the network, sent out a request for the nearest file server. This was sent back with an internetwork address containing a network number.

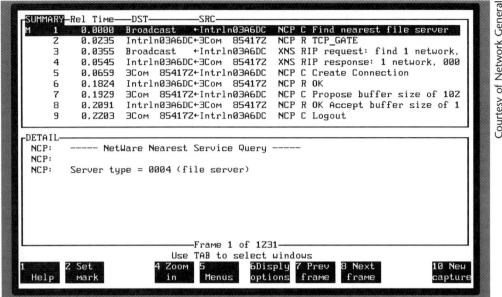

Fig. 4-21 General Service Query

Since the workstation had just joined the network, it did not know its network number. It therefore sent out a RIP request to find out the network for the file server and incidentally learned its own network number. The workstation then used NCP to send requests to set up a connection.

Figure 4-21 shows a SAP query that looks for the nearest file server. It is also possible to submit a general service query which may result in several responses. When a node receives either type of query, it sends a SAP response back to the requesting workstation.

Another type of SAP response is the broadcast. A server will periodically broadcast its available services on the network, allowing other servers to update their local database of available services. A special type of broadcast is the server shutdown advertisement, which indicates that a service will no longer be available. Broadcasts ensure that changes in the availability of services are eventually propagated throughout the network.

A service like SAP is useful but has limits in a large network. One large problem is the full replication of the namespace across the entire network. Every SAP database must know about every name on the network. In addition, there is no coordination of naming across different nodes—each node offers its own services.

A newer service from Novell, the NetWare Name Service, is a global name server. Different portions of the network each maintain a name server, which registers different services, such as the location of printers. If a service changes location, the name server updates the location of the service. Within an area,

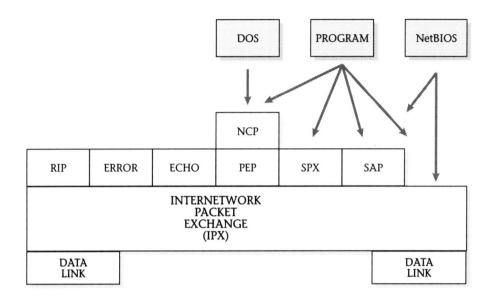

Fig. 4-22 IPX and SPX Clients

several name servers may exist. Mechanisms exist to make sure that any information replicated between two name servers is consistent.

IPX and SPX Clients

We have examined a variety of protocols that form the foundation for a Novell network (see Fig. 4-22). A program can use these services for building yet more complex services. For example, the NetWare Core Protocols build on top of the Packet Exchange Protocol. PEP provides the service of requests and responses. NCP provides an additional service of making a remote disk drive appear to be directly attached to a workstation.

In addition to the NetWare Core Protocols (discussed in the next chapter), it is possible for a program to make direct use of these services. A program can be written that mixes calls to NCP, SPX, SAP, and IPX, using each of the services as appropriate. We will see a variety of applications for message handling and database management that build on these foundation protocols.

A special type of user is the NetBIOS implementation from Novell, examined in the last chapter of this book. NetBIOS is actually another network architecture that has been grafted onto Novell networks. Novell provides a program that looks like a NetBIOS interface, but in fact it uses the services of IPX and SAP.

Key Points in This Chapter

- IPX is Novell's version of the Xerox XNS protocol. IPX is a network layer protocol—it determines which data link to use to forward a packet one hop closer to its destination.
- The Routing Information Protocol is used to inform routers (or *bridges*, in Novell literature) about changes in the network topology.
- The SPX transport layer provides gauranteed delivery of data across the network. SPX is used by third-party developers.
- The NetWare Core Protocols use a simpler transport layer, known as the Packet Exchange Protocol (PEP).
- SPX allows several packets to be unacknowledged; PEP requires each packet to be individually acknowledged before the next can be sent.
- The Error and Echo protocols are used for reporting errors and echoing data back over the network.

PART II

NETWARE

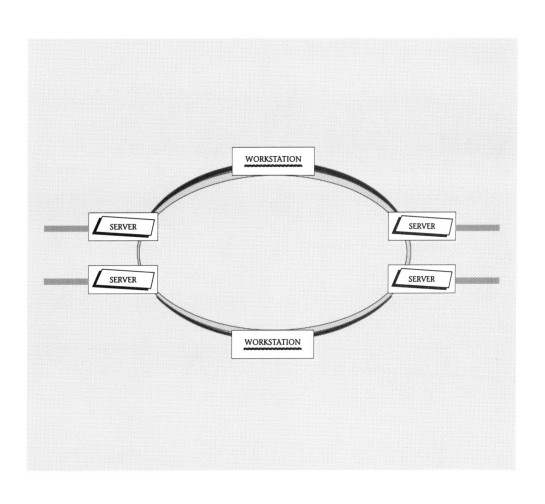

CHAPTER 5

NetWare Core Protocols

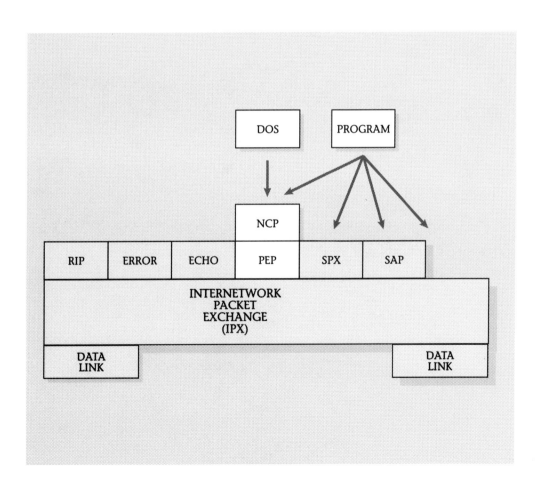

CHAPTER 5

NetWare Core Protocols

NetWare and Servers

In the last chapter, we began to look at the NetWare Core Protocols. The portion of NCP we examined was the mechanism used to specify a task to be performed. In this chapter, we look at what those tasks are—the functionality of the NetWare Core Protocols.

A NetWare environment consists of software on clients and servers (see Fig. 5-1). The server side is the NetWare operating system—a special-purpose operating system developed by Novell. The operating system has been designed to permit several server programs and many different workstations to share the resources of a single computer.

A server for the NetWare operating system is typically an 80386-based computer. We will see in Chapter 12 that Portable NetWare allows other computers to become NetWare servers. The 80386-based version is known as "native" NetWare.

The server is configured with a variety of peripheral devices. Disk drives, modems, printers, and asynchronous communications boards are all possible hardware devices. In addition, various software programs may be added to supplement the services of the NetWare Core Protocols. In this chapter we look at the functionality that comes with the basic NetWare operating system. Subsequent chapters will discuss optional applications, such as message handling and database access, which can be added to the basic services.

On the client side, the workstation, the NetWare software runs in conjunction with the workstation operating system—DOS or OS/2. This software, the NetWare shell, extends the services of the operating system onto the network. For example, the shell allows the extension of DOS file access over a network by intercepting calls meant for the operating system. If the resource requested is local, the shell hands it over to the operating system. Otherwise, it packages the request up in a packet and submits it to the IPX-based protocol stack.

Notice that the equipment in this network is all fairly generic. Workstations and servers can be any standard PC. The networking hardware is also generic—token ring, Ethernet, and ARCNET can all be obtained from a variety of different sources.

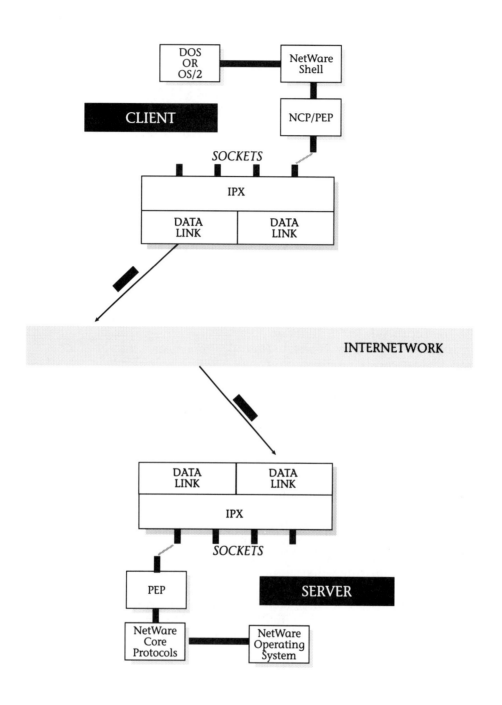

Fig. 5-1 Client and Server Portions of NetWare

Although one can buy all this hardware from Novell, there is no particular reason to do so aside from the convenience of buying as much as possible from one source. What makes this combination of equipment a Novell network is the NetWare operating system for the servers and the NetWare shell for the workstation.

In subsequent chapters, we will see that this network can be expanded greatly beyond PCs. The Apple Macintosh can be added as a workstation or client. Various types of minicomputers and mainframes can all be integrated, either as Portable NetWare servers or through communications gateways.

NCP Services

The services provided by the core protocols fall into the following categories:

- Basic operating system services
- Bindery
- Basic communications services
- File access
- Locking and synchronization
- Printer access
- Queue management

Some or all of these services are used by programs that reside both on servers and workstations. The services define what a Novell network does for the user, as opposed to the protocols in the earlier chapter, which are for the most part transparent to the user. The services listed above are basic building blocks, adequate for a series of programs to be explicitly designed for use on the network. Subsequent chapters will show supplemental levels of services particularly designed for database access and message transfer.

Other chapters will also deal with the provision of services to the user, but in a more general fashion. As will be seen in this chapter, the basic NetWare services are just that—basic. The programmer is forced to consider many of the details of the interaction of programs across the network. Chapters 9 and 10 will discuss how Novell and other companies are getting around these problems by making the network appear as just an extension of the workstation using remote procedure calls and STREAMS.

NetWare Operating System

A native NetWare operating system consists of a kernel that provides the core services and a variety of utilities used, for example, to add new users, control security, or to do installation. Additional software, such as a database management system, may be loaded and run on the file server.

On older versions of NetWare (i.e., NetWare 286 and Advanced NetWare), third-party programs and options to NetWare are called a Value-Added Process (VAP). On NetWare 386, for 80386- and 80486-based file servers, the optional software is called a Network Loadable Module (NLM). Network Loadable Modules are software programs that are dynamically loaded as required and actually become part of the kernel operating system.

Because an NLM is an integrated part of the kernel of the operating system, it has full access to all system resources. The VAP, by contrast, uses a set of protocols to obtain access to operating system resources, with the kernel arbitrating each request. Because of its integration, the NLM permits a higher degree of performance than the VAP.

A VAP is actually a user that logs onto the file server just like any other user. The VAP has a password and is defined as an object in the bindery, described in the next section. After the VAP has logged in, the program is loaded into the file server's RAM. The VAP then begins to provide services to its clients throughout the network.

The NLM, by contrast, is actually part of the operating system. Most of the NetWare services on NetWare 386 are actually implemented as NLMs, including the drivers for network boards and even the installation routine. This means that the configuration of the file server can be modified while it is in operation on the network.

In NetWare 386, all third-party programs, such as database servers, are implemented as an NLM. The NLM has full access to the operating system and could, if poorly written, corrupt important information maintained by other

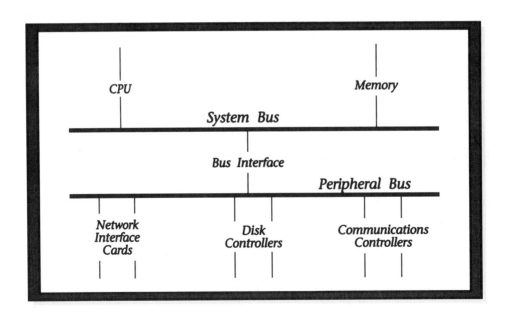

Fig. 5-2 Components of a Server

programs, including the operating system. The NLM must be well behaved, adhering to some very important rules that ensure coexistence among multiple programs. Novell offers a certification program for vendors writing NLMs. It behooves the network manager to test a new NLM before installing it on a NetWare server in a production environment.

A server consists of a computer with the NetWare operating system and a series of peripheral devices (see Fig. 5-2). By definition, the server must have one or more network cards. Multiple cards allow the computer to service clients on more than one network, and allow the server to act as a router for packets that cross the networks.

In addition, the server will probably have one or more disk drives. If the server is a file server, there can be a great many different disk drives. Other mass storage devices that are often seen on servers are tape backup units and optical disks.

The server may also have specialized peripherals, such as a board for wide area communications. A wide variety of other peripheral devices can be installed. For example, IEEE 488 boards could be installed on the computer, allowing it to monitor and control programmable controllers, as on a factory floor. Workstations would then access these services using a software program, such as a VAP, that runs on the server.

The NetWare operating system provides a variety of services for disk drives so they can be widely accessible on the network. NetWare supports much larger amounts of mass storage than are typical on a workstation using an operating system such as DOS.

In NetWare, users don't actually interact with a disk drive directly. Instead, the disk drive is partitioned into volumes. It is possible for a single volume to span several disk drives, allowing very large logical disk sizes for the user.

A special kind of volume is the mirrored volume, where data is actually duplicated and stored on multiple disk drives. That way, if one of the drives fails, the data is still preserved. This mirrored disk capability is known in the Novell marketing lingo as System Fault Tolerance (SFT).

A related feature is the Transaction Tracking System, which allows the programmer to structure updates to multiple pieces of data into a single logical transaction. The TTS software guarantees that if the system crashes in the middle of an update or the programmer decides not to proceed with the transaction, none of the updates take effect. The data is "rolled back" to its prior state. TTS is discussed again in the context of advanced data access services.

The Bindery

A central feature of any NetWare operating system is a special file called the bindery, which is used for security, accounting, and name management. Each NetWare server has one bindery, which contains a series of objects (see Fig. 5-3). Each object has associated with it a series of properties, which have property values associated with them.

An example of an object is a user who is allowed to log into this server. The username is the name of the object. The object has a property of PASSWORD

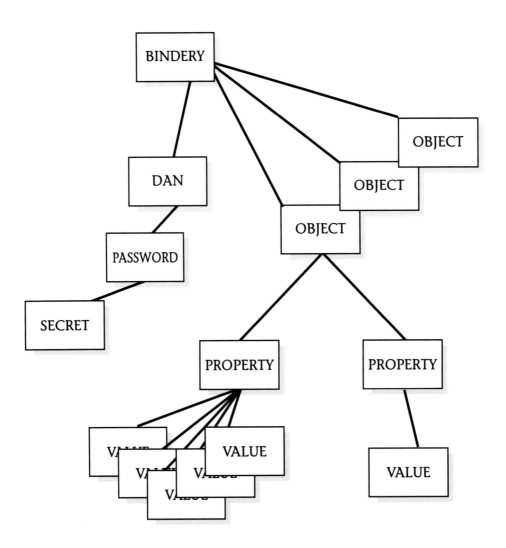

Fig. 5-3 Bindery Components

associated with it, with a property value of the user's current password. When a user on a workstation wishes to log in to a particular file server, a log in request is sent over the network (see Fig. 5-4). This screen shows that a workstation sent a message to server to verify Dan's password. This command (marked C on the screen) was given to the NetWare operating system on the server. The server checked the bindery to see if this was a valid password and sent back a response (shown in the detail section).

This was followed by a second exchange, also in Figure 5-4, where the verification worked. At this point the workstation finished a task it was working on (probably checking the password but possibly another) and logged out of the server. The workstation then logged back in as user DAN, presumably to get the higher level of access that user DAN would have.

The bindery is more general than just managing logging in a user with the right password. It serves as a central database for system information. The object *DAN* was an example of an object of type *USER*. Other types include:

- User group
- Print server
- File server
- Job server
- Gateway
- Archive server
- Job queue

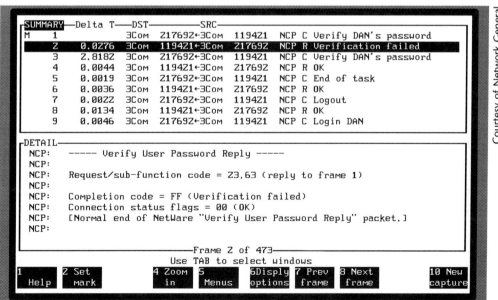

Fig. 5-4 Verifying a Password

Each object stored in the bindery has an object type code associated with it. A special type is "unknown," and it is also possible for programmers to define their own object types.

When searching the bindery, the user can look at objects that have a certain name or can search for all objects within a given type. For example, if we are unsure how *DAN* is spelled, a program or utility could issue a system call to search the bindery for all objects of type user that start with a D. Of course, while this specific bindery search would work, one wonders how this user got promoted to the job of system administrator.

In addition to the object type indicator, each object in a bindery has a unique 4-byte object ID, which can be used for subsequent references to that object. For example, it will be quicker to refer to the object ID that corresponds with DAN than it would be to have the system search each time for that particular name.

Once an object ID is found, the normal next step is to look at the properties associated with that object. A property can be single- or multivalued. An example of a multivalued property might be *GROUP_MEMBERS*. The values for this property would consist of a set of object IDs, which in turn correspond to individual users who are members of this group (or possibly, to other groups which are members of this group).

Verifying a password is a specific instance of searching the bindery. A more general call allows the programmer to find out what properties an object has and the values of those properties.

For example, Figure 5-5 shows how the bindery is used to maintain a list of valid users for a print server. In this call, the detail part of the screen shows that the program is requesting to verify that *SIMPSON* is a valid value for the property *Q_USERS*. Looking at the summary part of Figure 5-5, we can see that the call failed and that *SIMPSON* is not a valid user. The simple solution is to just add *SIMPSON* as a valid user using the print server management software.

As we can see, the bindery is a critical part of the NetWare security framework. Associated with each object in the bindery is a 1-byte flag that governs security for that object. One-half of the byte (1 nibble) governs who can search the object; the second half governs who can write to the object. Access to an object can be restricted to any one of five levels.

The lowest level allows anyone, including any objects not logged into the server, to access this object. Next, only people (i.e., objects) who are logged in can search this object. Third, only people who are logged in as the object being referenced can change the object. This is the most common level of access protection for the username and password, allowing the user to change his or her password.

Two additional levels are used to further restrict objects. The supervisor level of access allows only users who are logged in as the object *SUPERVISOR* to access this object. This level of access also allows an object that is logged in which has the security equivalence of supervisor in the bindery to access the object.

Finally, the NetWare level only allows the operating system to access the object. That means that any access to this object will be through a program that runs at the kernel level of the operating system.

Properties also have a security flag associated with them. This allows certain properties, such as the user's full name, to be available to everybody on the network while restricting access to other more sensitive properties, such as username.

Properties also have two other flags. One indicates if the property is static or dynamic. A dynamic property is only in effect while a program is running. For example, the fact that a particular service is now running is a dynamic property used for service advertisement functions.

The other flag indicates if the property is an item or a set. The item is a single-valued property value, while the set contains the object IDs of one or more other objects that make up the set.

NetWare is heavily dependent on the operation of the bindery, which is implemented as a set of two files. These files should be placed on a disk drive that has a quick access time, although it is hoped that large portions of the bindery will stay in a main memory cache on a busy server.

It is important to note that when performing bindery updates, there is no built-in mechanism that ensures that updates by different users will be properly synchronized. Programmers need to use the synchronization mechanisms discussed later in this chapter. If several users are simultaneously trying to update

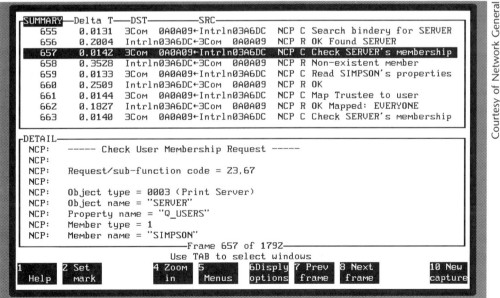

Fig. 5-5 Searching the Bindery

a group of objects in the bindery, it is possible for inconsistent updates to result if no precautions are taken to coordinate access.

Communications Utilities

A user logs into a file server as a bindery object. It is also possible for the user to access data on the file server without being logged in. This is known as being attached to the file server.

Each attachment or logged in user corresponds to a connection with a workstation on the network (or with a VAP running on the server). The file server keeps a connection information table in memory, which is used to keep track of the connection status, the connection number for each side of the connection, network addresses, and similar information. This status information is available to the programmer. Figures 5-6 and 5-7 show a message being sent from a workstation to a server to find out the current status of a particular connection.

A variety of other utilities are also available for use in programs. For example, the status of a particular volume on the network can be requested over the network (see Figs. 5-8 and 5-9). This call might be used by a programmer to see if there is enough room to save a file. If not, the program would then check other volumes to see if there was room. If not, the programmer would notify the user that the file is too big for that particular file server.

These basic utilities also allow the program to determine which versions of NetWare and the individual utilities that NetWare provides are being used. When a program attempts to connect to the NetWare file server, it first checks to make sure that it is able to support the version of the operating system on that file server. These calls can also return the type of file server—who manufactured it, how many volumes are mounted, and other descriptive information.

Configuration information about a particular server allows a program to be highly flexible. For example, a program can be written that, before logging a user onto a server, checks all the servers on the network to find out which one has the best service rating at that time and also has the resources necessary to carry out the intended task.

These basic calls also allow the workstation to coordinate the nature of its interaction with a particular server. For example, Figure 5-10 shows a workstation sending a request to the server to disable broadcast messages. These are messages that are broadcast to all workstations that have sessions with a server (or a group of workstations that are using a common service).

A broadcast message might be used to notify the user of the availability of the status of servers on the network. A message might appear on everybody's screen when a new server joins the network. Disabling these broadcasts can be quite useful if too many messages are being broadcast. The user can selectively turn off certain categories of broadcasts (assuming a program is written to do so).

Another coordination service is for the system clocks of two computers. The time on different computers is never exactly the same. By finding the clock time on a server (see Fig. 5-11), a workstation is able to calculate the differential in the clocks. It then uses that information to, for example, compare the update time of two different files.

It is also possible for programs that want to interact directly with IPX and SPX to do so using the communication services. For example, a program could use the IPX service to broadcast a datagram on the network. The broadcast would be directed at a specific socket number, which would correspond to the assigned socket number for that program.

This type of broadcast would be used by special-purpose servers to exchange information among themselves. For example, a distributed database would use this form of broadcast to inform the other database servers of its current status.

File Access

Rather than using IPX and SPX directly, most programs use network services that are built on top of the underlying transport layer. One of the key services offered by the NetWare operating system is the ability to access files on a server in a fashion transparent to the workstation.

The transparency of files across a network is a key feature. Transparency allows programs designed for a single computer environment to easily function in a network. This is done by mapping files on the file server to the local DOS file system on the workstation (see Fig. 5-12).

Accessing a local disk drive is the responsibility of the file system on a computer. The file system takes incoming requests for data and sends them down to a device driver, which actually accesses the disk drive.

For network-based access to data, the NetWare shell is used. This program is equivalent to the local device driver—it accepts requests and returns data. The file system registers which disk drives are being handled by which device driver. When the file system sees a disk drive that is handled by the network device driver, it sends the request to the network program. In turn, this program decides where the data is located, formats the appropriate packets, and sends the data down to a real device driver—one that controls an Ethernet controller, for example.

On the workstation, the NetWare shell maintains three tables to help it map a file request to the proper file server. First, there is a drive handle table, which contains an entry for each letter available for a disk drive. Each of these entries points to an entry in the drive flag table.

The drive flag table indicates if the drive being referred to is local or network based. If it is network based, it can be a permanent or a temporary mapping. Temporary mappings are used by a particular program, while permanent ones stay in effect on the workstation. The drive flag table also indicates if a local disk drive has been allocated by another workstation as a network drive.

If the disk drive is network based, there is also an entry in another table that contains the connection ID being used to communicate with that file server. A workstation may maintain a connection with several file servers, even if there is not a user logged into the file server.

When a request for remote data is received, the NetWare shell packages that request into a NetWare Core Protocol message, which is sent over the connec-

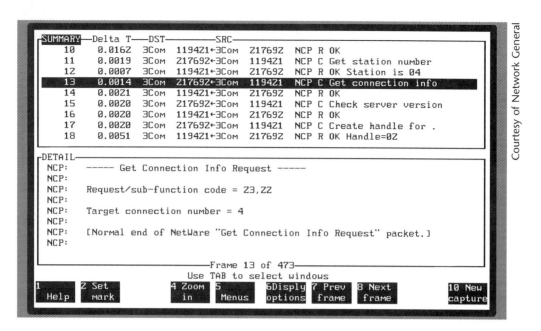

Fig. 5-6 Connection Status Request

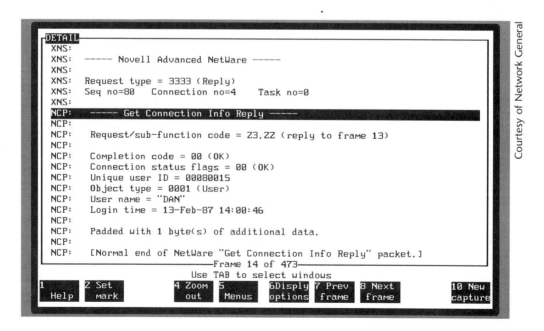

Fig. 5-7 Connection Status Reply

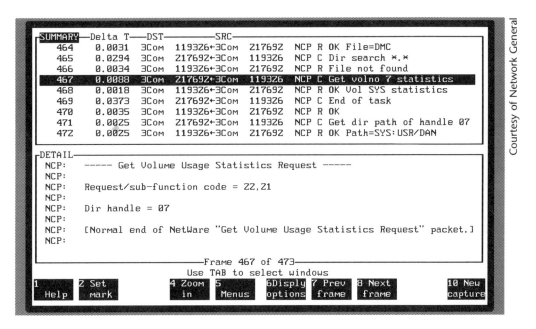

Fig. 5-8 Volume Status Request

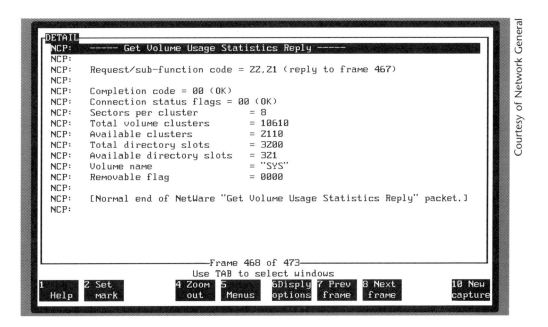

Fig. 5-9 Volume Status Reply

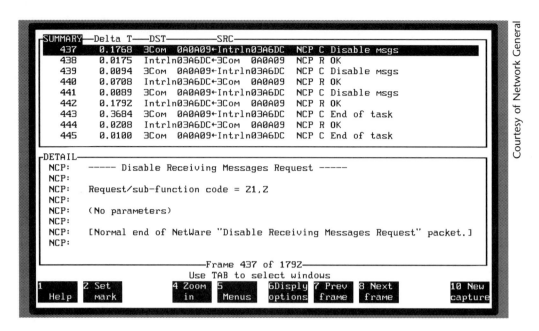

Fig. 5-10 Disable Broadcast Request

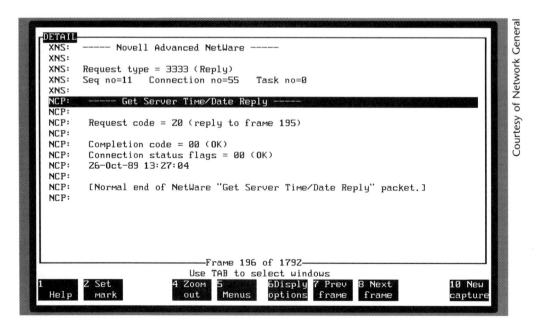

Fig. 5-11 Time/Date Reply

tion ID to the file server. The file server takes this incoming request and translates it into a request to the NetWare file system.

What looks like a disk drive to the workstation may in fact be just a portion of a disk drive on a file server. For example, the file server could take just the subdirectory that corresponds to a user's files and make that available to the workstation as if it were a disk drive.

The file server needs to take the incoming request for data from the workstation and decide what portion of which volume this request applies to. To do so, it consults several tables maintained for each connection that is active on the file server.

The file server maps the workstation's request for a disk drive into a local volume and directory path. It then takes the rest of the path provided by the workstation, such as additional subdirectories, and appends it. For example, a user refers to a file *H:archive\old_data.wp*. The workstation, after looking up the connection, sends a request for disk drive *H:*, subdirectory *archive*, and the file *old_data.wp*. The file server consults its table and sees that *H:* corresponds to *VOL1:\user\simpson*. The NetWare Core Protocols sends a request down to the local file system for:

VOL1:\user\simpson\archive\old_data.wp

When a workstation and a file server exchange requests for data, they use a handle, which is a number that identifies a specific portion of the file system on the server, such as a file or directory. A handle allows repeated requests for information to be exchanged without transmitting the entire path of the file each time.

Figure 5-13 illustrates the concept of a handle. In the summary portion of the screen, we can see that the workstation has created a handle to be used for a specific directory on the file server, *SYS:\DOS\V3.10*, which is presumably the location of DOS version 3.1 on the file server.

The detail section shows that the workstation is checking to see that the path of handle 06 is in fact correct. Figure 5-14, the reply from the server, confirms that the mapping took effect. After confirming that the mapping took place, the workstation then checks to make sure that the correct version of the server is being used.

This exchange of messages indicates that the traffic is from a workstation that is just booting up and is using the file server as the boot drive. The workstation has probably just been turned on and is loading DOS, after which it will log in the user.

Typically, after a directory has been assigned a handle, the workstation tries to look for files in the directory. Figure 5-15 illustrates a request from a workstation to return a directory listing of all files in the directory that correspond to handle *0D70*.

Figure 5-16 is the reply from the server. The name of only one file has been returned. NetWare has been implemented so that a directory search returns one file at a time, along with information on various attributes of the file, such as the security permissions.

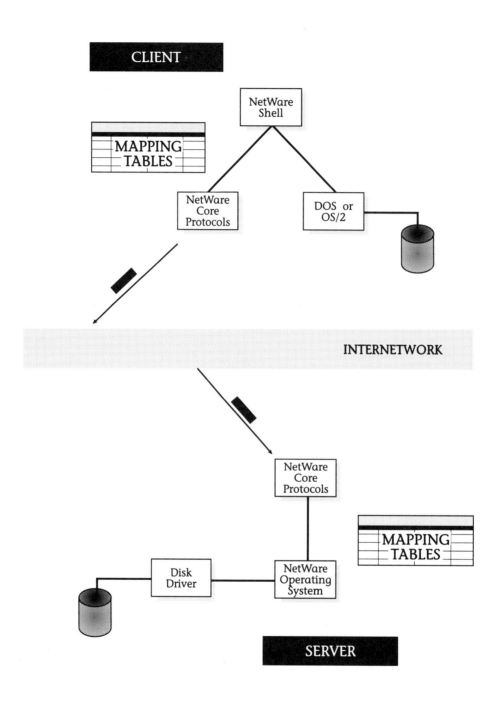

Fig. 5-12 Remote Data Access

If there is more than one file that meets the search request, the reply includes a search index value. The workstation then resubmits the request, along with the search index. When the last file is returned, the server indicates this by not providing a search index for the next packet.

Figure 5-18 shows this traffic on a Novell network. After the initial request there are many more requests for additional files. Each exchange consists of a request and a reply and is taking up to five-hundredths of a second, meaning that a directory listing of 200 files might take 10 seconds on this network.

Figure 5-17 also illustrates a new aspect of the Sniffer Analyzer. Notice that relative time is being used instead of delta time. Delta time, used in previous illustrations, shows the time between two adjacent packets. Relative time shows the time that has elapsed since a particular packet (which might be in the middle of the trace or at the beginning) was sent. Relative time makes it easier to see how much time has elapsed since a particular operation started. Delta time makes it easier to see how quickly events are occurring on the network.

Attributes and Access Rights

Figures 5-15 and 5-16 show that the directory search request included directory access rights. The reply, with the *IDEAS.AGA* file, included a set of attributes for a file. Security information, creation date, modification date, and other attributes are associated with every node of the file system.

The word *node* is used in a different context here than the concept of a network node. A node is a directory, a file, or a special kind of node known as a trustee, which will be discussed in a few paragraphs. Directory and file nodes store the attributes for that portion of the file system, including information such as the creation date. File nodes include a pointer to the directory that the file belongs in. A directory node includes a pointer to its parent directory.

An important set of attributes for directory and file nodes governs security in the file system. Security begins at the directory level. Security for a directory is specified two different ways. First, the directory has a maximum rights mask. This is the maximum level of access any user will be permitted, unless they are on a special privileged account. Second, there are trustees for a directory. A trustee is the object ID of a group or individual user on the system. There can be several trustees for a directory.

Both the maximum rights and the rights for a trustee are governed by an access mask, which is a list of the eight allowable operations that are permitted on this particular directory. These operations include:

- Search the directory
- Modify file attributes
- Delete files
- Open files
- Read data in files
- Write to files
- Create new files
- The right to administer security

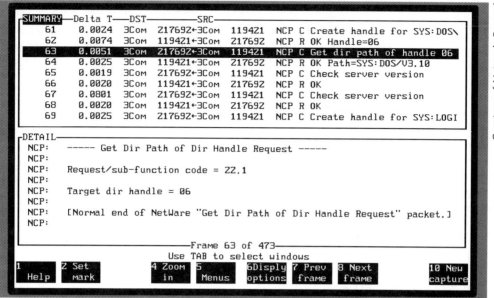

Fig. 5-13 Directory Handle Request

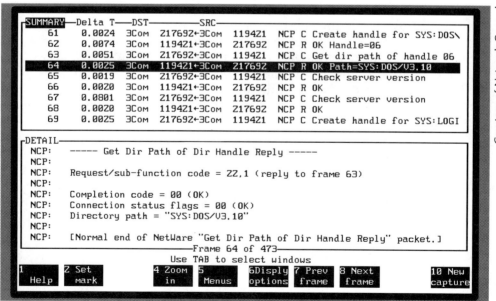

Fig. 5-14 Directory Handle Reply

```
┌DETAIL─────────────────────────────────────────────────────────┐
│NCP:   ----- Alternate Directory Search Request -----          │
│NCP:                                                           │
│NCP:   Request code = 63                                       │
│NCP:                                                           │
│NCP:   Volume number = 0                                       │
│NCP:   Dir access handle = 0D70                                │
│NCP:   Next search index = -1                                  │
│NCP:   Dir access rights = E7                                  │
│NCP:          1... .... = Modify/rename access                 │
│NCP:          .1.. .... = Search access                        │
│NCP:          ..1. .... = Parental access                      │
│NCP:          ...0 .... = No delete access                     │
│NCP:          .... 0... = No create access                     │
│NCP:          .... .1.. = Allowed to open existing files       │
│NCP:          .... ..1. = Write access                         │
│NCP:          .... ...1 = Read access                          │
│NCP:   Match file name = "*.*"                                 │
│NCP:                                                           │
│NCP:   [Normal end of NetWare "Alternate Directory Search Request" packet.] │
│NCP:                                                           │
│                    ─Frame 1451 of 1792─                       │
│                     Use TAB to select windows                 │
│ 1      2 Set       4 Zoom  5       6Disply 7 Prev  8 Next    10 New    │
│ Help   mark        out    Menus    options frame   frame     capture   │
└───────────────────────────────────────────────────────────────┘
```

Fig. 5-15 Directory Search Request

```
┌DETAIL─────────────────────────────────────────────────────────┐
│NCP:   ----- Alternate Directory Search Reply -----            │
│NCP:                                                           │
│NCP:   Request code = 63 (reply to frame 1451)                 │
│NCP:                                                           │
│NCP:   Completion code = 00 (OK)                               │
│NCP:   Connection status flags = 00 (OK)                       │
│NCP:   Next search index = 168                                 │
│NCP:   File name = "IDEAS.AGA"                                 │
│NCP:   File attribute flags = 00                               │
│NCP:          0... .... = File is not sharable                 │
│NCP:          .0.. .... = Not defined                          │
│NCP:          ..0. .... = Not changed since last archive       │
│NCP:          ...0 .... = Not a subdirectory                   │
│NCP:          .... 0... = Not execute-only file                │
│NCP:          .... .0.. = Not a system file                    │
│NCP:          .... ..0. = Not a hidden file                    │
│NCP:          .... ...0 = Read and write allowed               │
│NCP:   File execute type = 00                                  │
│NCP:   File length = 367280                                    │
│NCP:   Creation date       = 25-Sep-89                         │
│                    ─Frame 1452 of 1792─                       │
│                     Use TAB to select windows                 │
│ 1      2 Set       4 Zoom  5       6Disply 7 Prev  8 Next    10 New    │
│ Help   mark        out    Menus    options frame   frame     capture   │
└───────────────────────────────────────────────────────────────┘
```

Fig. 5-16 Directory Search Reply

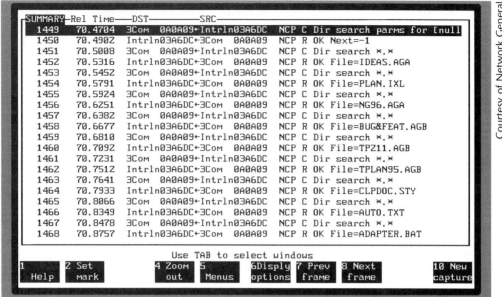

Fig. 5-17 Directory Search Traffic

Administering security includes adding new trustees to the directory or changing the rights mask of an existing trustee.

A trustee node on the file system consists of the name of the subdirectory that this list pertains to and up to five object IDs of users or groups. Each object ID has an access rights mask for that trustee. There is also a pointer to an additional trustee node, allowing more than five trustees to be defined for a given directory.

When trustee rights are granted, they are granted for all subdirectories below this directory. A particular user may also be in several different groups, all of which have some form of access defined for this directory or one of its parents.

The effective trustee rights are the sum of all the rights for the current directory and all the parent directories. To calculate this information for a given user, NetWare looks for all groups that have trustee rights to a directory and all its parents. If any of these rights masks give the user permission to do an operation, that permission applies to all lower subdirectories.

For example, users do not typically have trustee rights to the top level of the file system. In the *public* subdirectory, there would be a trustee right for a group *EVERYONE*, allowing members of this group to search and read files.

Below the *public* subdirectory would be a subdirectory called *demo*. This directory node would have a trustee right for a group *DEMO_ADMIN*. The trustee rights for this group would allow full access to the subdirectory.

If user *SIMPSON* is in both groups and attempts to delete a file, the file system would start by calculating the effective trustee rights. Since *SIMPSON* is in both groups, access would be allowed to any file in the subdirectory if the next two steps in the security calculation are not violated. Next, the file system checks the maximum rights mask for the directory. Only the operations permitted in the maximum rights mask are permitted, assuming that the trustee rights also grant the permission.

The system will never allow an operation that is not permitted in the maximum rights mask for this particular subdirectory unless the user is on a privileged account. If an operation is permitted at all, it then checks to see whether this particular user is able to perform the operation based on a trustee right.

The directory security governs which users may perform a given operation on a file. File attributes help define an additional level of security. The file system first checks the directory rights to decide if the operation should be permitted at all, and then it checks the file attributes to see if the operation will be permitted on this particular file.

One or more of the following attributes can be enabled for a particular file:

- Read-only
- Read-write
- Shareable
- Execute-only
- System file
- Hidden file

The execute-only attribute makes sure that the program is only executed on the file server and cannot be copied to another computer for execution. Since the file cannot be copied, only deleted, it cannot be backed up. It is a good idea to maintain an additional copy of this file on a floppy disk or hidden in some other directory.

A read-only file cannot be changed by a user. In order to change this file, the user would have to first gain the right to administer security for this file. This is limited to the creator or a trustee with equivalent security rights.

The shareable attribute indicates whether several users may share access to this file. If a file is shareable, the workstation that is doing remote operations on the file knows that there may be other operations occurring simultaneously.

If a file is shareable, it is not cached at the workstation. Normally, when the user asks for, say, 100 bytes of data, the workstation will request 512 bytes since the file server will read 512 bytes from the physical disk in any case. The workstation will then pass the requested 100 bytes to the user program but will keep the additional 412 bytes of data in memory. If the user then asks for the next 100 bytes, the workstation will be able to display it to the user without sending a request over the network.

If a file is shareable, the workstation will always resubmit the read request just in case the file has been changed in the meantime. This would seem to be the proper way to mark an informational file that should be available to many different users. The read-only attribute prohibits a user from accidentally changing the file. The shareable attribute, however, leads to interesting results on the network. When a user asks for the first record of data, the workstation sends a read request for 512 or 1024 bytes of data, starting at offset 0 in the file. After the first 100 bytes are displayed on the screen, the workstation then sends out another request over the network for 512 or 1024 bytes of data, this time starting at offset 100. The result is a tremendous amount of network traffic. The lesson is not to mark a file as shareable unless people will be simultaneously writing to it. A read-only, shareable file just wastes network resources.

File Operations

The workstation and file server typically go through several steps before actually accessing a file. First, the user is validated in the bindery. Then, a subdirectory on the file server is mapped to a drive on the workstation. Then, a directory handle is provided, followed by a search for a particular file. Then, assuming that the user has permission to access that file, a program typically opens the file. Opening the file allows the program to read and write data, modify the contents, or do any other operations on the file that are permitted by the effective rights mask.

Opening a file (see Fig. 5-18) allows the NetWare file system to see how the file will be used, allowing it to coordinate access among multiple users. The open file request indicates the desired access rights to the file. For example, the file *LOGIN* is being opened in single-user mode. If somebody else were already using the file, the request would be denied.

The reply to this request is shown in Figure 5-19. Notice that the request succeeded, and that a file handle is returned for further references to this file. The reply also returns the attributes of that file, such as the fact that the file is not shareable. The file attributes include the date and time of the file creation and other information that was returned with the directory search reply in Figure 5-16.

A typical exchange of network traffic to open a file is shown in Figure 5-20. Here the workstation has to try five times before it is able to successfully open the file. In the first three tries, the workstation is looking for a file named *USRLOG.COM*. It then tries *USRLOG.EXE* twice before succeeding.

This is happening because of the way the workstation operating system is looking for files. A workstation has a search path, which tells it where to look for a program when the user types in a command name. This allows a user to execute a command without necessarily knowing where the actual program is stored.

When the user types a command name, the workstation looks for the file in the first directory listed in its search path. It then proceeds to look for the command in subsequent directories until it finds the file. If it goes through all the directories in the search path and doesn't find a file, it tells the user that the command is unknown.

On DOS, there is a further refinement to the search. DOS will first look for files ending in *BAT*, then *COM*, and then *EXE*. When the user requests the command *USRLOG*, DOS will make up to three sweeps of the entire search path before returning the message *unknown command* to the user.

In this case, the search path includes network-based directories. In Figure 5-20, the workstation is searching several different directories and two different file types before finding the file. Looking into each packet in this exchange would indicate that a different directory handle was being submitted in each of the requests.

After the file is found and opened, the workstation begins to read data in the file. Each request is a separate packet (see Fig. 5-21). The request indicates where in the file to start reading and how many bytes to read. In the figure, the request is for 512 bytes of data. The next packet, shown in the summary window, shows that only 385 bytes were returned with the reply. In this case, the file happened to be only 385 bytes long.

The next screen, Figure 5-22, shows a workstation working through a file 1024 bytes at a time. The last exchange of data only returned 888 bytes, indicating that the end of the file had been reached. Notice that the workstation and the file server are exchanging 1024 bytes of data at a time, indicating that this exchange must be on a single Ethernet.

The maximum packet size permitted by IPX is 576 bytes. If the workstation and the server had been separated by an internetwork router, the read requests would have been for 512 bytes, the typical block size for disk drives. Likewise, if the two computers had been on an ARCNET or 4-Mbps token ring, the packet sizes would also have been smaller than 1024 bytes.

After a program is done reading a file, it can perform a variety of operations, such as writing new data or updating existing data. When the program is finished with a file, it closes the file (see Fig. 5-23), allowing other users to access it.

In Figure 5-23, several different operations occurred in rapid succession. The file was opened, the current size was found, a small amount of data was read, and it was closed again. This exchange of eight packets took 0.0483 seconds, most of which was spent in getting the 16 bytes of data. Each of these packets is very small, and the entire exchange could have easily fit into two Ethernet packets.

In NetWare, each command must be in a separate packet. There have been vague suggestions by Novell that future versions of NetWare will support multiple requests sharing a single packet. This will conserve network resources, and provide rapid response time for short transactions like the one in Figure 5-23.

Locking and Synchronization

Directory security and file attributes combine to define an allowable set of operations that can be performed on a given file, and the different levels of access permitted to different groups of users. It is possible, however, that two valid users may submit operations that could corrupt data.

An easy example is the case of an account balance at a bank. The ATM machines for a bank are the workstations, and the Novell file server provides all the account information (it's obviously a very small bank). Since a bank has multiple branches and ATM machines and a given account can have multiple names on it, it is possible for two operations to arrive at almost the same time at the file server.

Both operations want to take $100 out of the same account, which has a current balance of $100. To withdraw money, the workstation first checks to

```
DETAIL
NCP:     ----- Open File Request -----
NCP:
NCP:     Request code = 76
NCP:
NCP:     Dir handle = 03
NCP:     Search attribute flags = 06
NCP:                 .... .1.. = System files allowed
NCP:                 .... ..1. = Hidden files allowed
NCP:     Desired access rights = 13
NCP:                 000. .... = Not defined
NCP:                 ...1 .... = Exclusive (single-user mode)
NCP:                 .... 0... = Allow others to open for writing
NCP:                 .... .0.. = Allow others to open for reading
NCP:                 .... ..1. = Open for writing
NCP:                 .... ...1 = Open for reading
NCP:     File name = "LOGIN"
NCP:
NCP:     [Normal end of NetWare "Open File Request" packet.]
NCP:
```

Fig. 5-18 Open File Request

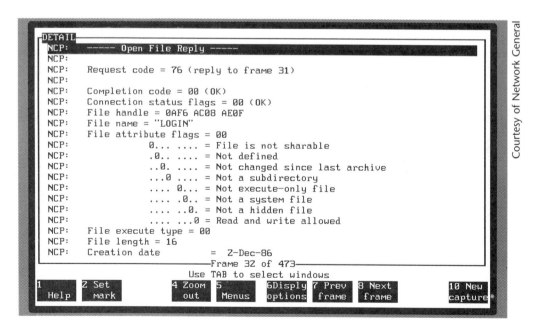

Fig. 5-19 Open File Reply

NetWare Core Protocols   135

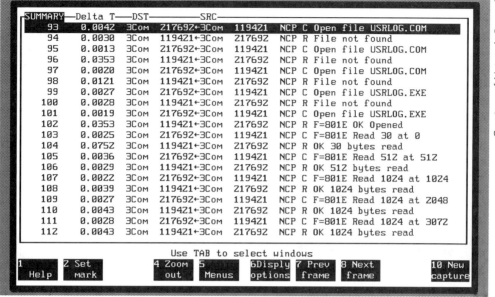

Fig. 5-20 Repeated Open Attempts

see if the balance is available, then dispenses the money to the user and updates the account balance record.

When each workstation submits its request to update data, there is a guarantee that all the operations of any one task will occur in the proper sequence, but there is no guarantee that the operations among different tasks will occur in any particular order.

In our example each workstation submits the request for the account balance, which returns to each an available balance of $100. Each workstation dispenses $100 and notifies the file server to subtract $100 from the balance. Not only is the bank in our example very small, but it will get significantly smaller if it continues this practice.

Locking a file ensures that other users are unable to access data that is being changed or about to be changed. In the bank example, the first workstation to submit the request would lock that record in the account file. Then, it would read the balance, dispense the money, and update the balance. When it was finished, it would release the lock. When the lock was released, the second operation would be granted its lock request on the customer record. It would see that the balance was $0, display some vaguely worded error message on the screen, and return the customer's card.

A series of system calls is provided in Novell networks to allow a program to lock a file or a portion of a file. The file can be locked for exclusive use or the lock can be shared. A shared lock is used to indicate that somebody is reading the file or a portion of a file and that an exclusive lock to write data should not be granted.

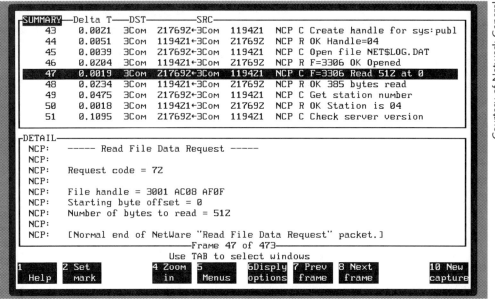

Fig. 5-21 Read File Request

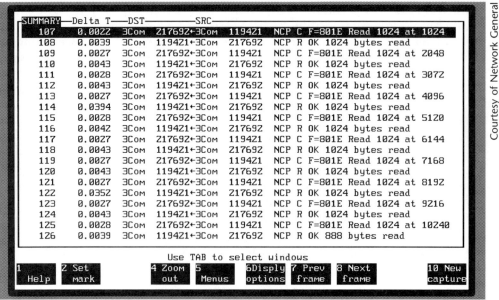

Fig. 5-22 Read Traffic

If a user currently has an exclusive lock on a file (known as a write lock), another user who requested a nonexclusive (read) lock on it would be denied. The request shown in Figure 5-24 would thus be denied.

Figure 5-24 also shows a timeout value on the lock request, in this case 0. A timeout value indicates how long the workstation is willing to wait before a lock is granted. If the file is currently busy, the lock manager on the file server will wait until the timeout value before returning with a lock unavailable status message in the reply.

A timeout value of 0 indicates that the workstation is not willing to wait. The file server should immediately decide whether or not to grant the lock and return a reply packet with the lock status. If the workstation is willing to wait, it is placed in a queue behind any previous lock requests waiting to be satisfied.

Novell allows files to be locked at the record or file levels. It is possible to have several exclusive record-level locks on a given file, as long as they are different portions of the file.

Normally lock requests are put into a log, which is a list of several lock requests for a workstation. The workstation decides which files and records to lock and submits the log request to the file server. The file server then sets about accumulating locks one by one. If a given lock is unavailable the server waits for the timeout value. If the timeout value expires, and there are still lock requests that have not been satisfied, the file server will release all the locks and return a message to the workstation.

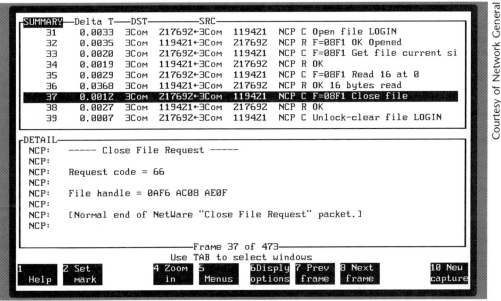

Fig. 5-23 Close File Request

A log of several lock requests is used to prevent deadlock, also known as a deadly embrace. If each workstation tries to accumulate several locks one by one, it is possible that one workstation will be holding a lock that another needs. If the other workstation is in turn holding the lock that the first workstation needs, they could easily wait forever.

Although NetWare does not, some operating systems have deadlock detection algorithms built into their lock manager. These algorithms cover the cases where the program doesn't know ahead of time all the locks it will need and accumulates them one by one. The lock manager detects the deadlock situation and notifies one of the user programs that its lock request has failed.

When a user program is done with a file, it must unlock it to allow other users to access it (see Fig. 5-25). If a user decides to go to lunch while a file is locked, no other users on the network can access that file. For this reason, many networks have a watchdog program that looks for any programs that have not submitted any activity for a long period. When the watchdog program finds such a user, it terminates the session, which frees up any locks held by that session. When the user came back from lunch, he or she would see a message on the workstation screen indicating that network access had been terminated. The user would simply restart the program, which would initiate another session.

In addition to record and file locks, the NetWare lock manager allows programs to define their own resources to lock, known as logical records. A logical record lock doesn't actually lock any data, it just locks a data structure in memory.

A logical lock might be defined by a database management system. The system could define a logical lock record that stood for the entire database. When a user program was performing administrative tasks on the database, it would take out an exclusive lock on this logical record. If another user tried to log into the database, the first thing the software would try to do would be to take out a nonexclusive lock on the logical record. Since an exclusive lock request had been granted, the lock would fail. This would indicate to the software that another user was performing an administrative operation, and it should not permit this additional user access to the software.

Semaphores

A lock allows a user to be included or excluded from a particular file or logical record. A semaphore is related to a logical record in that it doesn't apply to a physical concept—the software programs that are using the semaphore must agree on what the semaphore stands for.

Unlike the lock request, the semaphore is meant to control the number of simultaneous users instead of the kinds of simultaneous uses. When a semaphore is declared, it is given a value. Each user program that opens the semaphore will decrement that value by 1. When the value is 0, requests for the semaphore will be denied or put into a wait queue. A negative value indicates the number of users that are waiting to use the semaphore.

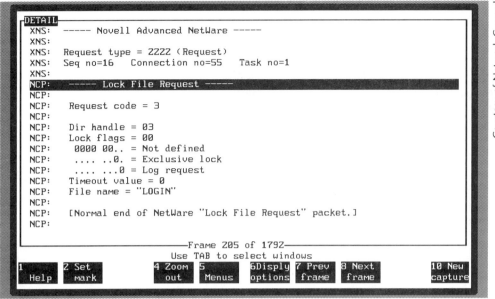

Fig. 5-24 Lock File Request

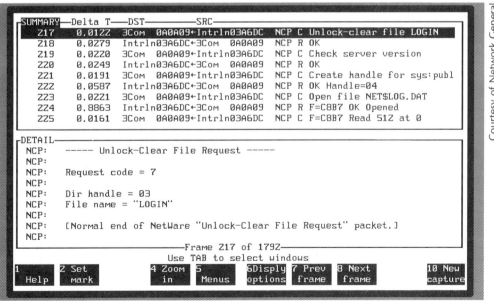

Fig. 5-25 Lock File Reply

A semaphore is ideal for limiting the number of simultaneous users for a particular software program. Some software is sold on the basis of how many simultaneous users will be allowed. These software packages can use semaphores to control the maximum number of users. When a user exits the software program, it sends a signal to the semaphore. This signal increases the value of the semaphore by 1, thereby permitting another user to log in.

Semaphores play a large part in software on Novell networks that rely on queuing for resources. For example, several users may be trying to access a printer. Or, there may be several users trying to access a database server. Semaphores are used to make sure that only a limited number of users access a given resource.

Print Services

The services previously described, file access, security, and locking, are all designed to make one kind of peripheral, the disk drive, transparently available over the network. Another kind of peripheral device, the printer, also needs to be made available to the workstation.

NetWare services for printer support are meant to allow a printer on a server to appear locally attached to the workstation. Because of the cost, a printer needs to be shared by several users, but DOS requires that the printer appear locally attached. The NetWare print services arbitrate access to the printer through a queuing mechanism.

On a PC workstation, printing is done by sending data to either a serial or parallel port. The Novell software allows the NetWare shell to "capture" output intended for a local serial or parallel port and send it over the network to a remote printer.

Several ports can be captured and routed to different printers on the network. Note that PCs have a limit on the number of serial or parallel ports they have, limiting the number of network printers available to a single PC at any one time. If the serial or parallel ports are in fact being used for something else, such as a mouse or modem, they are unavailable for use by Novell for printing.

We will see in Chapter 11 that this method is very different from the way Apple workstations treat printing. In an AppleTalk environment, printers are part of the network and an unlimited number of printers can be made available to the user. Apple workstations, even if participating in a Novell network, use the Apple printing architecture.

When a PC user has the OS/2 operating system, it is possible to have several different pieces of software running at the same time. The OS/2 version of NetWare allows the user to have a private capture of a parallel port that is used by only one piece of software. A plotter might be made available to a graphics package, for example. The OS/2 user can also have a global capture of a parallel port, which applies to all software packages running on the workstation. A laser printer, for example, might be the default printer for all software packages.

When a user captures a local parallel port, this includes designating the target printer across the network to use. The file server has a software program, known as a print server, that makes the printers available across the network. It manages all file server print resources, assigning each printer a number. It then makes the availability of its services known using the Service Advertisement Protocol and the bindery. The bindery stores the information on the printer's status, while SAP is used to make that information available to incoming requests.

When a job comes in, the print server puts it into a file in a subdirectory used as the queue for a particular printer. Note that the incoming data is not immediately printed. As soon as the print data is in the file, the application program is given an indication that printing is complete and returns control back to the user. The file eventually advances to the head of the queue and is then sent to the printer.

A variety of messages may go through the network used to control the particular characteristics of a remote print job. For example, the programmer can have the workstation portion of NetWare load in different banner pages, or forms, with each print job.

When a workstation starts up on a network, a program can use SAP to find out the availability of any print servers. Then, messages can be sent to the file server to find a description of the types of printers that it is offering. This information can include a verbal description as well as the capacity of the printer (i.e., maximum lines per page).

Next, the user chooses a remote printer and the local port to be captured. At this point, no network traffic is involved. The user can also choose things like the number of copies to print or the tab settings on the printer. When the user chooses to actually print, the capture begins and data is sent over the network to the print server.

While NetWare does provide a method for controlling who accesses which printer, standards on how to talk to a particular printer are not part of the network architecture. The print services are used to provide the basic connection to the printer. It is then the responsibility of the software package doing the printing to format the data in a way that the printer can accept.

An example of a language for describing how a page looks to a printer is PostScript, developed by Adobe Systems. Software programs, such as a word processor or graphics package, work with the user to develop the layout of a page. When the user wants to print, the software converts that page into a series of PostScript commands, which are sent to the printer (or put into a file for sending to a printer later). Other examples of page description languages are PCL, used in the Hewlett-Packard Laserjet, and Quickdraw, used in the Apple ImageWriter.

Job Servers

The print server is built into the basic core protocols and essentially provides a queuing mechanism for incoming requests. This queuing mechanism can also be made available in a more general sense to other software programs running on the file server.

These software programs could be a database management or corporate accounting system, or a wide variety of systems used to control peripheral devices.

For example, a server might have eight modems. A server program would be written that queued requests for the modems and then allocated them to the requesting users.

Another example would be controlling access to a local fax card on a file server. Users could send documents, along with a phone number, to the fax server. This server maintains a queue and sends the documents one by one over the telephone lines.

The NetWare Queue Management Services (QMS) are used by the job server as a way of managing incoming requests. (A program could also accomplish this task without the use of QMS. The program would perform queuing by using SAP, broadcasting its services, processing incoming files, and performing all the other steps used to manage incoming requests.) QMS allows the programmer to concentrate on the functionality of the software—such as how to convert the word processing document to fax format—instead of on how to make the services available via the network.

A queue presumes that there will be many requests coming in over the network to a limited resource. The resource can only service some finite number (usually one) of requests at once. QMS maintains a queue for a server with up to 250 requests in it.

Note that the nature of the request depends on the software program. QMS simply takes files and moves them around in a queue, keeping track of which task has which priority.

A particular queue maintained by QMS is then serviced by the server software program. The server software program submits a *get next job* call to QMS, which will return the number of the next job that the server should get.

It is possible to have up to 25 different software programs all sharing the same queue. Take the fax server example. If there are multiple fax cards on the computer, there would probably be one server for each card. Each server, after completing a job, would submit a *get next call* to QMS, which ensures that incoming jobs are fairly distributed in the order in which they came in.

A queue is actually defined on the file server as a bindery object. The bindery object is of type *QUEUE* and has a unique name. It also has four properties:

- The directory used by that queue
- A list of software programs that are servers for this queue
- A list of users that may use this queue
- The queue operator—a user (or group) who controls this queue

When a workstation submits a job to a queue, it submits two things. First, it submits the actual job, which is simply a file that will make some sense to the server program. Second, it also submits a work order for the job, which is used by QMS to control how the job is handled.

The work order can include the specific name of a server or simply the queue to be used. If a specific name is mentioned, QMS will wait until that particular software program requests a new job. If only the queue is mentioned, QMS instead gives the job to the next available server. The work order includes the name of the file (and a file handle) to be used when the server gets the actual job file. It may also include additional information, such as a target execution time for the job.

Later, the workstation can send a query through the network to find the current status of the job. QMS will examine the current status of the work order and determine if the job is being processed, in the queue, or finished. It can also determine which server processed the job.

Accounting Services

The last set of core services used by software programs is for accounting purposes. These services include a software program to charge a user's account for resources used. If the user's account falls below a certain amount (such as 0), the server might refuse to process a request.

Accounting can be used for a variety of purposes. The most obvious is to charge people money for the use of the computer. Many corporate networks, however, do not charge users directly for their use of resources. Instead, the networking budget is part of a separate department. In such an environment, accounting can still be quite useful. Sending people a listing of their usage of resources for a given period makes them much more aware of the impact of their activities on the network. Many networks send their users a bill even if no money is to be collected.

Accounting services in NetWare are based on the bindery. If an account is to be maintained for a user, two properties are added to the object corresponding to the user ID. The *ACCOUNT_BALANCE* property holds the current balance of the account. A second property is the *ACCOUNT_HOLDS*, which shows holds that have been put on the account but have not yet been charged.

A software program that wishes to charge for services is also put into the bindery and into a property of the file server object called *ACCOUNT_SERVERS*. The software program is then allowed to submit calls to the bindery that lower a particular user's account balance.

The actual charges to an account and any notes are stored in a file called *NET$ACCT.DAT*. Notes are used to describe the actions taken by a particular software server against an account. The charge record includes the ID of the server, the time that the record was inserted, the service performed, the ID of the client, and an amount to charge. The note record is just a long comment.

When a charge is made to an account, the account balance is adjusted in the bindery and one or more records are added to the accounting file to describe the nature of the charge. This accounting file continues to grow as charges are added. Periodically, the system manager has to move the data in the file to an archive. Typically, a system will move the accounting data to some special subdirectory, labeling each file by the time period to which it pertains.

The accounting file has the collection of information at a very high level of detail. This information needs to be processed to be made available to the user. Usually, this involves moving the data from an unstructured file into a database. If there are different Novell file servers on the network, the accounting files need to be unified into a consolidated accounting database before bills can be processed.

After the information is in the database, various types of reports are written. A bill, for example, is just a report listing individual charges and a few summary items, such as total charges. The Message Handling Service, described in the next chapter, can be used to mail the reports automatically to the users.

Other uses for this database are for the planning of network expansion. By tracking the usage of resources, the system manager is able to anticipate planned increases in use. If the system manager tracks the actual resources used (i.e., amount of CPU time, disk activity, or memory used), an increase in the number of users of one software program can easily be translated into the needed hardware resources to support the users.

Tracking resource utilization is an important aspect of managing a NetWare operating system or a Novell network. The accounting services should be supplemented by other types of information, such as security violations, the definition of each user (real name, phone number, log in directory, etc.), and any other information that helps define changes in the operating environment.

The network analyzer can also be used to feed information into the resource utilization database. Trace files can be used to show what types of operations are being performed on the network. Summary information of network utilization can be used to show the impact of certain periods of time or groups of software programs on available network bandwidth.

Keeping all this information in a relational database allows the system manager to use real information when planning budgets or trying to decide where a problem is. All too often, an organization will only add an accounting function to the network after it has gotten too large to handle. If the accounting function is added at the beginning, there is no need for the network to get too large to handle—managers will be able to plan and implement the network in a controlled, orderly fashion.

Key Points in This Chapter

- NetWare consists of the NetWare operating system on a server and the NetWare shell on the workstation. The "native" NetWare environment consists entirely of PCs.
- The NetWare shell intercepts calls from application programs and the operating system and packages them up as NCP requests for sending over the network.
- The NetWare server maintains a several connections with workstations. It maintains security using the bindery.
- The NetWare server maintains integrity among multiple users of data using a lock manager, which prevents users from making incompatible requests simultaneously.
- NetWare offers a variety of services in addition to data access, including printing, job management, and accounting.

CHAPTER 6

Message Handling Service

CHAPTER 6

Message Handling Service

Message Handling Services

A message handling service supplements the services of the basic file access mechanisms described in the previous chapter. Message handling services, typified by electronic mail, allow a user to send a message to another user. The second user is notified when the message is received. Although electronic mail is the typical application, message handling services have a variety of other uses. For example, messages can be sent from one database system to another, triggering updates of any data replicated between the two.

This chapter describes a particular message handling system, the Message Handling Service (MHS) from Action Technologies. MHS consists of a set of core programs that are used to provide the infrastructure for message transfer. The Novell subset of this technology is marketed under the name of NetWare MHS.

MHS has been bundled into the NetWare operating system, allowing the file server to also act as a message routing hub in a Novell network. Users still need to purchase a user interface—the program that presents messages to the user—or perhaps write their own. As will be seen, writing an interface to MHS is actually quite simple. A variety of vendors have written MHS-compatible user interfaces. These interfaces include electronic mail packages, such as Action Technologies' The Coordinator and cc:Mail's cc:Mail packages. They also include other applications, such as Ashton-Tate's Framework and Lotus's Agenda.

The combination of the user interface and MHS provides a complete message handling service. In addition, there are gateways out to other message handling services. MCI Mail, for example, is a commercial electronic mail service. By purchasing a gateway, it is possible to link an organization's local message handling environment with MCI Mail.

Of particular interest are gateways to X.400. X.400 is an international standard for message handling services. Many countries are building national electronic mail networks to supplement their telex, phone, postal, and other communications services. A gateway to X.400 allows users in a local organization to communicate with other users connected to the X.400 messaging environment. The MHS is like a PBX installed in a company. The PBX allows people within the organization to communicate among themselves and provides a variety of additional services, such as voice mailboxes.

The gateway is analogous to the link to the local telephone company, which in turn provides links to other telephone companies. X.400 is the standard that is used to connect to the messaging equivalent of the telephone company—a common carrier that is offering wide area transmission of messages (in many cases these services are indeed being provided by the telephone company).

It is possible that X.400 can also be used within an organization, just like an organization might install a private phone system. In the phone example, a PBX would be installed to permit local communications to be handled internally, bypassing the phone company. Similarly, an organization would use X.400 to route messages between different computer networks.

In a wide area example, an organization could run its own phone company—by leasing raw bandwidth from the common carriers or even laying their own cable. Similarly, an organization could use X.400 on top of common carrier packet switching networks using X.25 to build its own wide area messaging service.

MHS Message Structure

A basic message consists of three parts: the message header, the body, and zero or more attached files (see Fig. 6-1). The header includes, among other informa-

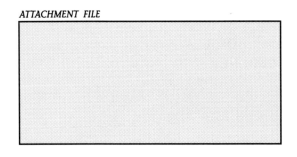

Fig. 6-1 Parts of an MHS Message

tion, the destination and source addresses for the message. The body is the text of the message. The attachment files can be in any format, including a DOS program to be mailed from one user to another.

The address for a message consists of four pieces of information, in the following format:

username.application@workgroupname.enterprise

First, there is the user's name. This name can be up to 64 characters long, but only the first 8 are significant. This means that the first 8 characters must be unique in a given group.

The workgroup name is a group of users on one or more computers. All of the users on one host must be in the same workgroup, and user names must be unique within a workgroup.

The application is the user interface that this particular message is going to. Each user has a preferred application, which is the default destination for delivering messages. The preferred application is usually an electronic mail user interface. Other applications might be a database system, scheduling software, or a word processor.

The enterprise name is an extension to the address added in Version 1.1 of the Message Handling Service. An enterprise is a collection of different workgroups and is known as a message handling domain. The workgroup is a subdomain of the enterprise.

The advantage in a domain naming system is that it simplifies message routing. When a host receives a message, it is responsible for routing it to the correct user. If the user is within that host's workgroup, the host will usually take responsibility for routing the message to the correct destination.

In large organizations, having every host know about every user would lead to considerable overhead, just as having every host on an internet know about every other host would also lead to overhead in the network layer protocols. When a host receives a message destined for another workgroup, the host does not even look at the username part of the address. Instead, it consults a routing table to decide which host is handling messages for that workgroup. Similarly, at the enterprise level, a host is not forced to know about every user in other enterprises. Instead, it routes the message over to a host that is part of that enterprise and lets it worry about how to get the message to the eventual destination.

Other Header Fields

In addition to the destination and source fields, the message header contains a variety of other fields that are used by the receiving application to decide how to handle this particular message (see Fig. 6-2). Note that this figure is not a real message header but merely a simulation for purposes of illustration.

The header begins with a variety of pieces of addressing information. For example, there is both a *to* and a *sent-to* keyword. The *to* address is the intended recipients of this particular message. The *sent-to* field is who this particular message was sent to. The reason for this distinction is that when mailing

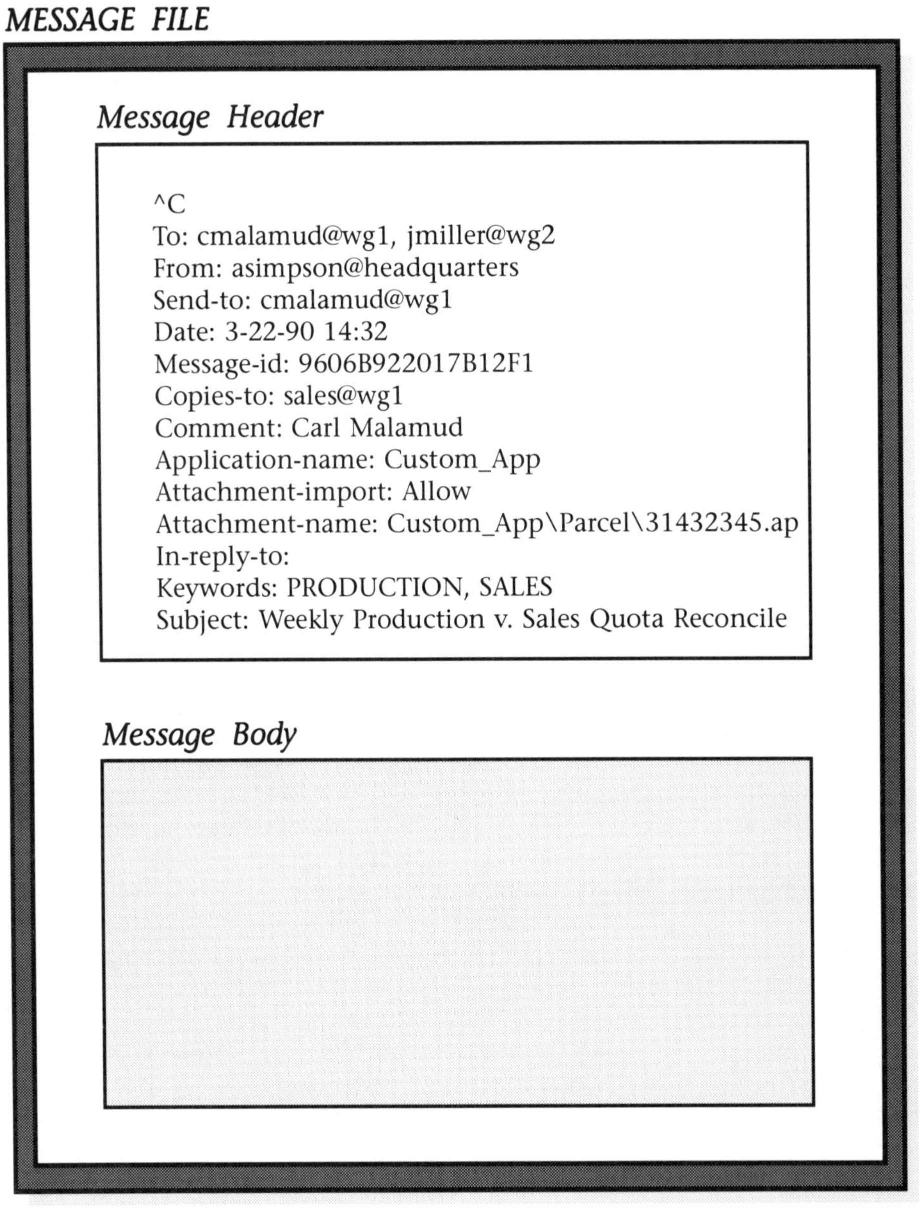

MESSAGE FILE

Message Header

^C
To: cmalamud@wg1, jmiller@wg2
From: asimpson@headquarters
Send-to: cmalamud@wg1
Date: 3-22-90 14:32
Message-id: 9606B922017B12F1
Copies-to: sales@wg1
Comment: Carl Malamud
Application-name: Custom_App
Attachment-import: Allow
Attachment-name: Custom_App\Parcel\31432345.ap
In-reply-to:
Keywords: PRODUCTION, SALES
Subject: Weekly Production v. Sales Quota Reconcile

Message Body

Fig. 6-2 Message Header

to several users, multiple copies of the message must be sent, one for each user. The *sent-to* field shows which of the multiple copies this one is. In the future, MHS may support the sending of a single copy of a message to multiple users on the same host, saving duplication of disk space and transmission time.

One extension to the address field is the comment keyword. By convention, this usually contains the full name of the sender. Most programs display the incoming message by first putting up the comment field, then putting the real address next to it in parentheses.

The message also includes a series of unique message IDs. The current message is identified by the *message-ID* keyword. The unique message ID is composed from the serial number of the sending machine plus an encoded value for the current date and time.

The *in-reply-to* keyword indicates the ID for a previous message. The application that is managing this mailbox could be designed in a way that allows the user to pull up the text of this related message.

An important point to note is that not all applications will respond to a given keyword in the header. Some keywords may not be understood by a given application, and it will not cooperate. For example, the sender of a message could include the importance keyword, which allows the sender to suggest that a message is of high priority and should go to the head of the user's message queue. A particular application may decide to ignore that keyword, putting the incoming message at the end of the queue.

The message may also have a *respond-by* keyword in it, containing a date that the recipient should respond by. An application that is sophisticated might enter a tickler in the user's calendar so on that day he or she is reminded to respond. Needless to say, even if the application handles the keyword, the user might decide not to honor it.

Each keyword field may also contain an option specifier, which governs how the receiving application is supposed to treat that field. For example, one option specifier tells the receiving application not to show the keyword.

Fields like the message ID are good candidates for not being displayed to the user. An application uses the option specifiers, plus its own convention, to decide what portion of the header the user will be interested in.

Other option specifiers govern whether the particular field should be saved or deleted from the header. One option is to discard the field before delivering a message to the user. This option might be used for the account number of the sender, which is needed by some intermediate system before it will forward messages.

If the keyword is delivered with the message, this option specifier indicates whether it should be returned in responses to this message. The subject field is a good candidate for a return message, for example. Returning the message ID of the message along with a reply is also a good practice.

The Message Body

The message body immediately follows the header and is contained in the same file. The message body is currently limited to ASCII printable text, plus carriage returns and line feeds. This guarantees that the message will be able to be transmitted over the widest possible variety of message handling systems.

The message body is limited to 8192 characters. It is usually recommended that messages be limited to a line length of 74 characters so they can be displayed on many different types of display stations.

It is possible that in the future MHS will support other types of message bodies, such as a program to be run or a graphics file. For the time being, the attachment file is the place to put those types of messages.

Message Attachments and Encoding

The attachment is a separate file that is transmitted along with the message. The file is limited to 32 Mbytes, although there is an additional constraint that the file must be smaller than one-third of the free disk space in all the hosts that the message will pass through. It can contain different kinds of information. Users can mail software or graphics images to each other. Files can be mailed between different kinds of computers, such as a Macintosh to a PC.

In order to handle the many different kinds of information, the sending application can specify how the attachment file is encoded. For example, text on a PC is stored as a 7-bit code. Each combination of the bits represents a character that can be displayed on the screen (or a nondisplayable character such as an escape code).

On the PC, this 7-bit ASCII representation is used by a program that is attempting to display the file. For example, a word processor would use the contents of the file to decide what characters are in a document. On the PC, this encoding scheme is the default for the message handling service. Microsoft Windows and the Macintosh both use a different encoding scheme than the standard IBM character set.

Since the encoding mechanism is specified, the receiving application knows whether or not it will have to translate the attachment. MHS supports many encoding methods, including binary files, and sets that restrict the characters to those that are printable on telex or other primitive display systems.

The encoding information is particularly important when the message is being sent among different message handling services. The gateway between the two domains is responsible for translating the incoming MHS message into a form readable by the other environment. Encoding is also important to applications that use MHS for delivering more than just electronic mail. For example, the attachment file might include voice or a fax that was being delivered to the user. The receiving application could then decide how to "display" the voice.

The User Interface

The user interface, or application, is a separate program from the Message Handling Service. MHS is responsible for delivering messages to a subdirectory designated as the mailbox for incoming messages. The application can do what it will with those messages. Normally, the application will take incoming messages and display them to the user. However, an application could take incoming messages and run them through a program, such as one that updates a database. A program can easily be written that takes incoming messages, processes them one by one, and submits updates to the corporate database. Presumably, the messages would have to be in an agreed-upon format, and the program would return any messages that it couldn't process properly.

The application can then send messages by depositing them in another subdirectory, that has been designated as the outgoing mailbox. The message handling service periodically cleans out that directory and sends any messages on to their destinations.

Several vendors have packages that interact with the MHS. Companies like cc:Mail and DaVinci Systems have electronic mail interfaces for MHS (in the case of cc:Mail, the interface is a gateway between their own message handling domain and MHS, along with the user interface). Database companies like Ashton-Tate, Lotus, Informix, and Paradox also have links to MHS. Action Technologies, the makers of MHS, also sell two user interfaces. MacAccess is meant for the Macintosh, and the Coordinator II is used on the IBM PC.

Figures 6-3 through 6-5 show the interaction between different programs via MHS. In our example, MHS is being used to coordinate a reconciliation between the current sales forecasts and the production schedules in place. The information will be used to adjust quotas of the sales staff so they sell what the factory is currently scheduled to produce. This is known as supply-motivated sales management—we schedule production at the discretion of manufacturing, then whip the sales staff into selling that inventory (or restrict them during times of low capacity).

The process begins with data being taken from the production database that reflects current manufacturing plans. Framework III from Ashton-Tate can be used to extract the relevant data. The information is then mailed to the sales manager, with the Lotus Agenda package put down for the receiving application.

Lotus Agenda imports the information, which is then compared to the current sales quotas. Revised sales quotas are generated, and the information is then mailed to the sales staff. The sales staff, in turn, uses a variety of electronic mail packages. The example shows cc:Mail and The Coordinator, but other uses could be using MacAccess on the Macintosh or WordPerfect Office or even a user interface they wrote themselves (during periods of low supply, one hopes).

The Message Transfer Agent

Up to this point, we have concentrated on what a message looks like and how it is used. The message transfer agent is responsible for taking that completed message and delivering it to its destination.

Two sets of protocols are involved in this change. First, the application and the message transport agent must agree on how messages are to be exchanged. Next, there is another set of protocols that govern how messages get transferred through the message handling service.

Submitting a message to be sent is actually a fairly simple matter. First, of course, the message must be in the proper format. The application must generate a message header and body that conform to the rules of MHS.

The application is then sealed, which puts a routing header on it. The routing header is used by the message transfer agent to determine the nature of this message. The routing header is 128 bytes long and contains fields that indicate the source and destination addresses, the size of the message, any attachment files, and the current delivery status of the message.

After the message is sealed, the application must put the message file and the attachment files into the proper location. The attachment is first put into a subdirectory called *mail\parcel*. Next, the message itself is put into a *mail\out* subdirectory.

The reason the message is put into the directory last is to coordinate with the software that will be collecting the mail for delivery. When the message transfer agent looks for mail, it does so by checking the out subdirectory. If a particular message has a file associated with it, that information will be included in the routing header.

In order to collect a message, MHS must be able to read it. If the application is in the middle of creating the new message file in the proper directory and writing into it, the MHS will be unable to read the file; MHS will bypass that message and come back to it later. A message is officially submitted to the MHS right after the message file is closed.

MHS delivers messages to a particular application by putting them into a subdirectory. There is one subdirectory in the MHS file structure for each

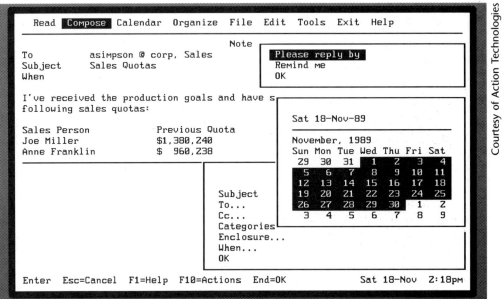

Fig. 6-3 ATI's The Coordinator

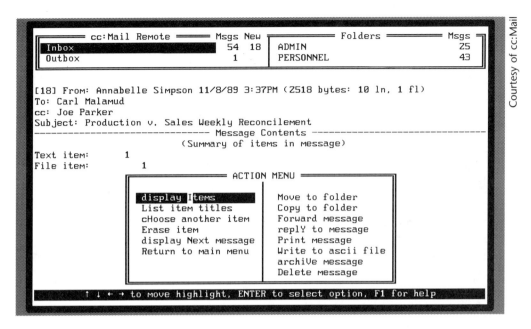

Fig. 6-4 Reading a Message in cc:Mail

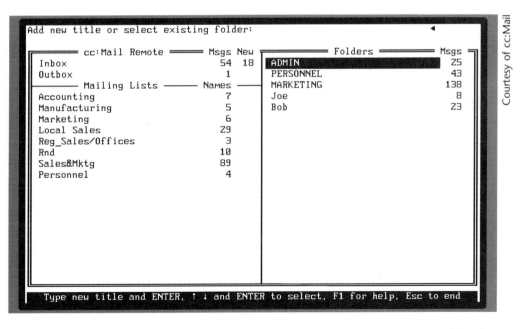

Fig. 6-5 Managing Mailing Lists

username. Subdirectories under a username are provided for each application, as is an incoming parcel subdirectory. The incoming parcel directory is used to hold all received attachment files. The application subdirectories are used for the delivery of individual mail messages. One of the subdirectories will be for the preferred application, which receives all messages that cannot be delivered to one of the application subdirectories.

If an application is sending mail to a local user, it is responsible for doing the delivery itself. In this case, the message would not need to be sealed with a routing envelope since messages are unsealed just as they reach the destination subdirectory.

The application would perform the local delivery simply by copying the message and attachment files into the appropriate subdirectories. The advantage of requiring applications to perform local delivery is that a message is instantly received. If the message were submitted to the message transfer agent, it would not be delivered until the MHS made its periodic rounds.

The Connectivity Manager and Hubs

The connectivity manager is the software program that is responsible for scheduling message delivery and the maintenance of routing tables. The transport server is the software program that takes care of the transfer of the message to another host.

Computers in an MHS environment are classified as hosts and hubs. A host is a computer that has users on it. A hub, which may also be a host, is responsible for accepting messages and sending them out to the appropriate host. Sometimes, a message will travel through several different hubs before it reaches the destination host.

Each workgroup has a special hub known as the workgroup-wide router. If a given host or hub does not know how to deliver a message, it will be sent to the workgroup-wide router, which is responsible for knowing how to find all users in that workgroup. A hub is just a special case of a host in that it routes messages out to other computers in the message handling environment. Each host has a connectivity manager on it that schedules the activation of connections to other machines.

The connectivity manager maintains a routing directory to enable it to decide which messages will go to which hub. The routing directory says which of the neighboring hosts are handling which workgroups. If the local connectivity manager does not know how to get to the destination address, it simply sends the message on through to another host that will know what to do with it, such as the workgroup-wide router. If none of the hosts in a particular workgroup know what to do with a message, it will be sent over to an enterprise-wide router. Eventually, the message will either be successfully delivered or it will reach a host that has no place to send the message.

Once the message reaches the end of the line and cannot be delivered, it is returned to the original sender as undeliverable. A good analogy is to a postal system. We can send a message that has a correct city and state but an incorrect street address. When the message is originally deposited, the local post office will determine that the message is going to a remote site. The post office doesn't try to look up the street address. Instead, it sends it to a city-wide post office, which in turn will know how to get it to the destination state. Once in the destination state, it will be sent to the appropriate city.

It is only when the message has reached the target city that somebody will be in a position to see that the message is undeliverable. At that point a new message is constructed that goes back to the original sender. This special type of message has the original message in it and additional header fields that indicate that it could not be delivered.

The connectivity manager has a scheduling cycle. It makes periodic sweeps of the incoming and outgoing mail areas. If it sees that there are messages that are bound for a neighboring host, it looks in its schedule and decides if the messages should be delivered now.

It is possible to configure a given connection for a specific cycle. For example, one neighboring host would be set up with a scheduling cycle of once per day. Once per day, the connectivity manager will activate a connection to that host. Other hosts are scheduled on demand. This allows the connectivity manager to request a connection when it has messages to send to that neighboring host.

Other neighboring hosts have a scheduling cycle of infinity, meaning that the remote host will be initiating all transfers. Even if this host is not activating any connections to remote hosts, the connectivity manager must still make periodic sweeps of the incoming mail area to see if there are any new messages that have been delivered.

The transport server is activated by one connectivity manager and is responsible for making a connection to the remote host, transferring outgoing messages, and processing incoming messages. Transport servers are able to use networks and asynchronous dial-up lines to do message transfer. Network transfer servers, such as the Novell version of MHS, use the underlying transport protocols on the network (IPX and SPX) to transfer messages to other hosts. In addition to NetWare, MHS supports network-based transport servers on IBM PC LAN, 3Com 3+, Banyan VINES, and AppleTalk local area networks. Asynchronous servers use modems to activate a call to the remote destination and transfer data. A third type of transport server uses the X.25 protocols to make the connection to the remote host.

The most efficient environment for message transfer is a local area network. In this type of environment, all the hosts can operate on demand because there is usually not enough message traffic to make a severe dent in available network bandwidth. In this type of environment, the connectivity manager will periodically activate and make a sweep of the incoming mail area. It will deliver all local mail to the appropriate directories. Messages that are destined for another host are placed in the outgoing mail area.

The connectivity manager then calls the transport server to make connections to all the appropriate neighboring host. The transport server will send all outgoing mail and receive any incoming messages. After the connectivity manager has called all neighboring hosts, it goes back to the incoming mail area. It again delivers all local mail and places any outgoing mail in the appropriate subdirectory. Then, the connectivity manager makes another cycle of connections to the neighboring hosts. Making the cycle twice provides a high probability that a route-through message will in fact make it through this host in one scheduling cycle.

Gateways

A gateway is a special kind of application that takes incoming messages from MHS and sends them out to another message handling environment. The gateway developer simply writes two programs, calling them *INPOST* and *OUTPOST*.

The gateway is then registered with the host in the network directory table. On each scheduling cycle, the connectivity manager will take all incoming messages bound for the gateway and place them in the appropriate subdirectory. Then, it executes the *OUTPOST* utility provided by the gateway developer, followed by *INPOST*.

INPOST is used by the connectivity manager to translate messages from the gateway's format into MHS format. The *OUTPOST* is used to translate any incoming messages from MHS into the proper format needed by the gateway.

Gateways have two main applications. The most obvious is to translate a message into another format and then send it back out through another message handling environment.

A less obvious use is for interaction with a database management system. In this case, the *INPOST* and *OUTPOST* utilities would be SQL-based programs that took the incoming messages and prepared them for updating the database. Outgoing messages could be reports that are generated for users automatically, such as current sales reports.

Gateways use an extension of the normal MHS addressing mechanism. The address extension allows gateway-specific address information to be embedded in the address. The gateway uses that information to decide how to continue to route the message. For example, a fax gateway takes an incoming mail message and sends it via the fax lines. The address extension in this case is used to decide what telephone number to dial.

The MHS specifications have provisions for several different kinds of gateways. Additionally, developers can specify their own format for the extended part of the address for special applications.

The predefined address extensions are used to provide a standard way of exchanging messages across a message handling domain. Figure 6-6 shows the different kinds of systems that have predefined address extensions.

One of the predefined types of extended addresses is for paper-based message handling services, i.e., the postal service, sometimes known as snail mail. There, the address extension consists of up to six lines of address information. Writing an outgoing snail mail gateway is actually a simple matter. The developer would only have to write the *INPOST* routine, since presumably messages could not be routed cheaply from the postal system into the electronic mail environment.

The snail mail gateway would be on a system that had access to a laser printer with at least two trays, or to two laser printers with one tray each: one for envelopes, the other for paper.

The *INPOST* routine would take the incoming message and submit two print jobs. The first would take the address field and submit a print job to print the envelope. A fancy system would print a return address, possibly even putting the name of the sender as well as the name of the organization. The second part of the *INPOST* routine would be to print the message body on the printer. Presumably, both printers would be in a location that is accessible to the corporate mail room. The mail staff would take envelopes, stuff them with the body, and then send them out.

Fax Gateways

A gateway to a fax system enables the user to send a message, which is translated by the gateway into the fax format and then sent to the appropriate telephone number. The advantage of this approach is that a document that is prepared on a computer does not then have to be printed out before it can be sent over the telephone lines.

Establishing a fax gateway is actually a fairly simple matter. Several vendors sell fax boards for PCs that can send and receive fax messages. The gateway is responsible for translating the incoming message from ASCII text or a popular word processor format such as WordPerfect or Microsoft Word to fax. Such a conversion can be done with several popular utilities, such as Hijaak from Inset Systems. Graphics images in several formats can also be translated into fax format.

Messaging System	Format for MHS Users
MHS	user.application@workgroup.enterprise
Telex	username@workgroup <X121:ESC8Telex-number;>
Fax	username@workgroup AX:Telephone-number
PDS (Postal Delivery System)	username@workgroup <PDS:line1|line2|line3|line4|line5|line6>
X.400	username@workgroup <X.400 Address>
Tandem	fam_name@gw_WG { correspondent_name@long_long_host }
3Com	username@workgroup { name:domain:organization }

Fig. 6-6 MHS Address Extensions

This gateway is registered just as any other would be, by putting an entry in that host's network directory. Users would send messages to the fax gateway using the extended addressing format:

TO: fax@sales {fax:14155551212}

The message would be routed to the appropriate host within the sales workgroup. There, the *INPOST* routine would be activated by the connectivity manager.

The *INPOST* routine, provided by the fax gateway developer, would do three things. First, it would examine the message header and determine the destination phone number. Second, it would translate the message body into fax format. Third, it would dial the telephone number and attempt to deliver the message. A sophisticated implementation would send a receipt back to the sender that gave the status of the transmission and what time it actually occurred.

This discussion does not, of course, mean that users have to write their own gateways. In the case of a fax system, several commercial systems are available that are compatible with MHS. Castelle, for example, has a network fax server called FaxPress. This system connects to a Novell network, and lets users send and receive fax messages over the network.

Commercial Gateways

A variety of vendors have gateways that interact with other message handling environments. Softswitch, for example, has gateways that link MHS with the following environments:

HP's HPDesk
IBM's PROFS and DISOSS
DEC's ALL-IN-ONE and VMSMail
Data General's CEO
Wang's Wang Office

The gateway consists of two dedicated PCs on the Novell network. The MAILbridge Server/MHS is the gateway to the other environment. A second PC has the MHS software on it (see Fig. 6-7).

Gateways also exist to commercial services such as CompuServe and MCI Mail. MCI Mail is especially interesting as a gateway because it allows outgoing messages to be directed to many other computer networks (such as CompuServe), as well as to fax, telex, and snail mail systems.

A gateway to MCI Mail allows the user to have access to people not connected to an electronic messaging environment while still retaining the benefits of word processing, message editing, calendar management, and other types of office automation.

The MCI Mail gateway consists of the M-Bridge MCI Mail Gateway, made by On-Site Communications. This software usually runs on a PC dedicated to MHS and gateway tasks but can be combined with a file server in a small environment.

Next, the user needs to subscribe to MCI Mail. This consists of an MCI Mail Remote Electronic Mail (REM) account, which allows an unlimited number of users in an organization to access MCI Mail. This is because MCI Mail allows the organization to register their enterprise name. MCI Mail then does not worry about the individual user part of the destination address. It routes the mail to the designated hub, which is responsible for final delivery (actually, the designated hub calls MCI Mail and picks up its messages).

X.400 and MHS

Of particular use to many computing environments are links between MHS and X.400-based messaging systems. X.400 is an international standard for messaging systems that has been widely supported by both national governments and commercial message handling providers. The term X.400 comes from the numbering system designed by the standard's developers, the International Telegraph and Telephone Consultative Committee (also known as the CCITT, which is an acronym for the French version of the organization's name).

X.400, like MHS, defines how a message handling service should be organized. It defines an address space—an organization of users into subdomains and domains. It defines a standard header structure for a message and how to encode the envelope. Finally, it defines actions that should be taken for the transferring of messages—the message transfer agent.

Note that X.400 is often referred to as an "MHS"—a message handling service. This should be distinguished from the particular product discussed in this chapter, Action Technologies' MHS. ISO has also adopted the 1988 CCITT revision of X.400. This ISO standard is often referred to as "ISO MHS," again distinct from the Action Technologies product.

X.400 and MHS are very similar in their functions but serve different purposes. Their similarity is in how messages are structured and addressed. The differences lie in how the different message handling services are typically used. MHS is meant for the administration of the organizational environment. This means knowing the exact location of each user and providing routing services within the organization. MHS also includes a specification of exactly how messages are to be delivered to individual users and applications.

X.400 focuses less on delivery to the individual user and more on the delivery of messages between organizations. As such, it is a standard that is being widely used by telephone companies, postal services, and other national administrations that are setting up electronic messaging services in a country or state.

MHS goes somewhat beyond X.400 in the services it provides to the individual user. It is tailored for a sophisticated electronic mail environment where different applications are able to exchange messages. There's no reason that X.400 couldn't provide some of these services, but because it is an international standard instead of a proprietary standard/software combination, it takes longer to change.

X.400 provides the links to the outside world. Receiving users might not have MHS but instead would have their own local electronic mail messaging system and user interfaces. On an IBM mainframe, for example, the user might

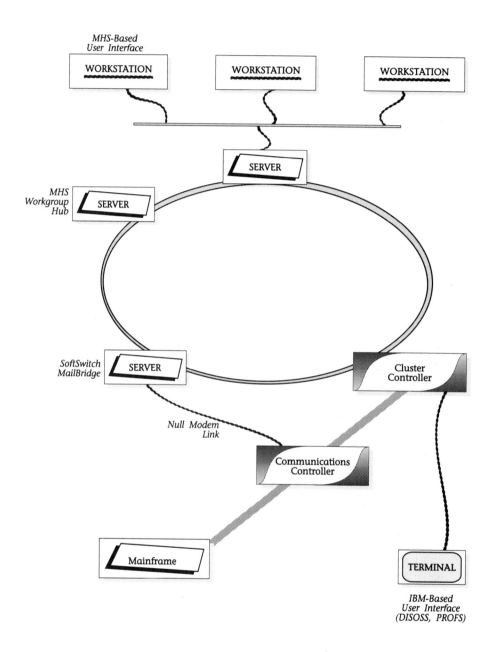

Fig. 6-7 Softswitch Gateway to IBM Mainframes

have the SNADS message handling system and the DISOSS user interface. On a VAX, the user would have DEC's Message Router and the All-In-One user interface.

Since X.400 is becoming the standard for connectivity, it is becoming unnecessary to install many different gateways, one for each of the different messaging environments that needs to be connected to the others, plus additional gateways to provide alternate routing for increased performance and reliability.

Routing also becomes more efficient in an X.400 environment. Routing is left to organizations with dedicated wide area message handling networks, such as telephone companies. If the commercial provider is unable to provide the performance needed, the organization can always install dedicated lines and use MHS or X.400 to combine two environments.

One of the significant differences between X.400 and MHS is the complexity of the address. X.400 supports a wider variety of address formats than the MHS basic address. To handle this problem, the extended MHS address includes the X.400 address:

username@workgroup <X.400 Address>

Before we describe what an X.400 address looks like, it is worth noting that most users will not have to concern themselves with either the basic or the extended part of the MHS address. Aliases are maintained either by the application or MHS that allow a user to refer to other people by their human names or by the name of a distribution list.

Mapping electronic mail addressed to human names is usually done by the administrator of the message handling environments. The administrator, also known as the postmaster, usually sets up mailing lists for all the major departments and groups in an organization. Administrators also set up aliases for all members of the organization in either the MHS network directory table or in the application's directory service.

An X.400 address needs to be more flexible than an MHS address because addresses will be used for an exchange of messages to many different locations and systems locations. An analogy to the telephone system is once again useful to see why this is necessary.

Telephone numbers vary widely in different countries, allowing each country to decide how it will configure its telephone system. The basic format of an address, however, is a series of domains and subdomains.

When an international telephone call is placed, the local telephone system first sees the international access code. It then looks at the international country code of the call. The rest of the number is sent on through to some central routing facility for the country in question.

Once the call request is received in the destination country, it looks at the next few digits of the number, the area code. The call is moved forward to the routing facility for that area, which puts the call through to the designated number (or is unable to place the call and plays a recording back).

One X.400 version of the address is actually almost identical to the telephone system. This is the telex address, which uses the addressing scheme set out in the CCITT X.121 standard. To send mail to a telex user (or other messaging system that is accessible via an X.121 address), the MHS user would enter the following address:

    username@workgroup <X121:ESC8Telex-number;>

Here, ESC8 stands for a standard escape character.

There are three basic address variants defined in the 1984 version of the X.400 standard, and others are defined in the 1988 version. Basically, each address consists of some required and some optional pieces.

In variant 1 of the address, the user puts in the country the message is going to, a private domain name (such as the name of a service provider like the telephone company), the name of the organization, a department within that organization, and a personal name. Additionally, the address can include any domain-specific attributes, such as the office location of the individual. Not all messages sent out using this form of address will include all the pieces. The sender must furnish enough pieces of the address that a computer that receives the message will be able to route it through to the next computer.

Like traditional mail systems, some are very good; others may not even send mail with extremely precise addresses to the destination. The collection of organizations and domains also varies by country. In the United States, for example, there are two different ways of setting up domains. The first uses the state as a subdomain, then the organization name as a sub-subdomain. The second method categorizes organizations as educational, governmental, military, or commercial. Each of those naming domains then organizes its addresses into various subdomains.

The most precise form of addressing is necessary when routers are not aware of the wider domains they participate in. As routers get smarter, addresses can become more and more flexible. For example, in routing mail to a user at Harvard University, one could probably leave off the city and state. Simply entering *Harvard.Edu* is enough to get the message to the central routing facility for Harvard.

The second and third variants of the X.400 address are based on numbers. One is based on the X.121 address and includes the name of the country, plus the X.121 number. The last variant consists of a country name and some other number as specified by that country or domain.

In an MHS environment, the X.400 address is specified by including a code for the particular part of the address that is being described, followed by a value. For example, in listing the country name, part of the address would be:

    CTA:USA

A personal name consists of the surname, the given name, any initials, and a generational qualifier, all separated by the | symbol:

    PN:Malamud|Carl|A|I;

The combination of the two would be the following MHS address:

malamud@X400 <CTA:USA;PN:Malamud|Carl|All;>

The MHS part of the address will vary with the way a particular organization is set up. The X.400 part of the address is sufficient to ensure that MHS delivers the message to the X.400 gateway (which would promptly return the message as undeliverable because the address did not specify enough information).

Action Technologies is working with several vendors to develop X.400 gateways, including projects with Touch Communications and British Telecom. It is also possible to run X.400 internally on the organization's Novell network, using the hardware and software from Retix.

Directory Services

One important issue, as can be seen from the discussion of X.400 addresses, is how to find somebody's address. Directory services allow a person to find the address of a user in a particular domain. There are two issues here. One is how you organize and present names to users in a way that allows them to easily determine where a message should go (or where it came from). This is a question for the application that is serving as a directory.

With gateways, there will be a broad spectrum of users to communicate with. A directory maintained by an application can only hold so many entries on a local workstation or file server. At some point, there needs to be a way of asking a remote domain about the addresses it maintains. This distributed naming service is an important issue in the future of message handling systems. The basic idea is to have a name server for each domain or subdomain keep track of the users within that area. A name server would be able to send a query to a name server in another domain.

This query could be used to verify that an address is correct or to perform wild-card searches on all addresses bearing certain characteristics. For example, a query might ask for all users with the surname of Simpson in the city of London in England. This particular query would probably generate a very large response. The response is sent back to the name server that submitted the query (and ultimately to the user that initiated the search). The message is sent back as an X.400 message and may include charges levied by any of the networks that handled the message.

The functions of these name servers are being defined in an extension to X.400, the X.500 directory services. Name servers in the underlying networking software are also important as they often provide the platform used to implement the X.500 service in a particular environment.

Key Points in This Chapter

- The Message Handling Service is a product developed by Action Technologies and available on a wide variety of networks, including NetWare. Novell bundles MHS into the operating system as NetWare MHS.
- There are two parts to MHS: the message transfer agent and the user interface.
- The message transfer agent moves messages from one user to another.

- The user interface can be any of several different applications, ranging from electronic mail to database systems.
- A gateway is used to connect MHS with other message handling environments.
- Gateways exist to fax, MCI Mail, CompuServe, and a variety of messaging systems including IBM's SNADS and DEC's MAILbus.
- X.400 is an emerging international standard for message exchange. MHS and X.400 do many similar things, but MHS is tailored for the PC environment while X.400 is more general.

CHAPTER 7

Data Access

CHAPTER 7

Data Access

Flat Versus Structured Data Access

In Chapter 6, we examined the method used in a Novell environment to access files. When a user specifies a remote file, the NetWare Core Protocols are responsible for accessing the file and delivering data to the requesting user. For NCP requests, no structure is defined for files. The user can read blocks of data by specifying how many bytes to read and at what offset to begin reading. Once the data is returned to the program, the program must interpret each record.

This type of file is known as a flat file (see Fig. 7-1). The file is made up of a series of blocks of data; each block is typically 512 bytes in DOS and NetWare environments. The programmer might want to define the file as being a series of 80-byte records. The 80 bytes would then be split up into fields—name, address, and telephone number, for example.

This approach is not suitable when the user wants a small piece of data out of a large file. If the user were looking for the address of somebody whose name is

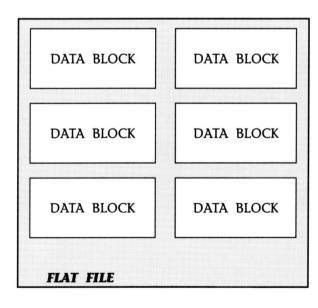

Fig. 7-1 A Flat File

Simpson, the program would have to retrieve all records until the desired one was found. Even then, the program would probably have to keep on searching in case there was a second record that had the same value for name. A flat file, therefore, is best suited for sequential access to data in which a program takes the file and reads all of the data blocks. This is suitable, for example, for a program that is going to be loaded into memory. For a data file, however, there may be instances where only pieces of the file are needed.

The flat file has two disadvantages. First, because more data is transferred, the operation is slower, especially over a network. Second, the programmer needs to write code that filters out the unneeded data.

This chapter discusses structured access to data—asking for data by the value of the information. This allows only the needed data to be retrieved, permitting faster operations and less programming. The chapter begins with a discussion of an alternate file structure, the binary tree (Btree). A Btree, and Novell's implementation of the Btree, Btrieve, allow a programmer to access data by specifying which rows are needed. Next, a higher level of structure, the SQL database, is discussed. Databases allow the programmer to refer to data by a logical name and not worry about programming the input and output. Support libraries provide this functionality, allowing the programmer to focus more on what the user wants and less on the mechanics of how to get the data.

The Btree File Structure

Btree is a method of structuring a file to permit direct access to specific records and is one of the more popular file structures, especially for PC-based database management systems. When data is loaded into a Btree file, it is sorted by an index value. An index is any part of the record that the programmer designates as the key part of the record. For example, we might have records of data that

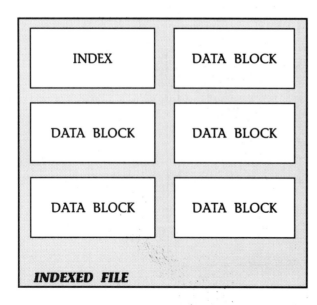

Fig. 7-2 An Indexed File

are each 80 columns long. The first 12 characters of the record are reserved for an employee's last name.

If we designate the first 12 characters as the index, or key, value, the data in the Btree will be sorted by employee name. Of course, the Btree file structure does not know that the first 12 characters happen to be the employee name field—only that it should sort based on the first 12 positions of each record.

The index is stored in a separate part of the file from the data blocks (see Fig. 7-2). If the file is frequently consulted, the blocks of the file that make up the index will be in the file cache—stored in main memory. Since the index is in main memory, there is little overhead in consulting the index because access to data that is in main memory is significantly faster than going to the disk to get it.

It would be possible for a programmer to implement this strategy even without Btree support on the file system. The programmer would designate the first several bytes of the file as the index. When the program started up, the index would be retrieved into main memory and then used for subsequent lookups.

Putting the Btree structure into the file system instead of having each programmer reinvent it has significant advantages. Of course, a big advantage is that programmers can skip writing this portion of the code. The second advantage is efficiency. The index is stored on the file server, meaning it doesn't have to be retrieved over the network for network-based programming. Even if the program is local to the file server, it is still more efficient to make the structured access a native part of the file system.

A file system that implements a Btree file structure is able to satisfy user requests for data by key value. With a flat file structure, the user can retrieve a specific record only if he or she knows its location—block 14, bytes 24 through 32, for example. In a Btree, the user is able to ask for all records that satisfy the condition:

    key_value = "Simpson"

This request is sent to the file system, which searches the file and returns zero, one, or several records. Because the indexing method is an inherent part of the file structure, this search is an efficient method for providing direct access to records by a key value.

It is possible that a user might not be interested in data that matches a key value. For example, the user might want to find all records that have a salary greater than a certain amount. Since the file is indexed by last name, the index will not be useful in finding records based on the salary field. In this case, the programmer would be forced to read the whole file, examining each record for the key value; the choice of which fields to make the index on is obviously a crucial decision.

Each Btree file has three parts: an index, leaf pages, and data blocks (see Fig. 7-3). The index and leaf pages are all stored at the beginning of the file. The data blocks then follow. The purpose of the index and leaf pages is to allow the file system to quickly find the address of all data by the value of the index field.

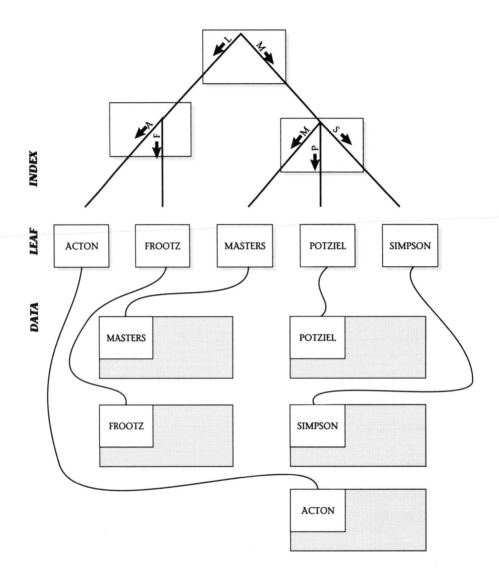

Fig. 7-3 Structure of a Btree File

The index is structured as a tree. Each part of the tree (known as a node) is used for a more and more precise definition of key values. The first level in Figure 7-3, for example, is used to differentiate between the first letter of names. If the name starts with M through Z, the file system consults the index pages on the right of the tree. If the name starts with A through L, the file system consults the index pages on the left part of the tree.

If we are looking up records based on a last name of Simpson, we will eventually end up at the bottom of the tree. This last level of the index is known as the leaf pages. The leaf pages are also an index and contain addresses for the data blocks that fall within that range.

The file structure, in our example, has *SIMPSON* as the value of the leaf page and pointers to four different data blocks. The file system would then read all four of the data blocks and return them to the requesting program.

The leaf pages have the important attribute of allowing sequential access to the data in sorted order. If the user had requested all names *greater than SIMPSON* (i.e., all names that fall later in the alphabetic sequence), the file system would have found the first leaf page that qualified. Then it would have read all the subsequent leaf pages, retrieving the data blocks as it went. The index provides direct access to data. The leaf pages then allow sequential access to data.

Novell's Btrieve

Novell's Btrieve product is an implementation of the Btree file structure on the NetWare operating system. This product is bundled in with the basic NetWare operating system and includes an access program for workstations. Companies like Informix sell similar products that allow Btree files to be stored on DOS or other operating systems. All of these products allow a programmer to define an indexed file and then access data by key value.

Btrieve consists of a library on the client side and two processes that run on the computer acting as the Btree server (see Fig. 7-4). The user can directly access the file using an interactive program or write a program that uses the Btrieve libraries. Interactive access to data uses a program called Xtrieve, which is used to access a Btrieve file.

On the server side, there are two programs. Both programs are implemented as Network Loadable Modules on NetWare 386. On older versions of NetWare, this file manager is a Value-Added Process.

The *BSERVER* process is used to access the files and is responsible for maintaining the indices on a file when it is updated. It also processes retrieval requests to search by index values. The *BSERVER* interacts with the Transaction Tracking System (TTS) to provide file recovery and rollback capabilities in the case of system crashes.

The *BROUTER* serves as an interprocess communication mechanism that allows a program on the server to request data from other file servers. It accepts a request for data and, if the data is on another server, sends the request to the *BROUTER* on that server. The *BROUTER* then sends the request down to the *BSERVER* process. Do not confuse the *BROUTER* process used for Btree file access

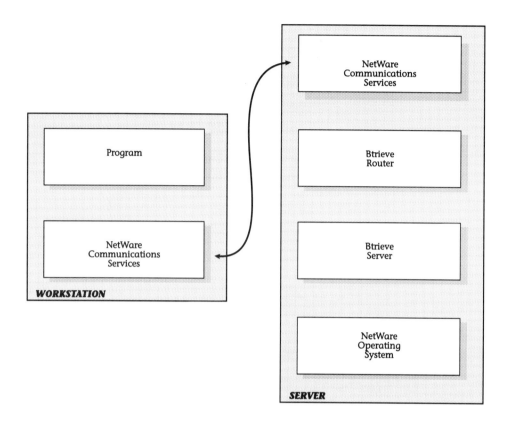

Fig. 7-4 Components of Novell's Btrieve

with the marketing term "brouter," which is used for a bridge that is able to function at both the MAC and network layers.

SQL and Databases

While Btrees provide efficient access to data from a computer's point of view, they are not necessarily efficient from the point of view of the user. This is because a Btree is still a file and requires the user to know what the data is in the records and how it is structured.

The Btree provides efficient access to the data based on a key value. That key value might be in positions 1 through 8 of an 80-column record. This definition, of course, raises an interesting question: What are we storing in positions 1 through 8? Is it last name? Zip code? Favorite food?

Any file raises the problem of what data is contained in it. The definitions are not apparent and must be stored someplace else. This typically means that a program must be written to access each file. The program contains the definitions of the data and provides some method for returning rows of data and displaying them.

Writing a program to do this might be justified for a large corporate accounting system but does not make sense when there are a variety of ad hoc spontaneous requests for data. Each time the requests for information change, a new program needs to be written.

Databases provide a further level of access to data. Often, the database is composed of a series of Btree files. However, the data files are supplemented by some additional files that define what data is stored. Instead of specifying which files to access and which key values, the user asks for data in a logical method. Data is structured as a series of tables, each with columns and rows (see Fig. 7-5). The user asks for certain columns of data and rows that meet certain qualifications. For example, the user might ask for the column *employee* where the column *salary* is less than a certain value. That request would retrieve zero, one, or several rows of matching data.

The language used to request this information is the Structured Query Language (SQL). SQL is an international standard for a query language. When a

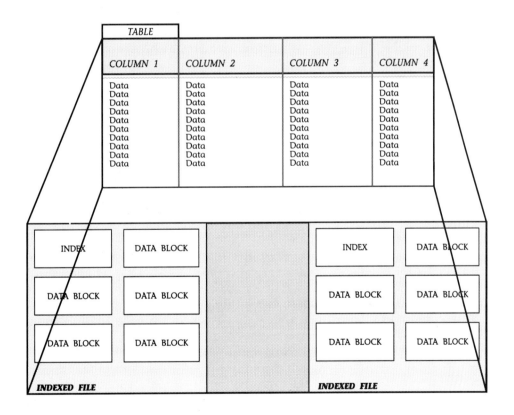

Fig. 7-5 Tables and Files

database server receives an SQL request, it looks at the underlying files, decides how to get the data, and returns qualifying rows to the user.

SQL permits logical access to data. The user doesn't have to worry about setting up a program that defines all the different columns in a particular file. That information is stored in the data dictionary for the database. The database server thus provides an increased level of transparency over the Btree file.

SQL has another important attribute as a query language. Inherent in the SQL language is the concept that a given query might retrieve several rows of data. The database server is responsible for retrieving all rows that match, then making them available to the user one by one. The user doesn't have to worry about finding the last valid row—the database will determine that.

Novell's XQL

Novell's XQL is an implementation of a subset of the SQL query language, together with programs to provide the function of the database server. XQL is the workstation software, while the server side is known as NetWare SQL.

The database consists of a series of Btrieve files. Some of the files contain the actual data. Other files, known as the data dictionary, contain the definition of the data files.

A table in XQL corresponds to one or more underlying files. A view is the definition of a table. The view consists of an SQL statement that defines what files make up this table. For example, one file might contain the last names of employees and their office locations. Another file might also contain the last names of employees, as well as personnel information.

A simple view would define two tables: *OFFICES* and *PERSONNEL*. An SQL statement could retrieve information from either one. Let's say, for example, that we want to look for the office location of all employees who make less than a certain amount but have large offices. The user would submit two SQL queries. The first query would look in the *PERSONNEL* table for all employees who make less than the target amount. This would return a series of values. Next, the user would submit a second SQL statement that looked at the size of the office for the targeted employees and returned the names of all those with offices greater than the target value.

It would be possible to combine these two operations into a single SQL statement, called a join, which would look for all office locations of employees that met both conditions of the query. The database server would be responsible for deciding how to figure out which rows met the query.

It is also possible to construct a view that is made up of several underlying files. For example, the two files could be combined into a table called *COMPLETE_INFORMATION*. This approach means that the user does not have to know about the two underlying tables and how to join them together.

The database server consults the data dictionary when an incoming SQL request is received. The data dictionary is a set of files that have a predefined format (see Fig. 7-6). The SQL request will start with the name of the table (or tables) to retrieve and look in a data dictionary table called *X$VIEW*, which contains the definitions of all views.

Name in XQL Dictionary	DOS File	Contents
X$File	FILE.DDF	Filenames and locations
X$Field	field.ddf	Field definitions
X$Index	index.ddf	Indices available for files
x$Attrib	attrib.ddf	Field attributes and masks
X$View	view.ddf	View definitions
X$User	user.ddf	Usernames and passwords
x$Rights	rights.ddf	User access rights

Fig. 7-6 Files for the XQL Data Dictionary

The database server would then look in *X$FILE* to see where the underlying files are stored and in *X$FIELD* for the definitions of all the fields in those files. If the user is asking for valid data, the database server consults the *X$RIGHTS* file to see if the user is allowed to access the data.

The server would then optimize the query—decide in which order to process it. For example, if there are indices on some of the fields specified in the search, it might be more efficient to first get that data and then go to the unindexed search values and look for them.

XQL Modules

The NetWare SQL server is implemented as a Network Loadable Module or a Value-Added Process, depending on the version of NetWare that is being run (see Fig. 7-7). The SQL server uses the services of Btrieve to actually store and retrieve data on disk.

On the client side, the NetWare SQL Requester is used to coordinate SQL access to data. The SQL Requester, in turn, uses the services of the NetWare Shell to communicate with the database server.

The user can access NetWare SQL through one of two means. The first is interactive access using the XQL Interactive (XQLI) interface. This allows a user to type in SQL statements and look at the answers on the screen. Interactive SQL access is usually only appropriate for debugging SQL statements and doing database maintenance tasks. Usually, a more user-friendly interface is needed. XQL provides two programming libraries to build SQL access into an application.

The XQL Manager (XQLM) provides the highest level of access, allowing the programmer to embed SQL statements into an application. The XQL Relational Primitives (XQLP) provide more control over data access at the expense of having to write more code. When the user embeds XQLM statements into a program, the statements are actually parsed into a series of XQL primitives that are then handed off to the NetWare SQL Requester, which sends them over the network to the NetWare SQL server. The SQL server finds the data using a series of Btrieve searches and sends it back.

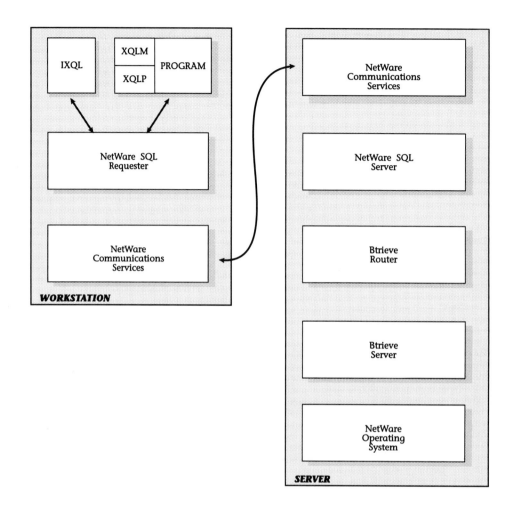

Fig. 7-7 Components of the SQL Server

Database Security

NetWare files have security associated with them, but at the file level. The user is permitted to read or write to certain files. In a database environment, the user does not see files, so the file level is not the appropriate way to handle security. Instead, security in an SQL environment is based on the concepts of databases, tables, columns, and rows. A user gains access to a database by being listed as a valid user in the appropriate data dictionary file.

After defining valid users, the database administrator would enable the security feature for that data dictionary. If security is disabled, users can still log into the data dictionary and have blanket access to the data. When security is enabled, the database administrator supplies a master password. This password is then needed to modify the security structure of the database.

After being defined, users are placed into groups, which form the basis for access to the underlying tables in the database. A catch-all group is provided for users not placed in a specific group.

When security is enabled, no group has access to any of the tables in the database. Access must be explicitly granted. The database administrator gives a group two levels of access to the database. The first level is table creation access. This privilege applies to the database as a whole and lets a user create new tables. That user then has full access to that table, including the ability to destroy it. The ability to access tables created by other users, however, must still be explicitly granted.

The second level of access is to individual tables. A group may be given read, write, or alter access to the table. Read simply allows the user to look at data in the database. Write allows the user to both read and write data. Alter allows the user to change the data dictionary definition of the table and implies read and write access.

Permission is cumulative within this framework, and a user may end up with several permissions. If the user has write and alter accesses to a table and the alter access is taken away, the user is still able to read and write to the table.

Locking and Data Integrity

Security allows a user to access a table. Security defines who may access a table. However, a further level of access control is needed to preserve the integrity of the data in the face of simultaneous access and in case of system failures.

A lock governs what types of simultaneous usage a piece of data might have. If a user is changing data in a row, for example, no other users should also be changing that same row or the changes might conflict. However, if two users are trying to read the same piece of data, there is no conflict.

The lock manager is provided by the Btrieve process. This lock manager handles locking for both native Btree access and for SQL-based access. Remember that SQL ultimately translates requests into a series of Btrieve calls.

There are three methods used to preserve the integrity of data:

- Preimaging
- Transaction Tracking System
- Record-level locking

Preimaging and the Transaction Tracking System are mutually exclusive—a file will use only one of the two methods.

Preimaging is used when the Transaction Tracking System is not active on a file. An SQL call can easily update several different files, or parts of a single file, in a single operation. A view update, for example, might translate into several different file updates.

Preimaging makes a copy of any pages of a file that are being updated. If the system crashes, the files are all restored to their prior condition. The preimage is actually another file on disk. Before Btrieve updates a file, it makes sure that the preimage of the data is already on disk. Then, if the system crashes in the middle of the update to the file, it is able to revert to the preimage.

A preimage does not guard against inconsistent data caused by multiple users. If two users are updating the same three pages of data, it is possible that half of the updates of each user will take effect. The record would then be inconsistent—it would have mixed data from two different updates.

The Transaction Tracking System is a software system used to provide a higher level of recovery. The TTS VAP or NLM is initialized along with the Btrieve and SQL processes on the file server. Then, the files that are to be tracked are flagged as transactional. It is not necessary to flag all files as transactional, since tracking adds overhead and thus slows down operation. Noncrucial files, or files that do not change and are backed up, do not need to be flagged as transactional. One Btrieve installation option is to automatically flag all files as transactional.

Transactions correspond to a piece of work, which may consist of many different updates, reads, or other basic file operations. The basic rule is that all of the steps in a transaction should take effect, or none of them should. If the file server crashes in the middle of a transaction, all the work that was done is "rolled back," restoring the file to its prior state.

A transaction starts when the user issues a *start transaction* command. For any access to a transactional file, TTS logs any operations that are accumulated. For files that are not marked transactional, the preimaging is used to ensure consistency. Note that preimaging consistency does not allow the user to manually roll back the changes later; it only guards against a system crash in the middle of that particular operation.

If the user does not issue a *start transaction* statement and the file being accessed is transactional, TTS will issue the statement for the user. This is known as an implicit transaction. When the user logs out, the transaction is completed.

When the user issues a *commit* command, the transaction is completed and all changes to files are logged. If the system were to crash, or the user to issue an *abort* command, the files would be restored to their original state.

TTS accomplishes this by taking a lock on all files involved in the transaction. While the file is locked, another user cannot access that file within a transaction. The second user will be delayed until the first lock is released.

It is very possible for two users to be waiting for each other, known as a deadly embrace or deadlock. For example, user 1 starts a transaction and locks file A. Around the same time, user 2 also starts a transaction and locks file B. Next, the users try to access each other's file. Neither program can continue until the other is finished (which won't happen). To guard against deadlock, Novell recommends that files always be accessed in the same order. This is satisfactory for certain applications, but many ad hoc query environments are unable to meet this requirement.

Both TTS and the preimaging method guard against failure by writing the data into a second file, which requires twice as many disk operations to update a single piece of data. While this ensures consistency, it comes at the price of performance.

An accelerated access feature allows the programmer to disable some of the overhead. Btrieve allows the user to open a file in accelerated mode, which bypasses the preimaging feature. Instead of writing the preimage data to disk, it guards it in main memory. It only writes to the disk when the main memory buffers are full. If the system crashes and there is no battery backup for main memory, data could be corrupted.

A second locking method is to lock individual records of a file. Note that the record locking and TTS-based systems are incompatible. A user cannot lock a record if the TTS has locked the file, and vice versa.

Two types of record locks can be issued: wait and nowait. A nowait lock returns immediately if the lock is unavailable, while a wait lock waits up to a user-specified timeout period for the resource to become available.

Typically, the user will submit a set of records to be locked. The lock manager will attempt to accumulate the locks one by one. If a lock request fails, the manager will wait for a specified period if it is in that mode. If it is unable to acquire all the locks, all the previously acquired ones will be released and control returned to the calling program.

A passive form of concurrency is used in case a record changes in between the time the data is fetched and the time when the user tries to update the record. Users can read data from a locked file, but when they try to do an update, if the record has changed, Btrieve will return a conflict status.

In this case, the program would retry the operation (or tell the user to try it again). Note that if the fetch is part of a transaction, and the file is already locked from another transaction or record lock, the fetch will not work. Only one transaction may be working on a given file at any one time.

Other Database Systems

Several vendors have alternatives to the NetWare SQL server. One is the Gupta Technologies SQLBase Server, which is also built on top of Novell's Btrieve mechanism. Other PC-based servers, such as the Ashton-Tate/Microsoft SQL Server, also run in a NetWare environment.

If the nature of the application is high-speed transactions processing, it is important to look at the speed of the locking mechanism. The transaction-control system needs to be able to balance the need for consistency with the need for performance. Most vendors allow record-level locking within a transaction instead of just table-level locking. Many vendors also provide mechanisms like automatic deadlock detection to provide high concurrency.

A second important area is the availability of a fourth-generation language (4GL) for application development. Tools like XQLM and XQLP allow SQL statements to be embedded in a traditional programming language like C or Basic, but require the programmer to write large amounts of code. A 4GL is specifically designed to retrieve sets of data from a database and present them to the user. A typical 4GL statement allows the programmer to specify a set of data to be retrieved; the 4GL automatically handles the details of presenting the data to the user. Presenting the data might involve putting the first row of data into a form and then putting up a default menu that allows the user to select the next or previous row of data. SQL provides only a subset of this functionality.

A third area is support for distributed databases and gateways. Although SQL is a common language, there are many aspects of communicating with a remote database that are not part of the standard. For example, the ways to set up a session, submit an SQL request, or communicate the results are all outside the scope of the standard.

A gateway allows a front-end program, such as Interactive XQL, to access other vendors' database systems. This is important because most organizations have several different brands of database management systems. Without a gateway, the user has to activate several different programs, one for each of the different database systems.

A distributed database is a way of combining several different databases, possibly of different brands, into a single logical database for the user. The distributed database server is responsible for coordinating transactions among multiple local database servers and for deciding how to access the data efficiently.

The Novell database offerings provide a rudimentary SQL capability. Advanced features, such as deadlock detection, 4GLs, gateways, efficient locking, and distributed databases are all missing from this environment. Sophisticated transaction processing, such as a bank or stock exchange, would thus need a more advanced environment.

Key Points in This Chapter

- Btrieve supplements the basic file system found in the NetWare Core Protocols. Btrieve allows data to be indexed in a file and then retrieved and modified by key value.
- XQL is Novell's implementation of a subset of the Structured Query Language.
- NetWare SQL is Novell's database server software. NetWare SQL builds on the services of Btrieve, using Btrieve to store its data.
- Many other database products are available from other vendors.

CHAPTER 8

Remote Procedure Calls

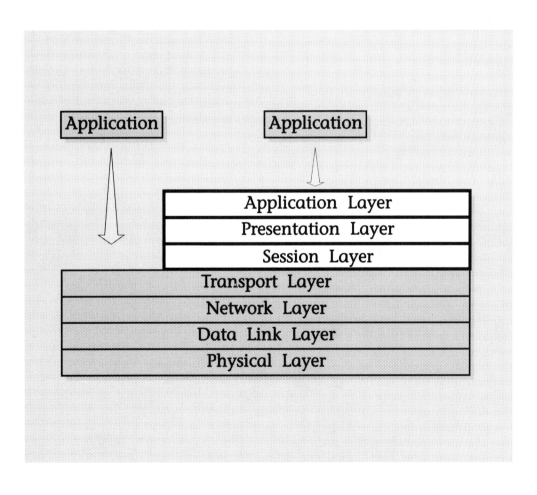

CHAPTER 8

Remote Procedure Calls

Upper Layers

In the last three chapters, we concentrated on a series of network services—the NetWare Core protocols, message handling, and database access. Each of these three sets of services operates at the application layer. The functions of the session and presentation layers are handled by the applications. For example, the Message Handling Service defines a presentation syntax—the format and encoding method for the message header and body. Session layer issues such as how to initiate the message transfer service are also defined by MHS. Initiating service by MHS consists of placing a message in a predefined location, then waiting for the next scheduling cycle of the connectivity manager.

For basic core services, this method works fine. However, it lacks generality. New applications, such as a distributed database, have to go through the issue of how to exchange data with other applications. Transport layers like SPX provide a foundation layer: the reliable transfer of data from one socket to another.

The session layer builds on the reliable transfer by specifying the type of work that is to be done—the management of the relationship between end-to-end transport entities. Different vendors build different types of tasks into this layer. For example, many put the security mechanism here to determine if a relationship between these two sockets is even valid.

While the session layer specifies the relationship between two sockets, the presentation layer specifies how to read the message. Each machine stores information differently and the presentation layer allows different machines to interpret data from each other. Text is stored as a series of codes on a computer. When a computer sees a code—255, for example—it translates that into a specific character. IBM PCs use a 7-bit ASCII code. Other computers, such as IBM mainframes, use an EBCDIC encoding scheme.

The presentation layer provides a way to represent text (and data in general) across different machines. It is the responsibility of a computer to translate any messages into this machine-independent format before sending it through the network. When its peer entity—the presentation layer at the destination node—receives the message, it is responsible for translating it into a machine-dependent format before delivering it to its client.

The last layer, the application layer, specifies what task is to be performed. The session layer sends up a series of messages (which may be larger or smaller than the underlying packet structure of the network). Each message specifies a task to be performed (or the continuation of a prior task) and the information needed to perform that task.

In the discussion of the NetWare Core Protocols, we saw an example of support for multiple tasks within an association (session) between two applications. NCP handles the specification of tasks for services provided by NetWare, but does not provide a mechanism for other programs to define and execute remote tasks.

This chapter discusses a general method for accomplishing this service, the Netwise RPC Tool (known as NetWare RPC when sold by Novell). This tool has been adopted by several companies, including Novell, as a way of allowing programs on different machines to communicate. The RPC Tool makes a network appear as an extension of the local computer.

Note that here we are not concerned with the type of work to be done. The application and presentation layers are concerned solely with sending commands. What the commands actually mean is an issue for the upper part of the application layer—the user program. The NCP application, for example, will take an incoming message as meaning "Open a file." Another application, such as a database management system, would not know what to do with such a command.

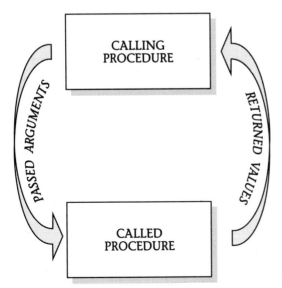

Fig. 8-1 Interprocess Communications

Interprocess Communication

To understand the Netwise RPC Tool, it is easiest to start with the way a program works on a single machine. A program is made up of several procedures (see Fig. 8-1). Each procedure performs a specific task.

A database management system provides a simple example. We might structure this program as two procedures. The first procedure would be responsible for managing the user interface. This includes displaying a menu for the user, providing help information, and deciding what information the user wants to see. The second procedure would be responsible for actually getting the information out of the files. This database server would accept a request from the user interface and deliver the data back.

The user interface would then be responsible for displaying the information. This might mean displaying data one row at a time, with a NEXT menu option to display the next row of data. When all the rows of data are displayed, the user interface would display a *no more data* message.

The database application thus consists of two procedures. The programmer would compile each of the two procedures. This takes the input program—C or Fortran, for example—and translates it into machine language. Next, the programmer links the procedures together, including any support libraries, into a complete program. Linking is the process of, among other things, registering all of the procedures in a table so they can find each other.

When the program runs, any procedure can call any other procedure, passing in the predefined arguments. By calling another procedure, the calling procedure is relinquishing control of the computer to the called procedure. The called procedure performs its tasks and then returns the appropriate data.

In this example, we have greatly simplified how a real DBMS would work. Instead of two procedures, there would be a great many, each performing a very specific task. The database server task would be several procedures, each one specializing in some aspect of retrieving data: security, query optimization, and network access, for example.

Whether we have two or many more procedures, the basic mechanism is the same. A procedure on a machine can call another procedure and ask it to perform its task. It provides the called procedure with information it needs (passed arguments) and reads the resulting information (return values).

Distributing the two procedures on different machines is very attractive in the case of a DBMS. The user interface is a natural candidate for the user's workstation. The workstation has a graphics controller, and the operating system is designed to be responsive to user input from the keyboard and the mouse.

The database server, on the other hand, is a program that fits best on a dedicated server. This computer has many disk drives and is optimized for data access instead of user input. The server can also accept requests from multiple user interface programs, allowing for significant economies of scale.

Several issues complicate separating the two procedures on different machines:

- Locating and forming an association (binding) with the remote procedure
- Representing the data in a common format
- Sending and receiving the data
- Handling errors that do not exist in a single-machine environment

A distributed environment can lead to errors that would not happen on a single machine. A distributed application often requires several steps to occur, one on each machine. In a distributed environment, each machine will fail independently. The distributed application must be able to decide the effect of a single component failure on the integrity of a transaction.

Single-machine communication between procedures is a special case of interprocess communication (IPC). When the applications are distributed, remote procedure calls (RPC) provide an extension of the IPC mechanism into a multi-machine environment. The RPC mechanism is the subject of the rest of this chapter.

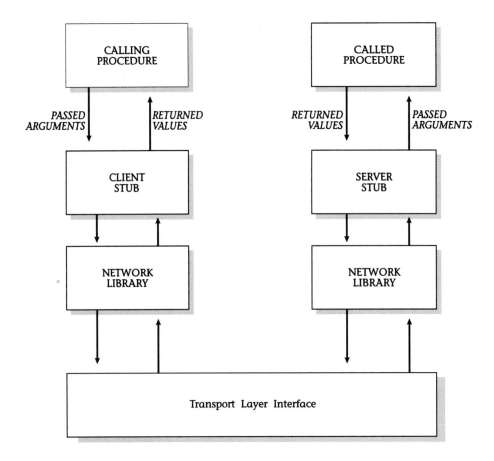

Fig. 8-2 Remote Procedure Call

Netwise RPC Tool

Netwise makes a compiler, the RPC Tool, that converts a series of procedures that run on one machine into a series of procedures that run on several machines. The compiler handles the issues of how the remote procedure is to be activated and how to pass and return complex data structures, as well as various miscellaneous issues such as the use of pointers and handling errors. The compiler provides a syntax to the programmer to use for registering, locating, and binding procedures.

The compiler produces a variety of procedures that are linked together with the original procedures program to form a network-ready program. The procedures that the compiler generates are used to fool the original procedure into thinking that it is communicating with a local procedure. The end result is two or more programs, one for each of the machines on which the distributed application will run.

The transparency of the code produced by the RPC Tool is a very important attribute. The programmer designs procedures without worrying about which ones will end up on which servers. Especially important is the fact that the underlying transport mechanism of the network is also transparent to the programmer.

The original, single-machine application consists of a series of user procedures. When the RPC compiler is finished, four additional types of procedures are contained in the program:

- Client and server stubs
- A dispatcher procedure
- Pack and unpack procedures
- Network and support libraries

The key elements from the programmer's point of view are the network library and the client and server stubs (see Fig. 8-2). Because many of the mechanisms in the RPC Tool operate by default (a programmer can simply provide a list of which procedures will be distributed), it is possible for programmers to be totally unaware of the distributed environment—the network is treated as if it were simply one large distributed machine. For complex applications, the programmer can modify each of the elements in the RPC Tool to provide better control or performance.

The client and server stubs emulate the single-machine interprocess communication mechanism. The client stub looks like the called procedure to the client application. It accepts the same parameters as the procedure and returns the expected values. It then delivers the request for a procedure call to the network library. The network library is responsible for delivering the request to the remote server. The network library does so by mapping the RPC Tool stub calls into transport layer calls, thereby providing the program independence from any particular transport layer.

Once the data is delivered to the remote machine, the message is delivered to the server stub. The server stub emulates the calling procedure. It calls the

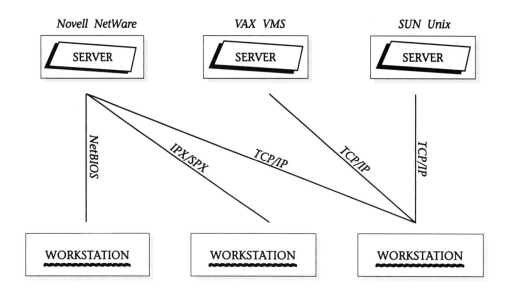

Fig. 8-3 Heterogeneous Environment

remote procedure, passing in the appropriate arguments. It then takes the return values and packages them into a message.

The server stub then delivers the message to the network library. Once again, the network library is responsible for delivering the data back to the client. There, it hands the reply to the client stub. The client stub takes the reply and packages it in the way that the calling procedure expects. It then returns to the calling procedure, just as if the local IPC mechanism had been used.

The Netwise network library allows the selection of different transport mechanisms at runtime (see Fig. 8-3). Thus, a program can be written that would distribute the user interface on a PC and the database on a PC-based file server. The application could be initially run in a Novell environment, using IPX and SPX as the network and transport layers. The network layer insulates its clients from the underlying data link, so that issue is not a concern here.

Later, the network could be changed to TCP/IP to allow greater flexibility in the choice of computers on the network. Additional user interfaces might be provided on Apple, Sun, and VAX workstations. Additional database servers might be provided on an IBM mainframe or other large computer.

Moving the application into this new networking environment would not be difficult. Supporting TCP/IP would simply be a matter of picking the appropriate network library.

Moving the program onto other computers would also not be difficult. The Netwise compiler uses the C programming language. Presumably, the program is also written in C. If the programmer used a standard version of the C compiler, moving the entire program would consist of recompiling and linking it on the new machine (assuming of course that a variety of pitfalls, including bit order, byte order, and word size, are not encountered).

The Netwise tool has been adopted by Novell as the RPC mechanism to use on its networks. What makes the tool especially attractive is that Netwise also supports a variety of other platforms. The computers supported by Netwise include all of the 80x86 computers, VAX, Sun, IBM, and many other machines. Supported operating systems include MS-DOS, Microsoft Windows, OS/2, DEC's VMS and Ultrix, and Unix.

The types of networks supported include NetWare, NetBIOS, TCP/IP, DECnet, and IBM's SNA/APPC. An IBM mainframe, for example, would probably use the SNA network protocols. A Novell workstation could communicate with a program on the IBM using the SNA gateway and the Netwise RPC Tool. Similarly, NetBIOS could be used to allow 3Com 3+ workstations to communicate with a Novell workstation that has the NetBIOS shell.

Version 3.0 of the Netwise tool also supports the Sun Remote Procedure Call Mechanism, which is the basis for the Network File System discussed in Chapter 14. The merger of the Netwise and Sun RPC mechanisms is discussed in more detail later in this chapter.

Procedure Declarations

The RPC compiler takes as input an RPC specification. This specification is a series of procedure declarations. The programmer prepares one entry for every procedure in an application that will be run on a remote machine.

The RPC specification is then used as input for the RPC compiler. The compiler takes the specification and generates a series of procedures which will be linked with the original program: client and server stubs and pack and unpack procedures.

All data shipped from one machine to another has to be packed and unpacked. Packing data means translating it into a machine-independent format. In the case of Netwise, this format uses the ISO standard known as ASN.1 BER. Unpacking means translating it back into a machine-dependent format. The client and server stubs call the pack and unpack procedures whenever a message is about to be sent or has been received.

The specification can be very simple, consisting basically of just a list of the procedures that will be accessed remotely. It is also possible to provide custom procedures, such as error recovery, in the specification.

When a procedure is defined to be remote, the programmer includes the definition of any passed arguments and returned values that the procedure will use. The programmer can also declare that certain variables are global—accessible to several different procedures without having to be explicitly passed. Global variables are supported in the RPC Tool because many existing applications make heavy use of this technique as part of their interface. Global variable support in the RPC Tool makes porting the applications to a distributed environment easier.

The definition of data structures uses the same method as the C programming language (which is the language used in the code generated by the RPC compiler). Simple data types, such as integers or characters can be defined. Several simple data types can be combined to form a data structure.

To illustrate the concept of data structures, take a hypothetical program that operates as a database server. It would need to receive requests from clients for data. The programmer would define a structure called *Data Request* with several elements. The first element would be the command type. In the case of the database server, this would signify whether the operation is a read, update, delete, or append of data to the table. This first element would probably be defined as an integer.

The second part of the structure might be the SQL statement itself, which would be defined as a string of characters. The third element of the structure might be the username of the user associated with the calling program, used to control what data is to be accessed.

For most data types, the programmer uses the same syntax in the RPC Tool that would be used in the ANSI standard for the C programming language. Two exceptions are the complex data types of arrays and unions.

An array is a set of one simple data type. An array of characters, for example, would hold all the individual characters of a text string. A database is well suited to an array. Each column of a table in the database would be defined as an array. The columns would then be combined together into a structure. Thus, by looking at the first element of each array, the user would be examining the first row of data in the database.

The problem with arrays is that often not all of the positions in the array are filled for a particular request. An array might be designed to hold 300 rows of data. A particular request might only retrieve 12 rows of data.

In a single-machine environment, unused space in an array is not a problem (assuming you have enough memory). Over the network, transmitting empty cells can dramatically affect the amount of network traffic produced by any one request.

Netwise handles this problem by allowing the programmer to specify a "termination expression" for the array. After the last unused cell, the programmer would insert the termination value (for example a NULL character) into the next cell. When the pack procedure packs the data, it will recognize the termination value and stop packing.

The second data structure is the union. A union consists of several elements, only one of which can be active at any one time. Again, in a single-machine environment, the only problem with a union is the use of memory space. In a networked environment, sending all of the members of a union through the network, even though only one is being used, is a waste of network bandwidth, memory, and CPU cycles.

To supplement the union definition, the RPC specification can include a choice expression. The choice expression is executed at runtime to determine which of the members of the union is active at that time. Only the active member is sent over the network to the remote procedure.

Process Binding

Binding specifies how the relationship between a remote procedure and the calling program will be established. A binding is formed when two applications have made a connection and are prepared to exchange commands.

If the procedure is called rarely, a nonpersistent style of binding is used. Nonpersistent binding means that a connection is set up on the underlying transport mechanism when the remote procedure is called. As soon as the values are returned, the connection is dismantled. Since connections on a network are a limited resource, the nonpersistent style is used to conserve those resources. Rather than keep a connection in place for infrequent communications, the connection is only set up when needed.

Nonpersistent binding means that each call has to set up and tear down a separate connection. The additional overhead involved in connection establishment makes nonpersistent binding inappropriate for remote procedures that are called frequently by the same caller.

For applications that make many repeated calls to remote procedures, a persistent style is used that lets several different calls all use the same connection. The connection is set up and then kept open. The connection ID is kept in memory, and that connection is used for subsequent calls.

When the application decides that it no longer needs remote resources, the last procedure call tells the server that the connection is about to be dismantled. The opening and closing of the connection are usually kept in the initialization and termination procedures of a program.

For both types of bindings, the address of the remote server can be determined at runtime. The address can be specified as a name or internetwork address. If the remote computer where the server will run is always the same, an internetwork address can be used to specify the target. Of course, it is hard to predict the future, and it is increasingly common for applications to move to different machines because the application is popular with users and a larger computer is needed to handle the increased demand.

Increased flexibility in moving procedures is available by using names. At runtime, the name of a server is specified, such as *DATABASE_SERVER*. The network library will use the appropriate mechanism to translate that name into an internetwork address.

In a Novell environment, for example, the RPC network library would use the Service Advertisement Protocol (SAP). In a NetBIOS environment, the network library would use the name management commands of NetBIOS to find the location of the designated target.

Using names allows the network manager to move a program from one computer to another without changing the program on either the client or the server. When the location of a server changes, the initialization procedure in the server control program for the application will inform the name service (i.e., the NetWare bindery) of its new location. Workstations requesting the remote services will be informed by the name service of the current location of the service.

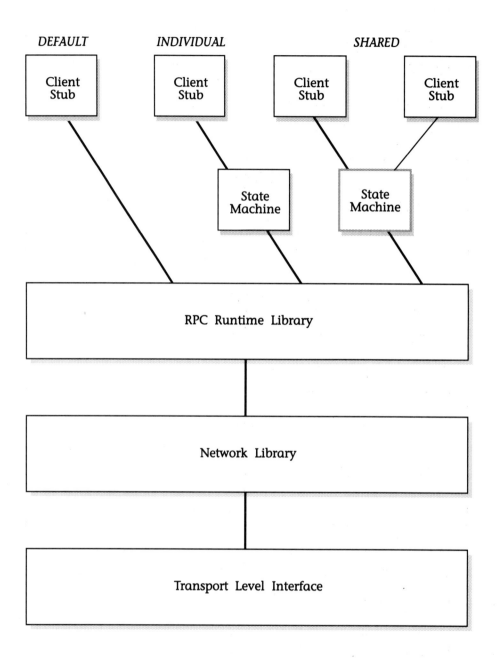

Fig. 8-4 Shared State Machines

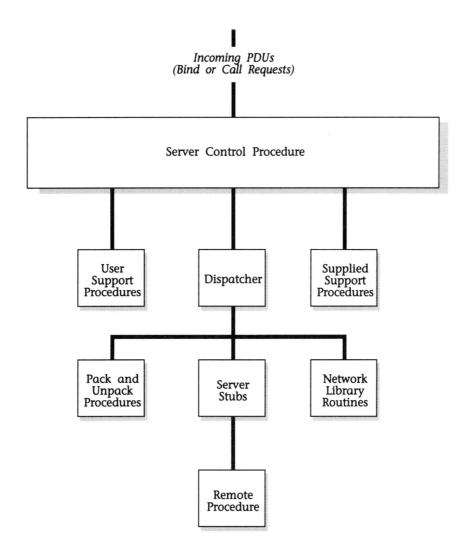

Fig. 8-5 Server Control Procedure

The Client Stub

To see how the code generated by the RPC Tool works, it is useful to begin with the client stub. The client stub is responsible for emulating the remote procedure—for accepting the passed arguments and then providing the appropriate return values.

The client stub is a piece of code that is structured as a state machine. A state machine is a program that goes through a series of states, one after the other. During each state it executes a certain set of instructions and then, if the appropriate conditions are met, proceeds to the next state.

The first state that the client stub enters is to start the state machine. The start state initializes any data structures used in the client stub. If necessary, the start state also initializes the network library.

Next, if the binding is based on a network name, the machine enters the find state, which maps the server name to a network address, using a support procedure in the network library. The network library will use whatever mechanism is necessary to perform the translation on that particular network.

Next, the machine enters the connection state. This establishes a connection with the remote server and provides the client state machine with a connection ID, which might be used for future calls if this is a persistent binding.

Next, the pack state is entered. Here, the client stub state machine calls pack procedures that were generated by the RPC compiler. The pack procedure returns a message known as a protocol data unit (PDU). The PDU is the equivalent of a sealed envelope in a messaging system and is ready to be submitted to the transport layer and transmitted over the network.

Next, the machine enters the send state, which hands the PDU off to the network library to be sent over the network. The client machine waits for the reply to be received and then enters the get state.

When the reply is received, the client machine unpacks the header of the incoming PDU to make sure that it is the answer to the request it sent, and not some stray that somehow reached this socket. The client machine then checks the reply to see if an error occurred during processing. If not, it unpacks the message and places it in the appropriate data structures.

If this is a nonpersistent binding, or the last call of a persistent binding, it enters the close state, which terminates the binding with the remote procedure. In the finish state, it stops execution and returns control to the calling procedure.

Many of the operations in these state machines can be shared among multiple procedures. Although the pack and unpack procedures are different, much of the remaining code can be reused.

The RPC compiler allows state machines to be shared among different client stubs, thus reducing the amount of memory used at runtime. In fact, if the programmer uses the defaults provided by the RPC Tool and does no customization of the RPC mechanism, the code uses a default state machine that is built into the network library support routines (see Fig. 8-4).

Server Control Procedure

There are several components on the server that are used to coordinate access to the various remote procedures. All of these components operate under the control of the Server Control Procedure (see Fig. 8-5).

The Server Control Procedure (SCP) accepts incoming messages and determines if they are bind requests for initializing a connection or if they are procedures that are to be executed. If the incoming request is a procedure to be executed, the Server Control Procedure hands the message to the dispatcher procedure. The dispatcher unpacks the header of the message to determine which procedure is to be executed and then hands over control to the appropriate server stub. The server stub unpacks the body of the request and places the data into the appropriate data structures. It then calls the remote procedure and waits for the return values.

The return values are placed into a reply message and submitted to the network library, which then sends the reply back over the network to the client stub. The client stub in turn hands the return values back to the calling procedure.

Netwise supplies three types of server control procedures with the RPC Tools. Each is suited to a different type of server:

- The single-binding control procedure can accept a single bind request at a time. It then executes the requests one by one (single tasking).
- The multiple-client control procedure is able to manage several different connections at once. It takes each incoming message and determines which dispatcher to use. Note that this is still a single-tasking solution—only one request is serviced at a time. If other requests come in, they are queued.
- The multitasking control procedure is able to have several active procedures over different connections. The multitasking nature of this control procedure only works on those computers that have a multitasking operating system.

Related to the multitasking control procedure is the multithreaded server control procedure. Unix is an example of an operating system that provides multitasking. For Unix, the programmer would use the multitasking SCP. For OS/2, the programmer would use the multithreaded SCP.

The server control procedure goes through several steps. First, it registers the name of the server using the network library. It is responsible for managing all process bindings. Finally, it is responsible for calling the dispatcher for routing incoming client requests.

The server is also responsible for managing shutdown of the server, including freeing all memory resources and terminating all active connections. As with other portions of the RPC code, it is possible to customize the server control procedure.

Custom Procedures

There are several mechanisms in the RPC Tool that allow the programmer to customize its operation. The customization might be used, for example, for debugging or providing more sophisticated error recovery procedures. At the extreme, it is possible for the programmer to modify the operation of the state machines or even use the network library directly.

Customization of the RPC code is done using four mechanisms:

- "Entry procedures" are executed whenever a state machine is entered. An entry procedure for a client stub is executed every time that the procedure is called by the calling application.

- "Exit procedures" are executed whenever the state machine is finished. In the case of the client stub, the exit procedure is executed whenever the reply is sent back to the calling procedure.
- "Hooks" are executed whenever a different state is entered within a state machine. The hooks are activated, for example, after a machine name is translated into an internetwork address (the *find* state) and before the attempt to set up a connection.
- "Traps" are executed whenever an exception condition occurs, which is usually when an error occurs.

A common customization is different error handling. For example, the programmer might put in a trap that looks for special errors caused by the network. The programmer would have the operation retried up to a retry limit instead of immediately returning to the calling procedure with an error.

Another type of error handling would be to handle application-specific errors. The server stub state machine would have a trap that looked in some portion of memory to determine what type of error occurred. For example, the database server might have refused to process an update because the user did not have the security level necessary to do so.

Netwise provides a series of macros (utility programs) to help the programmer determine what is occurring within the state machines. For example, the user can check which state the machine is currently in and even control the flow from one state to another.

Customization is available in several places in the control procedure on the server. First, the server control procedure will always execute any user-supplied initialization and termination procedures. For example, the user might log activation of the server upon initialization. When the server is shut down, a user-supplied termination procedure would log that fact and calculate the amount of time that the server was active.

It is also possible to provide more sophisticated control over the server using a server loop procedure, which is executed while the server is waiting for an incoming bind or remote procedure request. A user-supplied server loop procedure might be used to determine if the number of active sessions is approaching the capacity of this server. If so, another server could be initialized, possibly on another machine.

The most fundamental level of customization is to modify or bypass most of the built-in mechanisms, such as the dispatcher and the stubs. One possible use would be to change the nature of the RPC calls from synchronous to asynchronous.

Under the Netwise RPC model, when a calling procedure wants to use a remote procedure, it stops processing until the result is returned. This is synchronous processing—steps occur in a predetermined order—the model under which most RPC mechanisms occur. Of course, in a multithreaded environment, the master application can keep processing because it starts a new thread that waits for the result of the remote procedure.

Asynchronous processing allows the calling procedure to continue working while the remote request is being processed. A simple asynchronous model

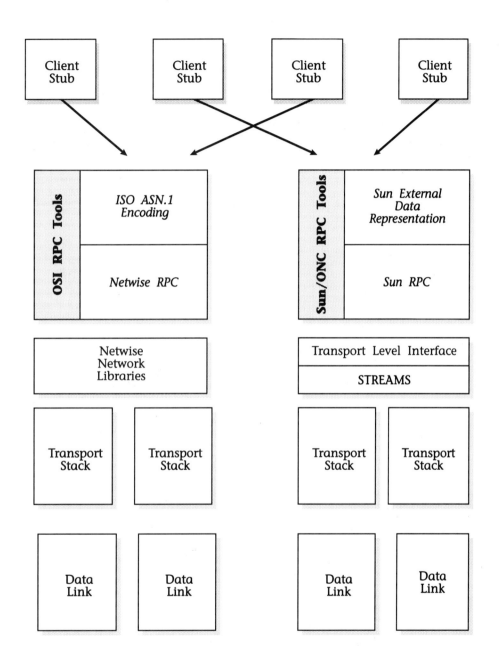

Fig. 8-6 Alternate RPC Mechanisms

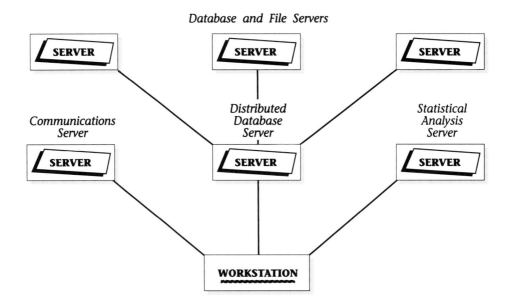

Fig. 8-7 Distributed Databases

might modify the client state machine to return immediately after the request is sent out.

With multitasking or multithreaded environments, there would be no need to modify the RPC mechanism. However, on a system like DOS, the programmer might wish to make such a fundamental change.

The next chapter, on the STREAMS interface, provides an example of asynchronous processing. Very few programmers would want to make such fundamental changes to something like the RPC Tool. Instead, they would pick an operating platform that had all the tools necessary—the RPC Tool, STREAMS, and a decent operating system.

ISO and Sun RPC Mechanisms

Version 2.0 of the Netwise RPC tool is based on ISO standard 8825 for the encoding of data, known as the Abstract Syntax Notation One (ASN.1) Basic Encoding Rules (BER). Built underneath that are Netwise mechanisms for providing session layer support. An example is the dispatcher that takes incoming messages and routes them to the appropriate server stub state machine.

Another RPC model has been developed by Sun Microsystems to support their Network File System. The family of protocols is bundled together under the marketing umbrella of Open Network Computing (ONC) environment.

Version 3.0 of the Netwise RPC Tool supports both the Netwise model for RPC mechanisms and the Sun Open Network Computing (ONC) model (see Fig. 8-6). The choice of the mechanism is decided at compile time and is transparent to the programmer. The Sun RPC mechanisms are important in TCP/IP networks, where they form the foundation for the Network File System.

Decided at runtime in Version 3.0 is the choice of the protocol stack to use. A variety of environments, including Microsoft's LAN Manager, TCP/IP, and Novell, are available. Most important, the RPC mechanism has been modified to support the use of the STREAMS interface, discussed in the next chapter.

Role of the RPC Tool

RPC mechanisms such as the Netwise RPC provide a machine and network-independent mechanism for designing distributed applications. These tools are not used directly by end users. Rather, they form a platform on which network-ready services can be built by developers.

An illustration of why platform-independent RPC mechanisms are important can be seen in the case of vendors of database management systems. As we saw in Chapter 6, most database processing now occurs on at least two machines—the user interface and the server.

It is important for the vendors to be able to code their database programs in a way that is not too dependent on the particulars of the networks and operating platforms. This is because users buy many different machines and networks and it would be impossible for the database vendor to code specifically for each combination.

RPC mechanisms are particularly important for distributed databases. In a typical distributed environment, there are several database servers, one for each type of information or department in an organization. The distributed database server is responsible for taking these separate database servers and making them appear as a single integrated database.

Figure 8-7 shows such a configuration. Three database or file servers are used to maintain portions of the database. The distributed database is responsible for providing a unified view of the information to the client applications. In other words, the client application should not have to worry about where a particular piece of data is stored.

The distributed database server is also responsible for maintaining consistency across multiple databases. If a user starts a transaction that involves multiple database servers, the distributed database server is responsible for making sure that all or none of the transaction was performed.

The last function of the distributed database server is efficiency. When data is being retrieved from many different sources, there are many different ways to get it. The distributed query optimizer is responsible for obtaining the data in an order that will minimize the response time and the impact on the network and individual machines.

All of these functions require processing distributed on many different machines, all able to send requests and replies. In addition to the database machines, this sample network might also include a statistics server used to further process the data and a messaging server to send the data to other users.

An RPC mechanism provides the foundation layer that allows the distribution of functionality on all these different machines. Rather than develop specific code for each system, a common mechanism can be used that ensures that all combinations of the different platforms work together on a variety of different networking protocols. The result for the user is flexibility in configuring the network and choosing equipment.

Key Points in This Chapter

- The RPC Tool is a remote procedure call mechanism sold by Netwise. It is marketed by Novell as NetWare RPC.
- The RPC Tool allows a programmer to distribute different parts of an application program on a network. The programmer specifies which procedures will be distributed, and the RPC compiler generates the code to make them work over a network.
- The RPC Tool is basically transparent to the programmer—no changes in programming are needed to distribute procedures over a network.
- The client stub, generated by the RPC Compiler, makes the remote procedure appear local to the calling program.
- A network library allows transmission of requests over different kinds of networks including Novell's IPX/SPX.
- The server stub interacts with the remote procedure, emulating the behavior of the calling program.
- In Version 3.0, Netwise integrates their RPC mechanism with the Sun Microsystems RPC/XDR standards used in the Network File System.

PART III

GATEWAYS

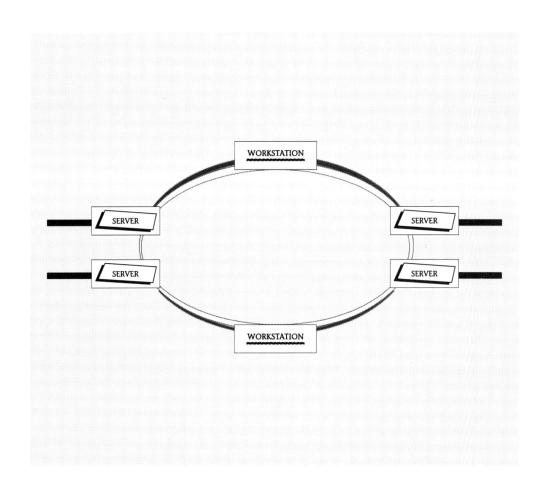

CHAPTER 9

STREAMS and Protocol Stacks

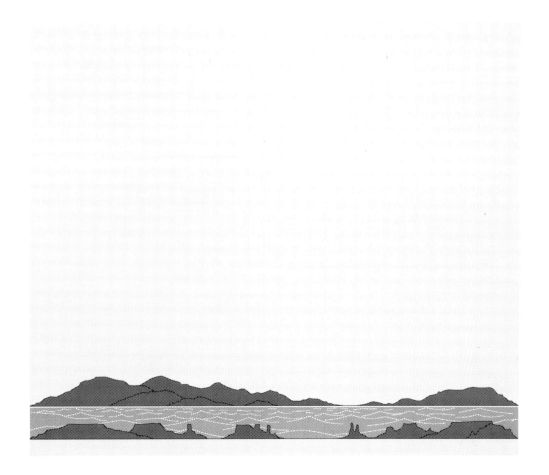

CHAPTER 9

STREAMS and Protocol Stacks

Protocol Stacks and the Operating System

Up to now, we have concentrated on the Novell networking protocols: IPX, SPX, and the NetWare Core Protocols. We have also examined three sets of services that are closely integrated into the Novell environment: the Message Handling Service, database access, and the RPC Tools.

While the Novell networks provide a great deal of functionality, there are occasions when users need to integrate other kinds of networks with the Novell environment. Most organizations use several kinds of networks. For example, a Novell network might be used in the departments, but the central data processing function might use an IBM mainframe.

The rest of this book examines other forms of networks and how to integrate them into the Novell environment. Just as the Novell networks are characterized by a protocol stack, so too are these other networks. The question is: How do we allow a user in one environment—a user on a Novell workstation for example—to access services in other networking environments?

This chapter discusses an important set of tools that allow a Novell file server to access other environments. The tools are based on AT&T's STREAMS interface, a method of providing a standard interface to protocol stacks on a server.

STREAMS is a service defined by AT&T as part of Unix System V Release 3. STREAMS is also a part of Unix System V Release 4, which merges several of the common mutations of Unix, including the Sun and University of California (Berkeley) strains, into one common operating system.

STREAMS provides a way of connecting different protocol stacks together. For example, different transport mechanisms can be used for different services such as message handling or database access. While STREAMS provides the basic technology, two additional mechanisms are needed that supplement the STREAMS tools. These mechanisms, the Transport Level Interface and the Link Support Layer, allow different combinations of protocols to be stacked together.

The Transport Level Interface (TLI) is a common interface defined by AT&T for user programs to communicate with a transport layer. An application that uses TLI is able to communicate with any network that presents a Transport Level Interface at the transport layer. For example, this would be a way to take the Apple file access services—the AppleTalk Filing Protocol (AFP)—and use the IPX/SPX transport layers instead of the AppleTalk transport layer.

The Link Support Layer (LSL) splits the protocol stack between the network and data link layers. Any data link driver that is written to support LSL can be used with any transport stack that supports LSL.

Both the TLI and the LSL depend on the STREAMS mechanism to work properly. The chapter begins with a discussion of STREAMS and then covers TLI and LSL. The chapter concludes with a discussion of a related mechanism, Named Pipes. Named Pipes are an integral feature of the Microsoft LAN Manager network and Novell has grafted the Named Pipes interprocess communication features on top of NetWare networks.

STREAMS and the other interfaces discussed in this chapter are not really networking tools in and of themselves—they are a standard interface on the operating system for accessing resources—both network-based and local. A standard interface does not provide interoperability by itself, but if used, it does make it easier for networking vendors to provide compatible equipment and software modules.

Character I/O Mechanisms

To understand STREAMS, it is best to start with the way input/output processing is done in a local environment. Any device to be accessed by a program, such as a modem or disk drive, has a device driver. This device driver is able to accept characters and output them to the device—sending data through a modem or writing data to the disk drive (see Fig. 9-1).

Each device driver has a set of commands used to signal the type of operation to perform. The disk drive, for example, has commands used to select the block

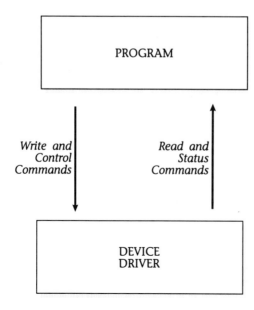

Fig. 9-1 Character I/O

of data to write. The idea behind STREAMS is to provide a common interface to all of these devices.

There is another significant enhancement in the STREAMS mechanism, support for message-based I/O mechanisms. Traditional device drivers are based on a character I/O mechanism—the user writes or reads one character at a time. In STREAMS, the user can dispatch a message, which will be put into a queue for the device driver. The device driver then processes the message when it has time.

STREAMS is thus message based and can queue the messages. As will be seen, this provides an ideal framework for a networking environment, which also shares those characteristics.

Basic STREAMS Components

A stream consists of three types of components: the stream head, modules, and a device driver (see Fig. 9-2). Modules are optional—all that is needed for a stream is the stream head and the driver. The stream head is what interacts with the program; it replaces the device driver as the interface the programmer sees.

A module is a software program that sits in between the stream head and the driver. In the case of LAN, the driver might be an Ethernet driver. A module might be a software implementation of IPX and SPX.

The device driver is any STREAMS-compatible device driver. It is responsible for accepting messages from upstream—from the stream head or any modules. It takes that message, translates it, and sends it out to the device that it is driving. If the device driver is a disk driver, it sends data to the disk. If the driver is an Ethernet driver, it sends data out onto the LAN. The driver also accepts data, which it sends upstream to the stream head, which in turn presents it to the user program.

The stream head is represented by a node in the file system, and thus looks like a file on the operating system. It is opened just like a file and can be used in that manner by using standard operating system read and write calls.

The stream head also supports an additional set of commands. When the stream is first opened, it consists of a driver and the stream head. The user can then push modules onto the stack between the stream head and the driver. Additional modules are pushed between the stream head and the highest-level driver.

When the user sends a command (i.e., an *IOCTL*) downstream to the stream head, it takes the data and packages it as a message. The first module downstream from the head examines the message and decides if it will take action. If it doesn't recognize the message, it sends it downstream to the next module. If it does recognize it, it performs whatever processing is necessary.

Message Types

The stream head communicates with the user program using a set of function calls. The function calls are translated into a message by the stream head and

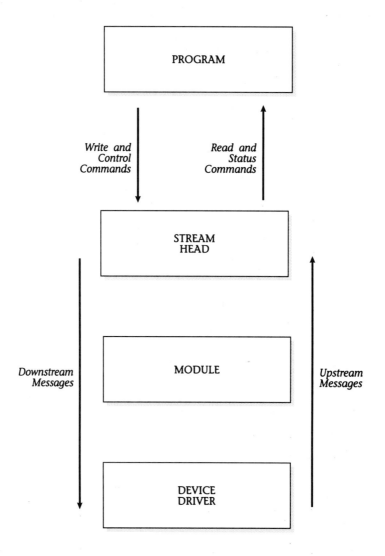

Fig. 9-2 Basic STREAMS Mechanism

passed downstream. Likewise, any messages received from downstream are passed back to the program in the form of a function call or interrupt.

Some basic messages are defined in the STREAMS interface. Additional messages can be defined as needed by programmers of modules and device drivers. The Transport Level Interface, discussed later in this chapter, is an example of some supplemental messages defined for a particular set of modules and drivers.

The way that a program interacts with the stream head differs among operating systems. Usually, function calls are provided for control of the stream's operation, for support of traditional I/O mechanisms, and for getting and putting messages to the stream.

The control of the stream allows the programmer to add and delete modules to and from from the stream. For example, in a Unix environment, the IOCTL (for I/O control) function call is used to control the operation of a device driver. Since the stream is represented by a file descriptor, the programmer can open the "file" and submit an IOCTL function call.

To add a module onto the stack, the programmer would use the *I_PUSH* argument to the IOCTL function call, giving the address of the module. To delete a module closest to the stream head, the *I_POP* option would be used instead.

If the stream head sees an IOCTL with the *I_PUSH* argument, it performs the task of adding the module to the stream. However, if the IOCTL function call has an unknown argument, the stream head will generate a message and send it downstream.

The first module downstream will examine the argument to the IOCTL and determine if it is a known type. We might define an IOCTL command for the transport module, for example, that was used to change the global retry limit for unacknowledged packets.

While the programmer might use the traditional I/O mechanisms (reading and writing strings), a more advanced approach for network protocol stacks is the message handling capabilities of the stream.

The programmer can issue a *putmsg* function call. That function call will alert the stream head that data from some location in memory is to be sent downstream. The stream head gets the data from the user's memory. The message has two parts: control and data.

The control part of the message indicates what kind of message it is. The data is what the interpreter of the message will use. Normally, the programmer would generate *PROTOCOL* messages. *PROTOCOL* messages are interpreted by modules on the stream, modified, and then sent along to the next module or driver. For example, the top level of the stream might be a transport layer that provides several service primitives, including establishing sessions and sending and receiving data.

This module would recognize a certain number of commands that could be in the command block of the protocol message. If the module sees an establish connection message, it copies in the data. Presumably, the data portion of this message would have the destination internetwork address of the desired remote host for this connection.

The transport module would then generate a message to be sent down to the network layer, which would add a routing header and send the message on down to the data link driver. In this way, each message is modified by the addition of a header and sent downstream through the protocol stack.

Message Queues and Flow Control

Each of the components on a stream has two message queues: one for incoming messages and one for outgoing messages (see Fig. 9-3). The queues provide flow control so messages do not overwhelm a module or driver, as well as providing expedited data services. A queue is simply an area of memory large enough to hold several messages. When a module wishes to send a message downstream,

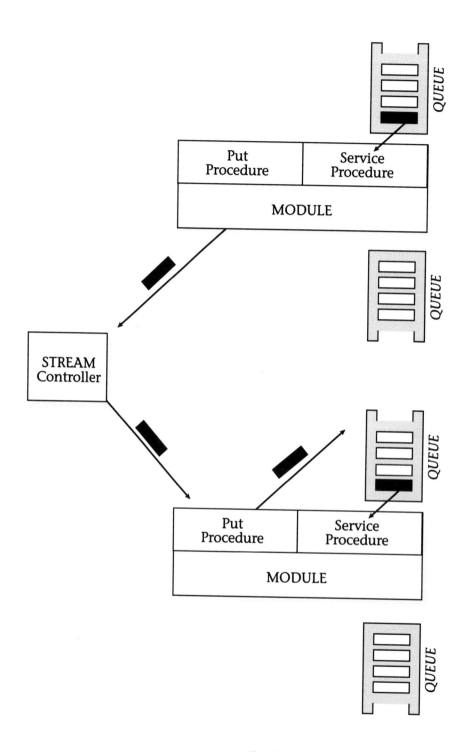

Fig. 9-3 Queue Management in STREAMS

it invokes the *put* procedure, which submits the message into the read queue of the next module downstream.

The queue consists of a series of linked messages. The head of the queue points to the first message, which in turn has the address of the next message. The last message, or the tail of the queue, has a pointer back to the queue head.

When a message is submitted, the STREAMS control procedure calls a *put* procedure that is associated with that queue. The put procedure is furnished by the module that is controlling that queue. It examines the message and decides if it needs immediate servicing. If not, it will put the message into the queue.

The message is queued by putting it into the appropriate position and adjusting the pointers so they are pointing to the next message block. Normally, the message is put in the tail of the queue, so the pointer is adjusted to point to the queue head.

A module also has a service procedure associated with it. Periodically, this service procedure is called, at which time it is responsible for trying to empty the queue of all messages.

There are times when a module will be unable to send a message downstream because the downstream module is unable to process it. When this occurs, the stream is blocked. If the downstream queue is blocked, the local module may not be able to empty its own queue, leading to a stoppage all up the line until the downstream queue unblocks itself.

Flow control is based on the size of the queue. Each queue has a high-water mark and a low-water mark associated with it. Upstream modules can add messages to the queue until it reaches the high-water mark. Then, all upstream modules are blocked until the queue reaches the low-water mark.

Normally, messages are submitted at the end of a queue. Certain classes of messages are known as high-priority messages; they are not subject to flow control and are not added at the tail of the queue. Instead, they are added at the head of the queue, behind any prior high-priority messages.

The STREAMS Multiplexor

A basic stream consists of one user, one driver, and optional modules. In most computing environments, it is necessary to share drivers among multiple users. Streams can be multiplexed, allowing several users to share a single stream. Multiplexed drivers are an essential component of the three STREAMS applications described below: the Transport Level Interface, the Link Support Layer, and Named Pipes.

A multiplexed stream is actually two or more streams stacked on each other (see Fig. 9-4). A multiplexing module is used to route data to the appropriate lower or upper stream. Note that the multiplexing can be in either direction: several upper streams sharing the multiplexing module or several lower streams under the control of the multiplexing module.

Multiple lower streams are created by first opening two separate streams. The first consists of the stream head and the multiplexing module. The second stream consists of a stream head and a driver.

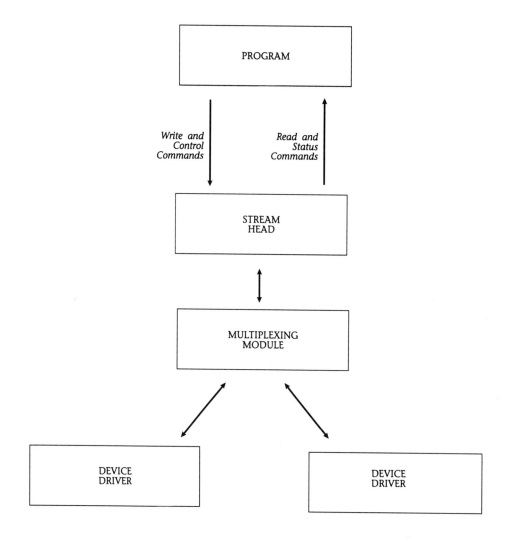

Fig. 9-4 Multiplexing Modules in STREAMS

Next, the lower stream is connected to the multiplexing driver using an *I_LINK* command. This linking instructs the stream head of the lower module to send all upstream data to the multiplexing module. All data from the multiplexing module is sent to the lower stream head and then passed to the driver.

Additional lower streams can then be added using *I_LINK* commands. In the Link Support Layer example discussed later in this chapter, multiple device drivers are connected to a single data link/network layer interface using multiplexing lower streams.

More streams can be added on top of this configuration using additional *I_LINK* commands. In the Link Support Layer example, different transport layer protocol stacks would all use the Link Support Layer for sending data over the network. The Link Support Layer would be responsible for routing the data between the appropriate upper and lower streams.

Transport Level Interface

As we've seen, STREAMS provides a general mechanism for sending messages from one module to another and finally to the driver. If a module doesn't recognize a message, it passes it on. If the module does recognize the message, it will perform some processing and then usually send a revised message further downstream.

STREAMS provides a mechanism for passing these messages but doesn't define what those messages are. The Transport Level Interface defines a common class of messages that are recognized by different transport layer service providers.

A module that is TLI compliant will provide service to any program that uses the TLI interface. Instead of programming directly to SPX, for example, the programmer would write an application that uses the TLI library calls.

At runtime, the program could be run using SPX, OSI, or TCP/IP protocol stacks. Since the issue is transparent to the program, it is possible to change the underlying transport mechanism without rewriting programs.

TLI has another portability implication. Since many vendors have adopted the Transport Level Interface, at least the networking version of the program will be highly portable. If the programmer used a standard version of the C programming language, the rest of the code will also be portable.

TLI consists of two components: a TLI library and a TLI module (see Fig. 9-5). The TLI library is linked into the program and becomes a support library, much in the same way that the RPC library was linked into the program in the prior chapter.

The TLI library accepts TLI calls that are in the main body of the program and performs the appropriate operations to deliver a message to the stream head.

The TLI module is opened when the stream is created. The module accepts requests from the TLI library and translates some of them into standard TPI messages. Below the TLI module are one or more different protocol stacks.

The TLI library allows the development of network-based programs without worry about what kind of transport stack is being used. For example, the programmer issues a *t_connect* function call to open a connection on any support transport stack.

The *t_connect* function call is translated into a *T_CONN_REQ* (transport connection request) message, which is passed down to the transport provider. The TLI module then waits until it receives a *T_CONN_CON* (transport connection confirm) back from the transport provider. It then returns the information to the stream head, which fills in the address of the remote connection.

It is also possible to send out the connection request and not wait until it is established. The program would immediately continue with other processing.

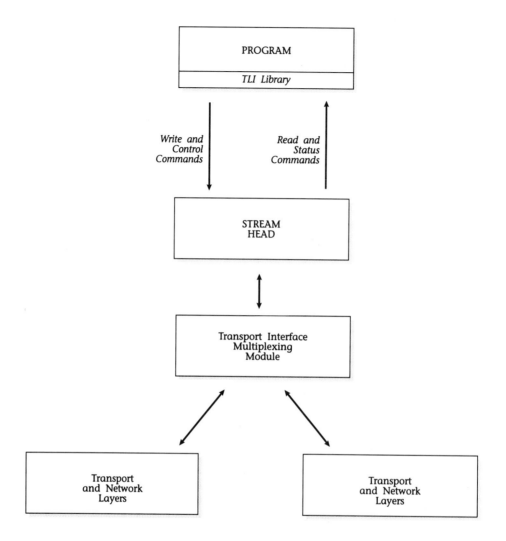

Fig. 9-5 Transport Level Interface

Then it would issue the *t_rcvconnect* call to find out if the connection request was successful.

A variety of TPI messages (and corresponding function calls) have been defined, including error handling and expedited data provisions. The basic functionality is the same as if the programmer was writing directly to the transport layer. The advantage of this approach is transparency—the programmer uses a single method to do network programming regardless of the type of network. Note that few users would be writing directly to the Transport Level Interface. Usually, the programmer would use a higher-level mechanism, such as the Netwise RPC Tool or Named Pipes (discussed later in this chapter).

Link Support Layer

The Transport Level Interface provides a bridge between different transport layer stacks and different session and application layer services. The Link Support Layer provides the same function as TLI, but between the network and data link layers of the network.

The Link Support Layer consists of three components: the link support layer itself and two interfaces (see Fig. 9-6). The Multiple Link Interface (MLI) is a standard interface for device driver developers. The Multiple Protocol Interface (MPI) is a standard interface for the transport stack developer.

In this environment, a transport stack has two standard interfaces. The Transport Level Interface ensures that its services can be used by any TLI-compliant network service. The Multiple Protocol Interface ensures that the transport layer can use any network driver that is compatible with the Link Support Layer.

One significant difference between TLI and the Link Support Layer is their origins. The TLI is a standard part of AT&T's standard Unix System V. Because of that, TLI has industry-wide support. The Link Support Layer (also known as the Open Data-Link Interface, or ODLI) is a joint venture between Apple and Novell and does not have widespread support.

The Link Support Layer serves a more specific purpose than TLI; it is a means to ensure that network cards designed for the Novell environment interact with it properly. TLI has the more general purpose of allowing different applications to be ported to different computing platforms.

The basic component that users see is network interface cards that are compatible with the MLI—known as a Multiple Link Interface Driver (MLID). When the MLID receives an incoming packet, it sends it up to the Link Support Layer, which then routes it to one of several protocol stacks.

The purpose of all this is to allow a single protocol stack to use multiple network cards in a transparent fashion and to allow a network card to be shared by several protocol stacks. This is accomplished by using a STREAMS multiplexor—the Link Support Layer.

The Link Support Layer is essentially a routing mechanism. It performs its task by registering all protocol stacks and MLI drivers that it will be servicing. Each protocol stack that will be serviced is entered in the network configuration file, along with a protocol ID.

An MLI driver also registers with the Link Support Layer, informing it which protocol IDs it is able to service. Note that a single driver might be servicing several physical interface cards. Each network boards is assigned a unique number by the Link Support Layer.

When the Link Support Layer receives an incoming packet from the MLI driver, it examines the header to determine which local service is needed. It then routes the packet to the protocol stacks that are registered for that type of packet. There is usually at least one stack that accepts unknown packet types (which will probably be thrown away as an error).

The Link Support Layer mechanism should seem familiar to the reader—it is very similar to the goals of the Logical Link Control layer discussed in Chapter

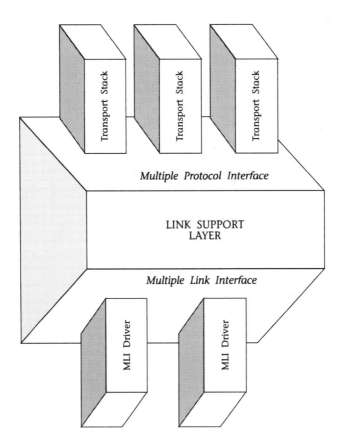

Fig. 9-6 Link Support Layer

3. The basic idea is to allow multiple protocol stacks to use a single driver and a single protocol stack to use multiple drivers.

The Logical Link Control, an international standard, defines a standard way of sending and receiving data on a network. The Logical Link Control in turn hands data down to the Media Access Control (MAC) sublayer, which sends the data out over the network. The single protocol stack is thus able to access many different kinds of data links.

The goal of allowing multiple protocol stacks to share a driver is also supported in the LLC model. The LLC header contains a field called the Local Service Access Point, which identifies one of several users of the data link service. When a packet is received, the Logical Link Control layer looks at the incoming packet and delivers it to the appropriate protocol stack.

So why use the Link Support Layer when an international standard essentially serves the same purpose? In addition to the basic operation of routing packets, the Link Support Layer provides a few services that can be used by the device driver writer. For example, the device driver can submit a procedure to be run by the Link Support Layer after a specified interval elapses.

From the user's point of view, the intent of the Link Support Layer is to make more network cards available by making it easier for vendors to port their controllers over to the Novell environment. Novell has said the company will write device drivers that are compatible with the Link Support Layer for its cards and for LAN adapters from IBM and 3Com.

Named Pipes and STREAMS

Named Pipes are interprocess communication mechanisms that make the network look just like a file. The program can read and write data from a virtual file, the network, the same way it can from a local file.

A pipe takes data from one end of the pipe and delivers it to the other. A pipe is a full-duplex communications mechanism. Each end of the pipe can simultaneously send data. To illustrate the utility of this approach, take the problem of printing over the network.

Most software is designed to print to a local printer or to a file. The user selects the print option and directs the output to one of the LPT ports on a PC or to a specified file name.

A named pipe looks like a file name. It has the following syntax:

\\machine-name\pipe\pipe-name

When this file is opened, a connection that is transparent to the user is set up over the network with a program that uses that remote pipe. If that pipe is being serviced by a print spooler, printing to the "file" is actually submitting a file to a print spooler. All of the network-based operations are transparent to the software, which acts as if it is just printing to a normal file.

Named Pipes thus combine the transparency of the STREAMS environment with the advantage of using names to request resources. These services are then available network-wide simply by opening the pipe.

A system that offers pipe services to the rest of the network is known as a named pipe server. The system that is attempting to open the pipe is the named pipe client. Figure 9-7 illustrates how this environment is implemented in NetWare.

When a named pipe client opens a pipe, this establishes a stream to a module called npmux. The npmux module is responsible for interacting with the named pipe clients and servers. It also interacts with a helper process, which is used to provide support services.

When the stream is established to npmux, the first thing it does is pass the name to the helper process, which is responsible for name translation. The helper uses the Service Advertisement Protocol to find out the network address of the desired pipe.

The helper process sends a SAP request for the named pipe. The helper processes on other computers (named pipe servers) listen to the broadcast and respond when they are able to offer that service.

When the helper process has found a machine offering that particular named pipe service, it attempts to establish a connection by sending a request to the helper process on the other machine. The remote helper process accepts the

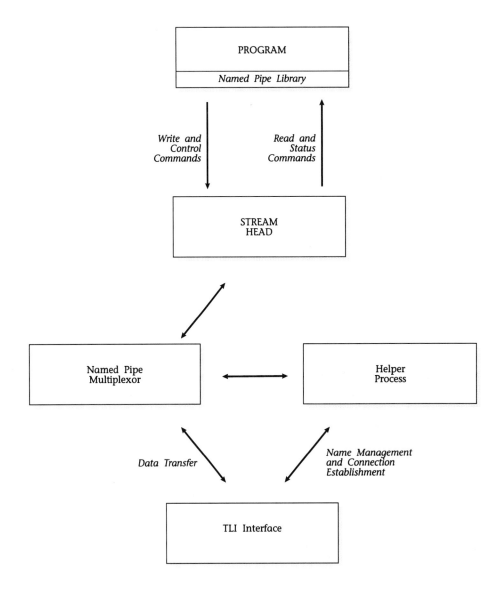

Fig. 9-7 Named Pipes (Client Side)

incoming connection request and notifies the pipe server—the program that registered itself as providing this particular service (i.e., a print spooler).

Once the connection is established, the calling program is notified and control of the connection is returned to the npmux process. Npmux is responsible for taking incoming data and routing it to the appropriate named pipe server or client. The npmux module is responsible for translating incoming read/write calls into the Transport Level Interface messages, which will be passed downstream.

A single npmux process can handle several instances of the same named pipe. When a program issues the *Make Named Pipe* function call, a stream is opened to the npmux module, which checks to make sure that it is able to service an additional instance of a named pipe.

The named pipe library provides a variety of function calls to the program developer, such as the ability to connect to a named pipe or to peep into the pipe to see what data will be coming out next. Connection establishment requests are available, such as the ability for a client to wait until a particular named pipe becomes available.

STREAMS and NetWare Environments

The Open Link Interface (the marketing term for the Link Support Layer and its two interfaces) was jointly developed by Apple and Novell. OLI is similar to Apple's AppleTalk Link Access Protocol. Presumably, Novell is committed to this particular interface.

Novell is also committed to providing at least three protocol stacks for NetWare: IPX/SPX, OSI, and TCP/IP. In addition, DEC's LAT protocols, AppleTalk, and other protocol stacks are potential candidates for this environment.

The STREAMS environment is also being used in computers that run Novell Portable NetWare, a way of allowing general-purpose operating systems to provide services to NetWare clients. STREAMS has been packaged into a machine-independent set of code, known as the Portable Streams Environment (PSE).

Novell has used PSE in implementing the STREAMS environment for the NetWare 386 operating system, as well as OS/2 and DOS. Note that these services on DOS operate different than in other environments because of the single-tasking nature of DOS. The Portable Streams Environment is also available as part of the Portable NetWare operating system, discussed in Chapter 12.

This chapter examined the general mechanism used for network-based communications (STREAMS) and several specific interfaces, including Named Pipes, the Transport Level Interface, and the Link Support Layer. All three interfaces have the goal of making the network seem transparent. Services that are network-accessible become available to the user without having to know the details of this particular network.

Key Points in This Chapter

- STREAMS is an operating system feature that allows messages to be passed among different software modules.
- The top of the stream is a stream head, which interacts with the user program. The end of the stream is a device driver, such as an Ethernet device driver.
- Multiplexing streams allow a device driver to be at the end of several different streams.

- The Transport Level Interface is a standard developed by AT&T. TLI is a standard interface to different protocol stacks (from the transport layer on down). A programmer who writes a network-based application that relies on TLI will be able to use a variety of transport stacks.
- TLI and STREAMS are also used in the Remote Procedure Call mechanism discussed in Chapter 9. The Netwise RPC Tool can use the TLI interface as the means of accessing different transport services.
- The Link Support Layer is a Novell-developed standard for a link between the transport stack and the data link. The Link Support Layer sits between the network and data link layers.
- Named Pipes allow users to communicate with foreign resources in the same manner they read and write to files.

CHAPTER 10

AppleTalk

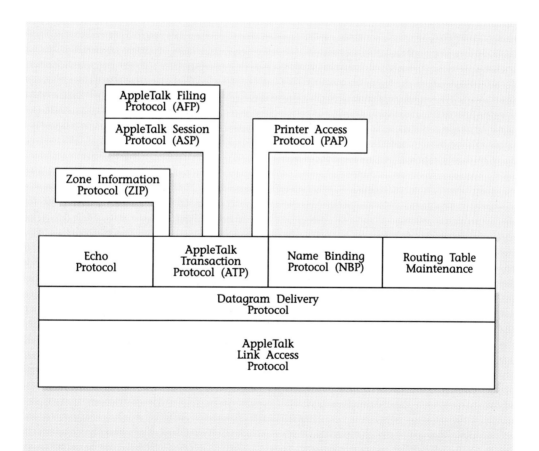

CHAPTER 10

AppleTalk

Novell and AppleTalk

The Macintosh was absent from discussions in prior chapters, despite its frequent appearance in Novell networks. The reason for this is that Apple workstations do not use the Novell network architecture. Instead, they maintain their use of AppleTalk, a network architecture developed by Apple specifically for the Macintosh and other workstations.

To network a Macintosh workstation in a Novell environment, a file server is installed that supports both IPX/SPX and AppleTalk (see Fig. 10-1). Incoming calls from DOS or OS/2 workstations are handled using the NetWare Core Protocols, with IPX as the network layer.

For the Apple workstation, communication with the file server is through the AppleTalk network, transport, and session layers. Once a message is received by the server, it is translated into a local file access command. The NetWare operating system gets the data (or sends the request out to another server using NCP to get the data). Once the data is received, it is repackaged into the AppleTalk format and delivered to the requesting workstation.

Figure 10-2 shows a basic configuration for such a network. Note that Apple workstations support both the Apple LocalTalk and Ethernet data link layers. The file server in this example has three network interface cards. The LocalTalk and one of the Ethernet cards are being driven by the AppleTalk network layer. The third card, the Ethernet card, is being used for the traditional IPX communication with DOS or OS/2 workstations.

In addition to access to a NetWare environment, there are a variety of other methods for allowing PC and Macintosh workstations to coexist. One of the more popular is TOPS, a network sold by a subsidiary of Sun Microsystems.

It is also possible to run AppleTalk and provide gateways to other environments. For example, there are a variety of ways to gateway AppleTalk networks into TCP/IP, DECnet, and IBM networks. If the user is simply trying to allow PCs to access printers over a network, a low-cost solution is to use AppleShare for the PC. AppleShare PC allows a DOS workstation to access a LaserWriter printer and supports several data link boards, including the 3Com Etherlink series, the IBM Token-Ring Adapter, and an Apple LocalTalk PC card.

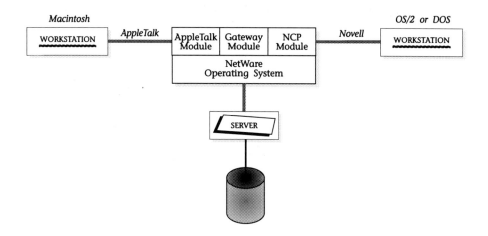

Fig. 10-1 NetWare Support for Macintosh

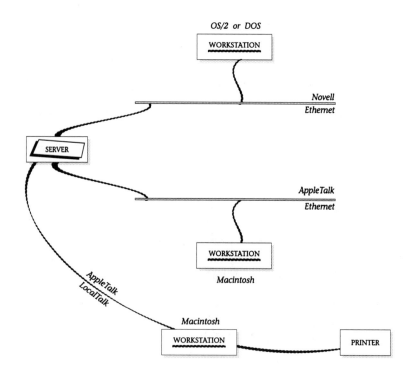

Fig. 10-2 Basic AppleTalk Configuration

Lower-Level Protocols

Before discussing the AppleTalk filing protocol, it is useful to briefly describe the lower support layers in the AppleTalk network architecture (see Fig. 10-3). In addition to Ethernet and token ring, AppleTalk supports Apple's LocalTalk interface. LocalTalk is extremely slow—about 2.5 percent of the speed of the Ethernet interface.

This low speed is compensated for by several factors. First, the typical Apple network has only a few computers and printers on it. Because of the simplicity of the LocalTalk interface, printers can go directly on the network—many typesetters, plotters, and advanced graphics devices have built-in LocalTalk interfaces whereas Ethernet or other LAN interfaces are fairly rare.

Names and Zones

AppleTalk subdivides the internetwork into a series of zones, each corresponding to one or more data links. Within a zone, computers share resources such as printers or disk drives. Most traffic is localized within a zone. Typically, for example, the user prints on a printer within the local zone. When necessary, however, resources in other zones are available.

All of the resources within a zone have a name, much as resources in a Novell network have a name. The Name Binding Protocol (NBP) is used to translate that name into an internetwork address. Printers, file servers, communication

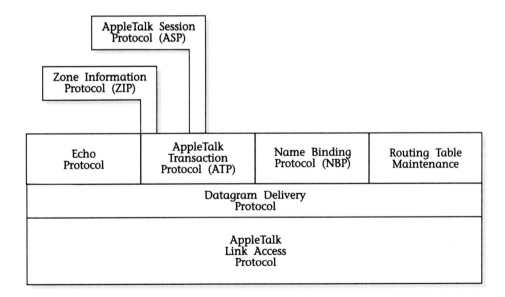

Fig. 10-3 AppleTalk Low-Level Protocols

servers, and other peripherals—represented by a socket at the network layer—are all network-visible entities and may register a name.

Figures 10-4 and 10-5 show some NBP traffic on a network being shared by Apple and Novell computers. In Figure 10-4 a request is being sent out from an Apple workstation. The request is sent to another computer, presumably a designated file server running the NetWare for Macintosh software.

Eventually, a result is sent back to the requesting node (see Fig. 10-5) that identifies the resource *TechWriter* as a particular network address. The word *TechWriter* is the name given by this particular organization to one of their laser printers.

NBP is similar to Novell's Service Advertisement Protocol. For example, a designated socket is used in both environments to listen for name lookup requests. The computer maintains a list of all entities currently on that computer.

In the figures, a lookup is being performed on NBP. First, a request was sent by the workstation to an NBP listening socket. This socket first searched its own name table, then sent out a broadcast request to other NBP sockets on the network asking them to return all names that match the description given in the request.

One way that NBP differs from the Service Advertisement Protocol is that an Apple network can be segmented into zones. NBP requests are broadcast only within a specific zone. A zone can span more than one data link and the collection of zones then makes up the internetwork. In a small network, there is no overhead for supporting zones since all requests default to the current zone unless otherwise specified.

If a node wants to find all resources in another zone, a broadcast request is sent to a router on the network. The router is responsible for working with other routers on the network to convert the broadcast request into a series of lookups, one for each of the data links in the target zone.

A special protocol, the Zone Information Protocol (ZIP), is used to maintain zone membership. Routers on the internetwork periodically send ZIP packets to each other that contain information on which networks belong in which zones at the given time.

To find a remote resource, three types of messages might be exchanged. NBP is used between the workstation and the local router. The local router uses broadcast requests to other routers to find out about resources in foreign zones. Finally, ZIP is used between routers to keep informed about which zones exist.

Network, Transport, and Session Protocols

The lower layers of the AppleTalk are similar to the Novell environment. We saw that Ethernet and token ring data links are supported in addition to the LocalTalk networks. At the network layer, the same basic operation of networks, nodes, and sockets is performed.

As in Novell, routers are used to move data between different networks, allowing the nonrouting nodes to be unaware of the topology of the network. A Routing Table Maintenance Protocol (RTMP) is used to maintain routing tables, much as RIP is used to maintain tables in the Novell environment.

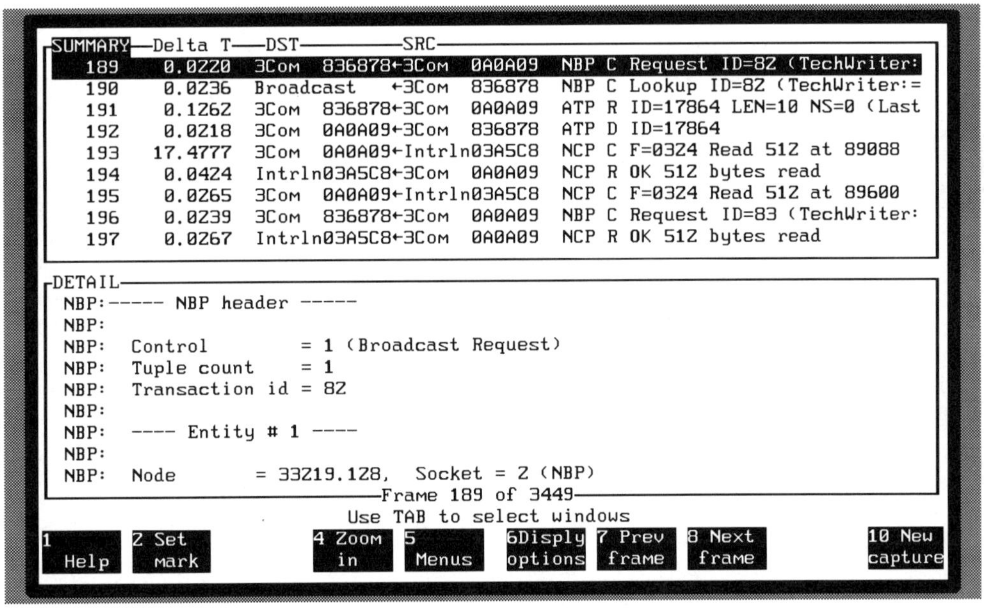
SUMMARY—Delta T—DST—SRC—
189 0.0220 3Com 836878←3Com 0A0A09 NBP C Request ID=82 (TechWriter:
190 0.0236 Broadcast ←3Com 836878 NBP C Lookup ID=82 (TechWriter:=
191 0.1262 3Com 836878←3Com 0A0A09 ATP R ID=17864 LEN=10 NS=0 (Last
192 0.0218 3Com 0A0A09←3Com 836878 ATP D ID=17864
193 17.4777 3Com 0A0A09←Intrln03A5C8 NCP C F=0324 Read 512 at 89088
194 0.0424 Intrln03A5C8←3Com 0A0A09 NCP R OK 512 bytes read
195 0.0265 3Com 0A0A09←Intrln03A5C8 NCP C F=0324 Read 512 at 89600
196 0.0239 3Com 836878←3Com 0A0A09 NBP C Request ID=83 (TechWriter:
197 0.0267 Intrln03A5C8←3Com 0A0A09 NCP R OK 512 bytes read
DETAIL
NBP:----- NBP header -----
NBP:
NBP: Control = 1 (Broadcast Request)
NBP: Tuple count = 1
NBP: Transaction id = 82
NBP:
NBP: ---- Entity # 1 ----
NBP:
NBP: Node = 33219.128, Socket = 2 (NBP)
Frame 189 of 3449
Use TAB to select windows
1 Help
2 Set mark
4 Zoom in
5 Menus
6Disply options
7 Prev frame
8 Next frame
10 New capture

Courtesy of Network General

Fig. 10-4 NBP Traffic on an Ethernet

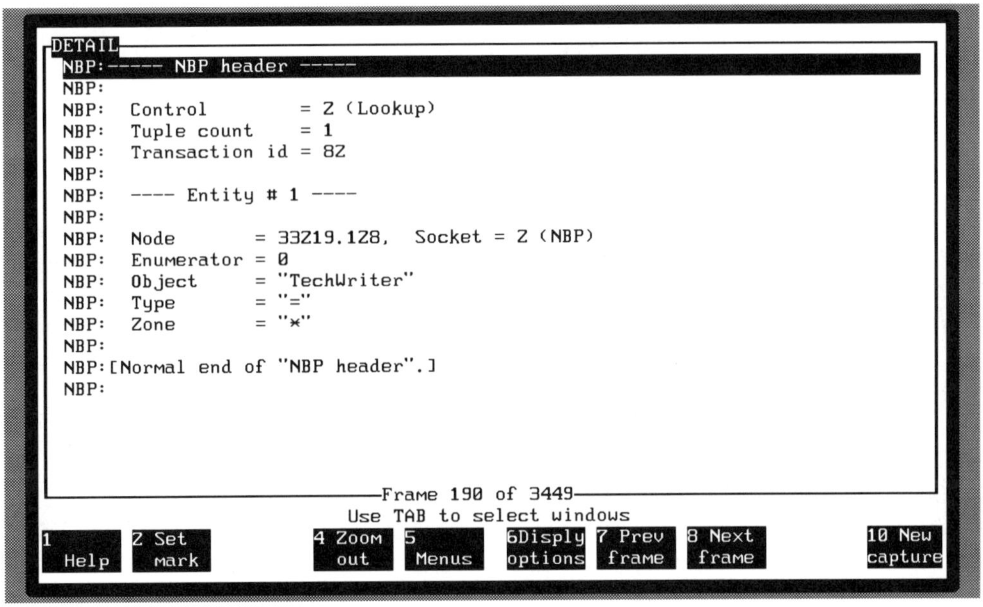
DETAIL
NBP:----- NBP header -----
NBP:
NBP: Control = 2 (Lookup)
NBP: Tuple count = 1
NBP: Transaction id = 82
NBP:
NBP: ---- Entity # 1 ----
NBP:
NBP: Node = 33219.128, Socket = 2 (NBP)
NBP: Enumerator = 0
NBP: Object = "TechWriter"
NBP: Type = "="
NBP: Zone = "*"
NBP:
NBP:[Normal end of "NBP header".]
NBP:
Frame 190 of 3449
Use TAB to select windows
1 Help
2 Set mark
4 Zoom out
5 Menus
6Disply options
7 Prev frame
8 Next frame
10 New capture

Courtesy of Network General

Fig. 10-5 NBP Request

At the transport layer, we see a slightly different mode of operation. Remember that Novell offers two different transport alternatives, SPX and PEP. SPX provides a stream-oriented transport protocol—all data sent from one end of a logical connection will be received at the other end in the order sent. PEP, which is bundled into NCP, is a ping-pong type of delivery mechanism—each packet sent requires a response, whereas SPX allows several packets to be outstanding.

The AppleTalk Transactions Protocol (ATP) is also a ping-pong type of arrangement, with a significant difference. Several response packets (up to eight) may be sent in reply to each request.

Figures 10-6 and 10-7 show some ATP traffic. In Figure 10-6, an exactly-once transaction is being sent to the destination. This means that the transaction is guaranteed to be delivered once and only once to the destination client (in contrast to the at-least-once mode, which may send several packets).

Figure 10-7 shows the response, which in this case is only a single packet. In the response is a bitmap, which indicates how many responses are to be expected and which one this is. When the original requesting node receives the response, it looks at the bitmap. Once it has received all of the responses, it sends a release packet (the third packet in the summary portion of Figure 10-6).

It is possible for a node to send a bitmap, along with a transaction ID, that specifies that certain parts of the response were not received properly. In this way, the node that sent the response is able to send back those pieces that didn't make it through the network. The responding node is also able to see which pieces did make it and can therefore be freed from the buffers.

The session layer interface in AppleTalk is the AppleTalk Session Protocol (ASP). ASP is used to verify that a user is allowed to access a given resource and to establish and tear down the connection. Afterward, ATP is used for the actual data transfer.

Figure 10-8 shows an ASP packet for establishing a session. Notice in the illustration that there is a series of tickle packets being sent to keep a connection alive. A program can send a transaction down to ATP with infinite retries, which is used to send out a "keep alive" packet when there is no other traffic on the network. The program, once it has sent down this request, can be assured that the session will not be terminated for lack of activity on its part.

The function of the tickle packet is accomplished in a NetWare environment with the NCP keep alive packet. This packet is sent by NCP periodically to prevent a connection from being torn down because a user has been idle.

AppleTalk Filing Protocol

From the point of view of a Macintosh workstation, the basic service provided by a NetWare file server is to support the AppleTalk Filing Protocol (AFP). As seen in Figure 10-9, AFP uses the services of the Session and Transaction protocols in AppleTalk. In addition, a server uses the Name Binding Protocol to publicize the availability of its services.

To use AFP, a user must first establish a session with a file server. Typically, the workstation will first issue two calls: It will use NBP to find the internetwork

```
┌SUMMARY─┬─Delta T──┬─DST───────┬─SRC──────┐
│ 3024   │ 4.8447   │ 3Com  0A0A09←3Com  836878  ATP C ID=2481 LEN=6
│ 3025   │ 0.1348   │ 3Com  836878←3Com  0A0A09  ATP R ID=2481 LEN=10 NS=0 (Last)
│ 3026   │ 0.4623   │ 3Com  0A0A09←3Com  836878  ATP D ID=2481
│ 3027   │ 8.9265   │ 3Com  0A0A09←3Com  836878  ATP C ID=612 LEN=0
│ 3094   │ 30.0646  │ 3Com  836878←3Com  0A0A09  NBP C Request ID=86 (TechWriter:
│ 3095   │ 0.0226   │ Broadcast   ←3Com  836878  NBP C Lookup ID=86 (TechWriter:=
│ 3150   │ 8.8001   │ 3Com  836878←3Com  0A0A09  ATP C ID=50177 LEN=0
│ 3221   │ 9.5257   │ 3Com  836878←3Com  0A0A09  NBP C Request ID=86 (TechWriter:
│ 3223   │ 0.0237   │ Broadcast   ←3Com  836878  NBP C Lookup ID=86 (TechWriter:=
└────────────────────────────────────────────┘
┌DETAIL──────────────────────────────────────┐
ATP:───── ATP header ─────
ATP:
ATP:  Client            =
ATP:  Function          = 1 (Request)
ATP:  Control field     = 2X
ATP:       ..1. ....    = Exactly-once transaction
ATP:  Request bitmap    = 01
ATP:       .... ...1    = Request bitmap
ATP:  Transaction id    = 2481
                 ─Frame 3024 of 3449─
                 Use TAB to select windows
 1      2 Set       4 Zoom   5        6Disply  7 Prev   8 Next           10 New
 Help   mark        in       Menus    options  frame    frame            capture
```

Fig. 10-6 AppleTalk Transaction Protocol

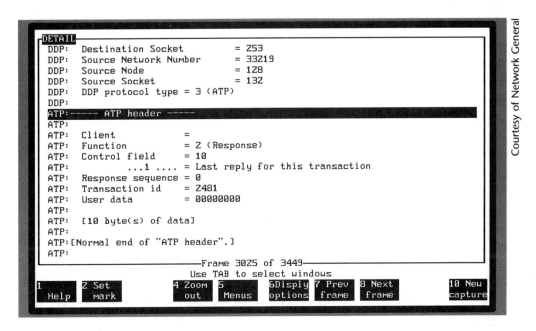

Fig. 10-7 AppleTalk Session Protocol

address of the file server, and then it will issue a *Get Server Parameters* call to find out what version of AFP is being supported.

Next, the user logs into the file server (see Fig. 10-10). AFP supports different User Authentication Methods to verify that the user is allowed to access this particular file server. In the illustration, a clear-text password is being sent over the network, meaning that the password is actually in the log in request packet.

Two alternatives exist to the clear-text method of logging in. One method is no security—no password is needed. In this method, the file server relies on the normal file and directory level security on the server. The other, more secure, method is a random number exchange. Instead of the clear-text USAM, the workstation tells the server that it will be using the random number UAM. The server then sends a random number to the workstation, which is used to encrypt the password. The encrypted password is then sent to the server, which decrypts it and checks it against the value stored.

After logging in, the user is able to access resources on the file server, much as a Novell user uses NCP to access those same resources. In order to support DOS, OS/2, and Macintosh workstations, the NetWare file system is expanded over the entities found in a DOS-based file system (see Fig. 10-11). The entities found in a DOS environment—the server, volume, directory, and file—are still present in this expanded file system, allowing a DOS workstation to access the same files as a Macintosh.

The concept of a file is expanded, however, under the AppleTalk Filing Protocol. Instead of a monolithic file, the file is split into two portions: the data and resource forks. For a Macintosh, the resource fork contains the icon for the

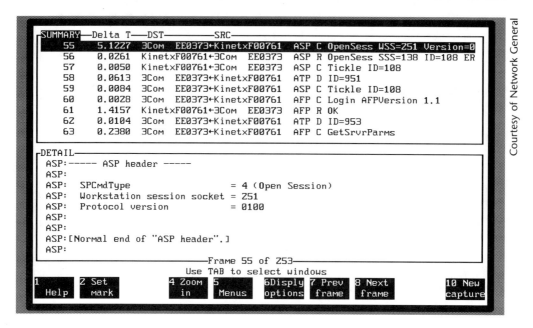

Fig. 10-8 AFP Open Session Request

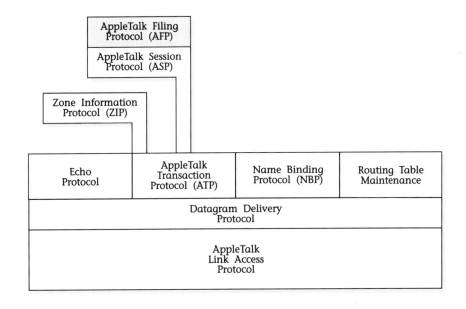

Fig. 10-9 AppleTalk Filing Protocol

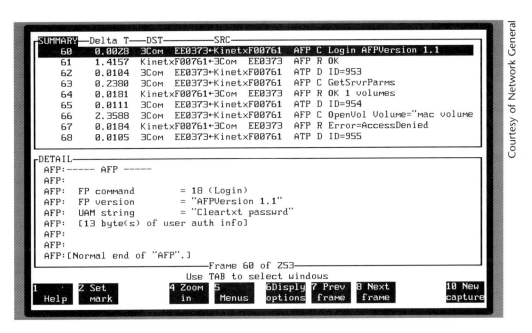

Fig. 10-10 AFP Open Session Request

application and executable code. The data fork contains the data for the program. If a DOS program stores a file, both code and data are contained in the data fork.

In addition, the Novell server maintains a desktop database. This database, used by the Macintosh Finder, helps the Macintosh maintain the iconic interface on the workstation. The desktop is used, for example, to find the appropriate application when a user points to a document. This means that a user doesn't have to specify the program name—only the document. The Finder will determine the creating application of that document and then start that application.

As in the DOS environment, the AFP operation begins by opening a file—in this case a fork of a file (see Fig. 10-12). If this were a DOS open, the Novell file system would automatically open the data fork only.

As with the DOS environment, NetWare maintains security information for files and directories. Access privileges are used to control who may access a particular directory (known as a folder on the Macintosh) or a file. In addition, access modes govern simultaneous access to that file.

The NetWare file server looks just like an Apple server to the Macintosh workstation. To the PC, it looks like an extension of the local DOS environment.

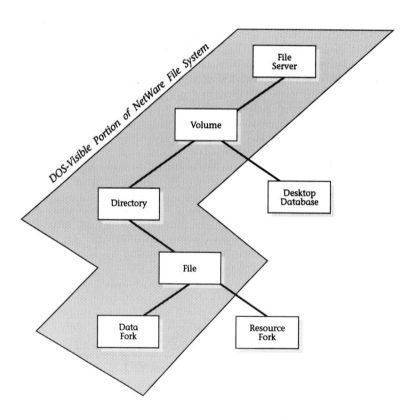

Fig. 10-11 NetWare/AFP File System

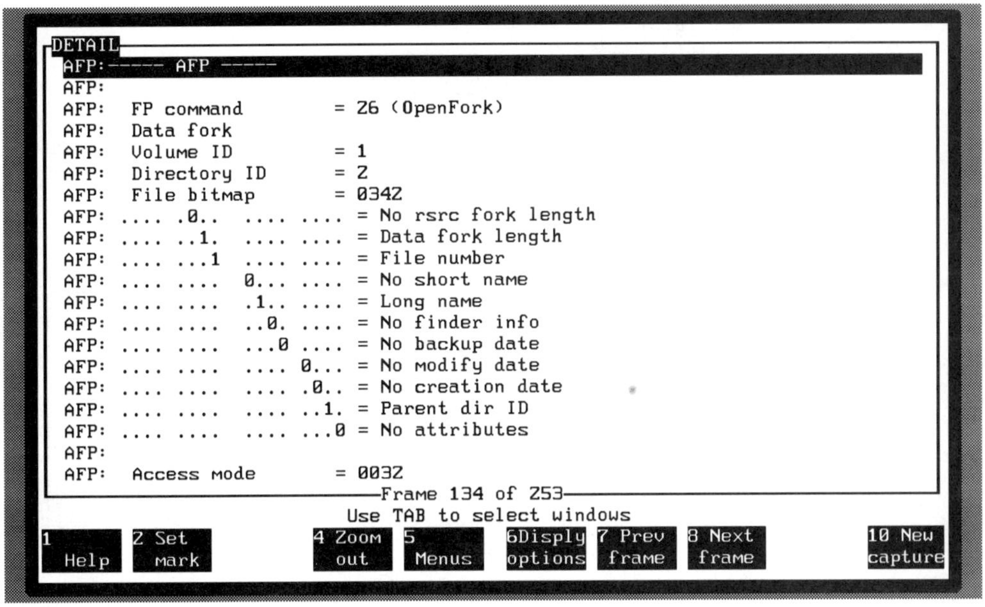

```
DETAIL
AFP:----- AFP -----
AFP:
AFP:   FP command        = 26 (OpenFork)
AFP:   Data fork
AFP:   Volume ID         = 1
AFP:   Directory ID      = 2
AFP:   File bitmap       = 0342
AFP:   .... .0.. .... .... = No rsrc fork length
AFP:   .... ..1. .... .... = Data fork length
AFP:   .... ...1 .... .... = File number
AFP:   .... .... 0... .... = No short name
AFP:   .... .... .1.. .... = Long name
AFP:   .... .... ..0. .... = No finder info
AFP:   .... .... ...0 .... = No backup date
AFP:   .... .... .... 0... = No modify date
AFP:   .... .... .... .0.. = No creation date
AFP:   .... .... .... ..1. = Parent dir ID
AFP:   .... .... .... ...0 = No attributes
AFP:
AFP:   Access mode       = 0032
                     Frame 134 of 253
                 Use TAB to select windows
 1       2 Set         4 Zoom  5       6Display 7 Prev  8 Next          10 New
 Help    mark          out     Menus   options  frame   frame           capture
```

Fig. 10-12 AFP Open Fork Request

The NetWare file system is actually a superset of the AFP and DOS file systems, allowing both types of workstations to store information on the file server. The file system in NetWare is actually more general than this.

NetWare has support for a variety of naming conventions used to access files. Normally, the file system can maintain at least two names for a file—one for DOS and the other for the Macintosh. Since the Macintosh allows 31 characters per name (instead of 8 for DOS), this multiple name space allows different operating systems to use the file server.

It is also possible in NetWare 386 for other file systems to be designed and stored on the file server. A Network Loadable Module is used to translate incoming calls from the remote system into the underlying calls to the NetWare files.

Printer Access Protocol

The Printer Access Protocol (PAP) is the other main service supported in NetWare for Macintosh, allowing a Macintosh to use a printer located on a Novell file server. Instead of using the session protocol, PAP is a direct user of the transaction protocol (see Fig. 10-13). This is because PAP is actually a session-level protocol, responsible for maintaining a session between a print server and a particular user.

As with the AppleTalk Filing Protocol, a session begins by using the Name Binding Protocol to find the address of the server. Next a session is opened with that file server (see Fig. 10-14).

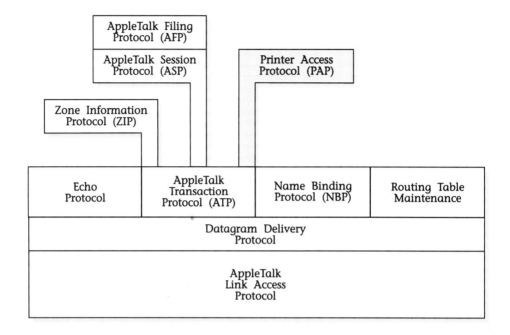

Fig. 10-13 Printer Access Protocol

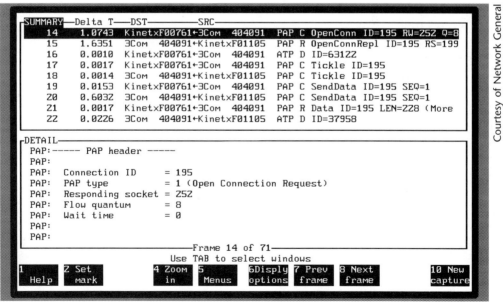

Fig. 10-14 PAP Traffic on an Ethernet

In many cases, there will be several users attempting to open a connection to a printer. If that printer is servicing another job, it returns a busy message to the user. In order to ensure that a user who has been waiting for a long time is able to access the printer, PAP maintains a sort of queue. Instead of having the server maintain the queue, the requesting workstations actually maintain information on who requested service first.

When users attempt to open a session, they indicate how long they have been waiting. If the printer is busy, that request is periodically resent by the user program to the PAP server on the printer. When the printer becomes free, it waits for a period before accepting a new request. During that time, it examines all incoming requests to determine which one has been waiting the longest.

A printer usually has a limited buffer space. Because of this, it controls the operation of the PAP session. A workstation is not able to send data until it receives a *send data* message, which gives it permission to send a specified amount of data. Once permission is received, the workstation can send the data, as shown in Figure 10-14.

Other Features

The expanded filing system maintained by the Novell file server is also accessible to DOS and OS/2 clients. This allows a DOS workstation, for example, to maintain a file name of 31 characters. In order to do so, a program is written that uses the Novell programming services to open resource forks, specify long names, and perform other operations outside the scope of normal DOS calls. These calls are not transparent—normal DOS file operations will not work with these extended attributes.

It is also possible for the programmer on a Macintosh to use NetWare services, such as queue management, or other services specific to the NetWare operating system. A set of application programming interfaces (APIs) is available to the Macintosh programmer. These calls are transmitted to the file server using the AppleTalk Filing Protocol. A special "sideband" is used to distinguish these Novell-specific commands from the more general AFP commands.

Key Points in This Chapter

- Novell uses the AppleTalk protocols for communicating between a Macintosh and a NetWare file server.
- The NetWare file server provides file and printing services to the Macintosh.
- The file server maintains multiple file spaces. For a PC, it observes the convention of eight-character names. For the Macintosh, the file has both a resource and a data fork as well as a longer name.
- The NetWare server and the Macintosh can be connected together using a variety of data links, including ARCNET, Ethernet, and LocalTalk.

CHAPTER 11

DECnet and Portable NetWare

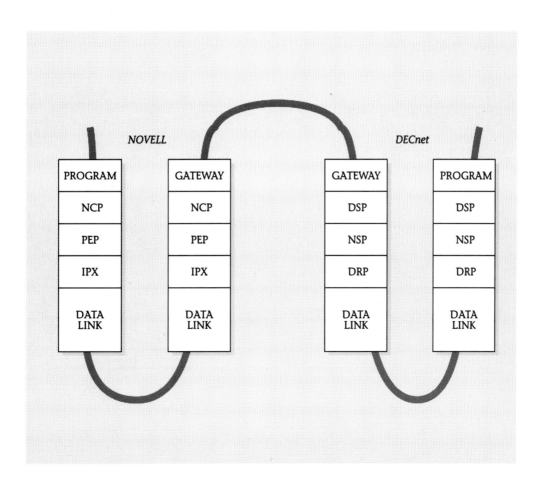

CHAPTER 11

DECnet and Portable NetWare

Portable NetWare

Portable NetWare allows a general-purpose operating system, such as DEC's VMS or AT&T's Unix to offer NetWare Core Protocol services to workstations. The advantage of this approach is that the users can the same services from another operating system that they can get from the native NetWare-based servers. Portable NetWare thus gives the Novell user a little more flexibility in configuring the network. In addition, Portable NetWare serves a gateway into these other computing environments, which offer a broader range of services.

Figure 11-1 shows how the NetWare services are added onto a host operating system. Known as Portable NetWare, this is a program that is compiled on the host operating system, and uses the IPX and SPX protocols to communicate with workstations.

Incoming requests from workstations are routed to one of three different modules. NetWare Core Protocol requests, such as data access, are routed to the NetWare server, which then interacts with the host operating system to gain access to resources.

In addition to basic NetWare operations, users may want to log onto the host operating system, just as a terminal user would want to. The terminal emulation package allows the user to appear to the host as a locally attached system.

Finally, the user may want to execute a program running on the host operating system. In this case, the remote procedure call mechanisms explained in Chapter 9 are used to tell the host operating system which remote procedure to execute. Of course, the programs on both the workstation and the server must have been written to use the RPC Tool or some other RPC mechanism.

Portable NetWare can be thought of as a series of modules, each dedicated to a different task (see Fig. 11-2). On some operating systems, these modules are in fact separate processes that are loaded as needed. In others, the modules might be procedures within a single program.

PEP (the header portion of NetWare Core Protocol packets), SPX, and NetBIOS are examples of networking support modules. NetBIOS, for example, uses the NetBIOS networking architecture on top of IPX to communicate with a workstation. PEP is used as support for the NetWare Core Protocols.

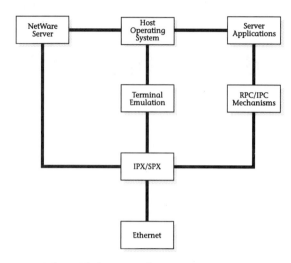

Fig. 11-1 Portable NetWare Structure

Two special modules are the multiplexing modules used to support multiple sessions from workstations. The NCPMux module is used to distribute incoming requests for resources to various processes on the host operating system. The RLogin Mux module allows multiple incoming requests to be handed off to the host operating system as if each one were a separately connected terminal. The RLogin terminal module is then responsible for communicating with the host operating system as if it were a local terminal.

Note that the two terminal modules provide a foundation protocol that allows characters to be delivered to and from a workstation. In addition, the user would run a terminal emulation program that allows the incoming data from the host to be properly interpreted. For example, in a DEC environment, the user would run a VT200 emulation program so that incoming escape sequences from the host can be translated into appropriate actions, such as reverse video or other attributes of the display.

The core of a portable NetWare environment is a process called *NWDAEMON*, which is the parent and creator of all other modules. This process is responsible for creating shared memory on the host, returning resources to the host operating system when done, and spawning NetWare engines.

The NetWare engine handles incoming NCP packets and formulates responses. The engine uses the NCPMux module (using a STREAMS interface) to communicate with its individual clients.

When an incoming connection is created, NCPMux assigns that connection to a particular engine, which then interacts with the host operating system. The way that an engine handles clients depends on the operating system. For example, in a Unix environment, an engine services each of its clients serially. In a multithreaded environment, it might be possible to service several clients simultaneously.

The engine is the basic NetWare file system code. Its responsibility is to translate an incoming file access command into the file system of the host operating

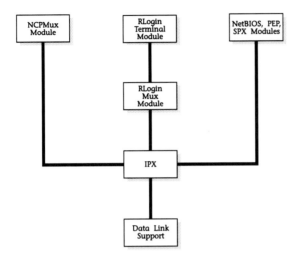

Fig. 11-2 Portable NetWare Modules

system. The engine is also responsible for keeping track of any file attributes that are not provided in the host file system but are needed in NetWare.

When Portable NetWare is installed on a system, it has a configuration file used to determine its access to resources. This file includes information such as the amount of shared memory that Portable NetWare is allowed to access, the maximum number of simultaneous connections allowed, and the number of processes allowed at once. This file also tells NetWare how many extra engines it should spawn ahead of time in preparation for incoming connection requests.

Portable NetWare is supported by several vendors. Some vendors, such as Prime and NCR, are doing the port themselves and then directly selling Portable NetWare to their clients. In other cases, such as DEC, third-party vendors are providing the software. The DEC software, NetWare for VMS, is the only one remarketed directly by Novell.

Novell provides the Portable NetWare environment by rewriting their core services in the C programming language. Any operating system that provides a standard C compiler, multitasking operating system support, and shared memory is a potential candidate for a Portable NetWare environment.

The communications function, the protocol stack, is isolated using the Portable Streams Environment discussed in Chapter 10. STREAMS isolates the NetWare services from the underlying communications details.

Portable NetWare is just one of many solutions available for integrating the PC with other operating systems. The advantage of Portable NetWare is that it makes the host look just like a Novell file server, making it easier for the user to adjust. The disadvantage of Portable NetWare also stems from the fact that the host looks like a Novell server—there are times when users will want to take advantage of the services offered on other systems and not be limited by the functionality of NetWare.

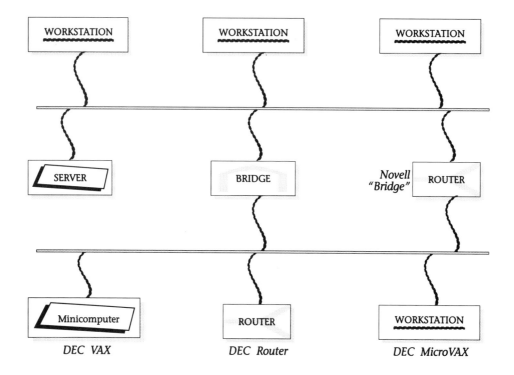

Fig. 11-3 Basic NetWare for VMS Configuration

NetWare for VMS

NetWare for VMS is the precursor of Portable NetWare for DEC minicomputers running the VMS operating system and is the ancestor of the more general Portable NetWare concept. In the basic configuration, the VAX is used as a supplementary file server for Novell workstations (see Fig. 11-3). The server on the upper Ethernet is a native NetWare server and can be used for normal operation, including tasks such as diskless workstations booting from the network.

Both a Novell router and a MAC-layer bridge are used to connect the two networks. The router, or network-level bridge in Novell terminology, is able to accept IPX packets from the workstation and forward them out the other Ethernet to the VAX. The bridge can perform the same task, based on the data link instead of network layer protocols. To avoid duplicate data delivery, one of these two devices would be configured to not forward data. For example, the MAC-layer bridge could filter out all Novell packets.

Separating the two networks is a strategy often used. The Novell traffic is localized on a workgroup network. Connection to broader resources is done on the corporate backbone. Each workgroup essentially gets its own private network, and still has access to organization-wide resources.

The Novell traffic is able to stay within the local traffic, ensuring good response time for the Novell users because they don't have to compete with backbone corporate traffic. Likewise, the corporate backbone doesn't have to be affected by transient loads in the Novell environment, such as the transfer of large graphics images or the remote booting of several workstations at once.

Once a Novell user has access to the VAX, running VMS, it is also able to access the services of DECnet. For NetWare services, IPX, NetWare Core Protocols, and all the services examined in prior chapters are used between the VAX and the workstation. However, once the user has logged onto the VAX (using the RLogin module), the user looks just like any other DEC terminal.

The rest of this chapter discusses what DECnet is and what services it might provide to the Novell user. Portable NetWare gives the user the Novell services on the VAX. The RLogin module, in conjunction with DECnet, gives the Novell user access to other resources that the VAX user has access to.

DECnet

DECnet is represented by a protocol stack, just as the Novell architecture is (see Fig. 11-4). Note that the illustration is for DECnet Phase IV networks. DEC began their migration toward an OSI-based protocol stack, known as DECnet

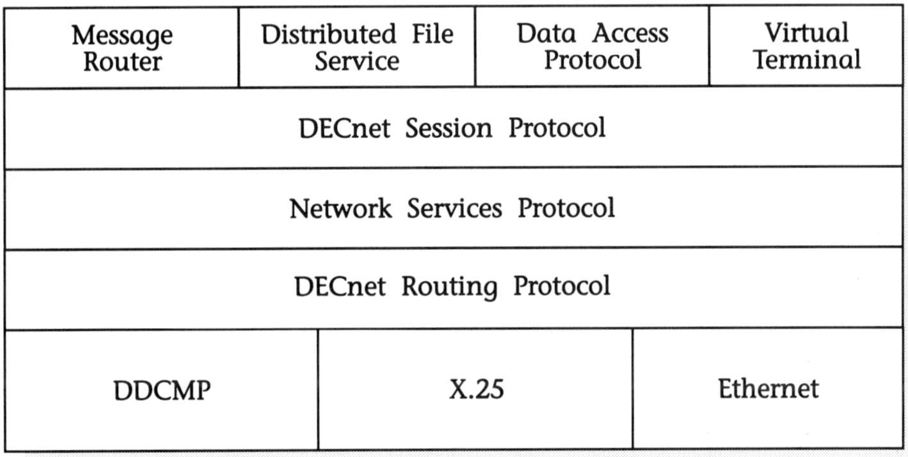

Message Router	Distributed File Service	Data Access Protocol	Virtual Terminal
DECnet Session Protocol			
Network Services Protocol			
DECnet Routing Protocol			
DDCMP	X.25		Ethernet

Fig. 11-4 DECnet Architecture

Phase V, in early 1990. They will maintain compatibility with the Phase IV networks shown here.

At the data link level, DEC supports their own synchronous communications protocol, DDCMP, for wide area communications. DDCMP is usually used to connect dedicated routers together for high-speed data transfer.

DEC also supports X.25, a packet-switched network discussed in the next chapter, and Ethernet. Both Ethernet Version 2.0 and the IEEE 802.3 versions of Ethernet are supported.

At the network layer, DEC uses the DECnet Routing Protocol. Figure 11-5 shows a packet used in this protocol. In this illustration, a router is making its presence known on an Ethernet with a *Router Hello* packet. End nodes, which are typically workstations and nonrouting VAXs, use this information to route packets through to other networks.

In a DECnet network, the topology is often much more complex than in a Novell network. This is because DECnet is targeted at large organizations, and DEC thus encourages and supports large, complex networks. This is not to say that there are not large Novell networks. Compaq, for example, runs its corporate network on the Novell protocols.

The DEC network divides a network up into routing domains, known as areas. Level I routers are responsible for routing data within an area. Level II routers are responsible for routing data between areas. Letting a router concentrate on only part of the topology of a network is the same strategy used in the Novell internetwork. The difference here is that there are two levels of segmentation, allowing better routing decisions to be made.

The routing algorithm in a DECnet is also more complex, given the fact that many DEC networks use complex topologies that combine a variety of wide area and local area links.

At the transport layer, DEC uses the Network Services Protocol (NSP), which provides the same form of reliable, end-to-end delivery of data as SPX. Unlike PEP, it allows windows of packets to be unacknowledged for a while, allowing more network bandwidth to be used for data instead of acknowledgment packets.

The session layer, as in the AppleTalk network, is responsible for the initial establishment of a session. Afterward, NSP is used to deliver data between programs. Instead of using sockets, the DEC network uses a concept of network objects. A VAX registers a variety of objects. When an incoming session establishment request is received, it specifies the object that it should be connected to (see Fig. 11-6).

Notice that DEC does not use a service advertisement protocol to perform this function but does have a distributed name server, which will play a key part in Phase V of DECnet. In Phase IV, however, broadcasting the availability of objects is not possible, except using the LAT protocols discussed below or some program-specific arrangement.

Many different applications are available at the application layer of the network, from distributed videotext systems to complex messaging environments

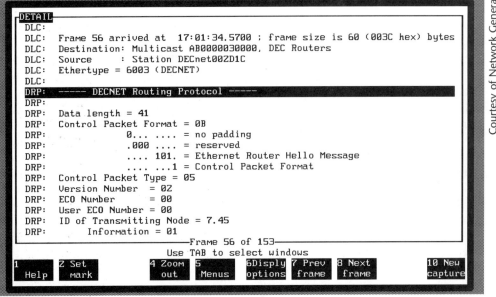

Fig. 11-5 A Router HELLO Packet

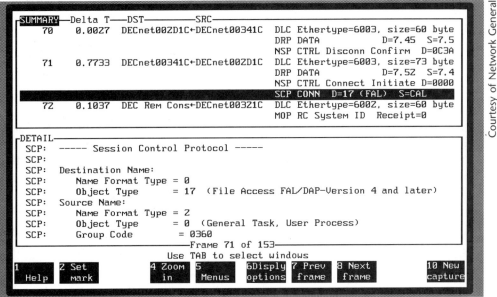

Fig. 11-6 DECnet Session Protocol

and distributed file systems. A Novell user first logs onto the VAX using the remote log in capabilities and then activates one of these services.

Two DECnet services used for data access are the Data Access Protocol (DAP) and the Distributed File Service (DFS). DAP, like the NetWare Core Protocols, is used to access data on a computer somewhere on the network.

For a Novell user to access files on the VAX with Portable NetWare, the standard mapping of the VAX disk drive to the workstation drive mapping table would be used. To get data on the rest of the DEC network, the user would go through a two-step process. First, the user would log onto the VAX. Next, the user would use the DECnet copy command to move the data from the remote DECnet node to a VAX that had NetWare for VMS. Once the data was received on the local VAX, it would then be available to the workstation using the NetWare Core Protocols.

An alternative to this approach is the DEC Distributed File Service. DFS is used to make remote files appear as if they were locally attached, much as NCP does for a DOS or OS/2 workstation. DFS would be used to make the remote DECnet resources available to the local VAX. In turn, NetWare would be told to map this "local" data to a workstation.

Two other major services in a DECnet environment are the Message Router and the Virtual Terminal service. The Message Router is used to route messages, much as MHS from Action Technologies does. Message Router, like MHS, has gateways out to many key environments, including IBM's SNADS and the X.400 protocols.

The virtual terminal service is used to log a user onto a remote computer on the network. Note that this remote computer can be many hops away from the source and use various data links.

For a Novell user to log onto a remote computer on DECnet, a two-step process is used. First, the user logs onto the local VAX running the NetWare for VMS. This makes the Novell workstation appear as a DEC VT-series terminal. Next, the user types the *SET HOST* command, which makes a VAX user appear to be locally connected to a remote DECnet node.

A wide variety of other services are also available in this environment, such as videotext or other protocols. These protocols are built on top of the session layer provided in DECnet. Many specialized programs, such as distributed databases, are also available with DECnet support.

LAT Protocol

A separate network architecture, the Local Area Transport (LAT), is used by DEC to connect terminals (or PCs acting as terminals) to a VAX. Figure 11-7 shows a possible configuration for such a network. Terminals are connected to a terminal server, which in turn is connected to the Ethernet network. Terminal servers that use the LAT protocols only support Ethernet. A variety of other devices such as printers or modems can be connected to the terminal server.

The LAT architecture is a direct user of the Ethernet. This means that it bypasses the routing function usually found at the network layer. Since all the nodes are on an Ethernet, there is no need for a routing function.

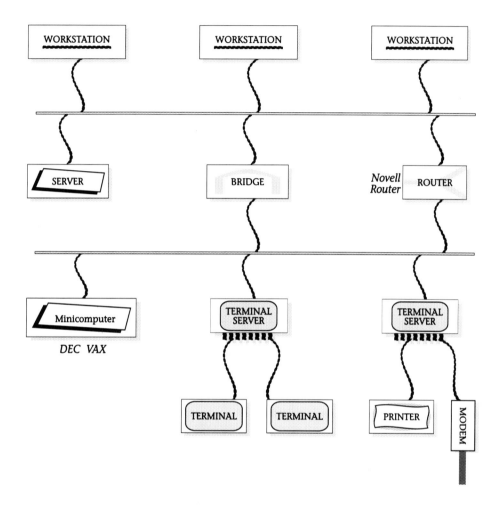

Fig. 11-7 Terminal Server Configuration

The LAT protocols allow the LAT host, usually a VAX, to receive connections from LAT clients, usually a terminal or PC connected to the terminal server. It is also possible, however, for the LAT client to be a PC that has LAT support and an Ethernet controller.

It is also possible to reverse the roles. For a VAX to use the services of a modem for outgoing calls or a printer, the terminal server becomes the host and

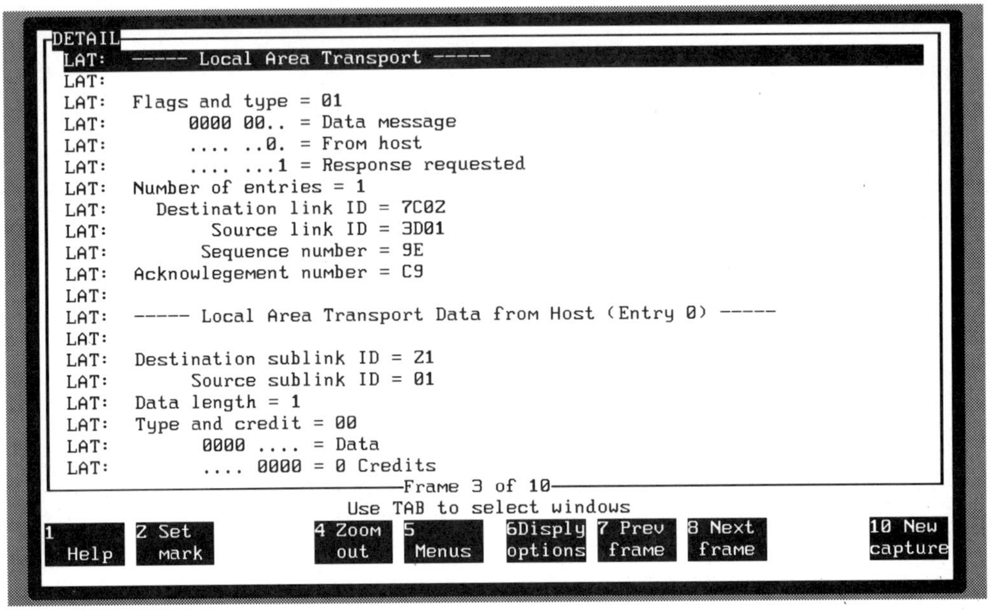

```
┌─DETAIL──────────────────────────────────────────────────────┐
│ LAT: ------ Local Area Transport ------                     │
│ LAT:                                                        │
│ LAT: Flags and type = 01                                    │
│ LAT:      0000 00.. = Data message                          │
│ LAT:      .... ..0. = From host                             │
│ LAT:      .... ...1 = Response requested                    │
│ LAT: Number of entries = 1                                  │
│ LAT:    Destination link ID = 7C02                          │
│ LAT:         Source link ID = 3D01                          │
│ LAT:        Sequence number = 9E                            │
│ LAT: Acknowlegement number = C9                             │
│ LAT:                                                        │
│ LAT: ------ Local Area Transport Data from Host (Entry 0) --│
│ LAT:                                                        │
│ LAT: Destination sublink ID = 21                            │
│ LAT:      Source sublink ID = 01                            │
│ LAT: Data length = 1                                        │
│ LAT: Type and credit = 00                                   │
│ LAT:      0000 .... = Data                                  │
│ LAT:      .... 0000 = 0 Credits                             │
│                      ─Frame 3 of 10─                        │
│                   Use TAB to select windows                 │
│ [1    ][2 Set ][4 Zoom][5     ][6Disply][7 Prev][8 Next][10 New  ]│
│ [ Help][ mark ][ out  ][ Menus][options][ frame][ frame][ capture]│
└─────────────────────────────────────────────────────────────┘
```

Fig. 11-8 A LAT Packet

the VAX the client. Because the roles of terminal server and host are reversed, this is known as a reverse LAT configuration.

Figure 11-8 shows a LAT packet on the Ethernet. Notice that the packet can have multiple entries in it. One of the characteristics of LAT is that it does not send a packet when a user is ready to send data. Instead it waits, typically 80 milliseconds, before sending it. During that time, it sees if there is other data going to the same destination. For example, two users might be logged onto the same VAX on the Ethernet. By multiplexing data on the Ethernet, the LAT protocols conserve bandwidth.

One of the features of LAT is the concept of a service advertisement. Any LAT service provider periodically broadcasts the availability of services it provides. LAT clients, such as terminal servers, record these service advertisements in a local database.

Users who want to log onto the network are presented with a list of available services. When the service is advertised, a node broadcasts a current service rating. For example, a VAX bases its service rating on the number of idle log in slots, the total number of log in slots, and the idle CPU time.

It is possible for several different LAT hosts to offer the same service. When a user picks a service, the LAT terminal server will connect the user to the service provider that has the best service rating at the time.

In this way, LAT is able to provide load balancing among multiple service providers, which is particularly important in VAX Clusters, discussed next. Load balancing is also useful for several stand-alone machines offering the same service, such as word processing or graphics.

Note that the load-balancing capability of LAT dovetails very nicely with the distributed file service. DFS allows files on the network to be remotely available in a transparent fashion. When a user logs onto any machine on the network, the "home" files are mounted on that machine. In this way, a network can consist of a variety of specialized servers. If a particular service is used more, the network simply adds another server. LAT then picks the server that has the best service rating on a dynamic basis. DFS then makes sure that the user's files are always available.

VAX Clusters

A VAX Cluster is somewhat similar to DFS, in that users on different computers all think that a group of files are locally attached. However, the VAX Cluster provides a much tighter integration of different computers.

Figure 11-9 shows a VAX Cluster configuration. The Hierarchical Storage Controller (HSC) is a dedicated special-purpose computer that serves as an intelligent disk controller. In addition to the HSC, the VAX Cluster includes any of the VAX minicomputers.

Up to 32 of these nodes (HSCs or VAXs) can be connected together in a cluster. The cluster operates at 70 Mbps, or 7 times faster than the Ethernet. The main purpose of this network is to allow all the computers to access the same disk drives.

To allow this, the VAX Cluster has a distributed lock manager that allows record-level access to data to be tightly coordinated among different computers. The distributed lock manager is designed so that if a computer fails, the cluster can continue to operate (although sometimes there is a significant pause in processing while the cluster tests the integrity of the lock space).

In Figure 11-9, there are disk drives connected to two different HSC controllers. Dual-porting disk drives ensures that if one HSC fails, the data stays available. In addition, as in Novell NetWare, a disk may be mirrored—all operations on one disk drive will occur on another one. Mirroring assures that if data on one drive is corrupted, the data remains available and online.

This network thus consists of a variety of redundant pieces—disk drives, computers, and disk controllers—all operating at a very high rate. This redundant operation is known in Novell terminology as System Fault Tolerant (SFT) Level III. Level II mirrors data and allows continued operation when a disk drive fails; Level III allows continued operation in the case of a CPU failure.

Novell and DECnet

Novell cites the high availability of the VAX Cluster as one of the primary benefits of NetWare for VMS. The user is able to store files in an environment in which files are guaranteed to be available almost all of the time.

Many organizations use DEC as a corporate backbone (others use SNA or TCP/IP, discussed in Chapter 14). With NetWare for VMS, the user is able to access this corporate backbone and thus use the wide area networking capabilities of DECnet to access remote resources.

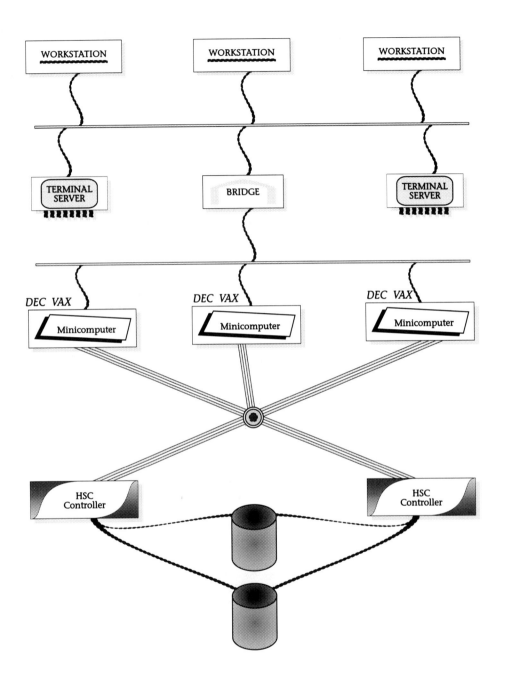

Fig. 11-9 A VAX Cluster

Often, Novell will be used as a local networking solution, providing the workstation user with local mail, data, and printing services. This network is then connected to a larger one, which is used to provide access to remote resources, such as Videotext, remote files, organization-wide messaging, or other services.

What is important here is not which network is better. In many environments, different kinds of networks are the rule. The important point is how to connect the different environments together at an adequate level of service. It is one thing to provide a bulk data transfer utility; it is quite another to make the data available transparently.

Key Points in This Chapter

- NetWare for VMS is Novell's original product for allowing another operating system (here DEC's VMS) to provide NetWare Core Protocol services for workstations.
- NetWare for VMS has been superseded by the more general Portable NetWare. Portable NetWare will, if vendors choose to support it, allow other systems such as Unix minicomputers to provide NCP services for NetWare workstations.
- Portable NetWare is a guest of the operating system. It allows multiple workstations to set up connections and access data and printers. Portable NetWare also allows the user to log onto the remote host.
- The remote log in feature gives the user access to all the features available on that remote system. In the case of a VAX and NetWare for VMS, the user has access to DECnet resources.
- DECnet is a very different network architecture from NetWare. DECnet is intended for the large corporation-wide network, while NetWare is aimed at the smaller workgroup.
- The basic DECnet architecture allows a variety of services similar to NetWare, such as remote access to data. It also allows other services, such as distributed file, naming, and queuing services.
- DEC uses two other network architectures: VAX Clusters and the Local Area Transport. VAX Clusters are a high-speed (70 Mbps) network for integrating disk drives onto several different VAX systems. LAT is a protocol that allows hosts and terminal servers to communicate.
- NetWare for VMS provides a gateway between NetWare and DECnet. NetWare for VMS uses IPX/SPX to maintain a connection to the workstation.

CHAPTER 12

X.25 and Wide Area Networks

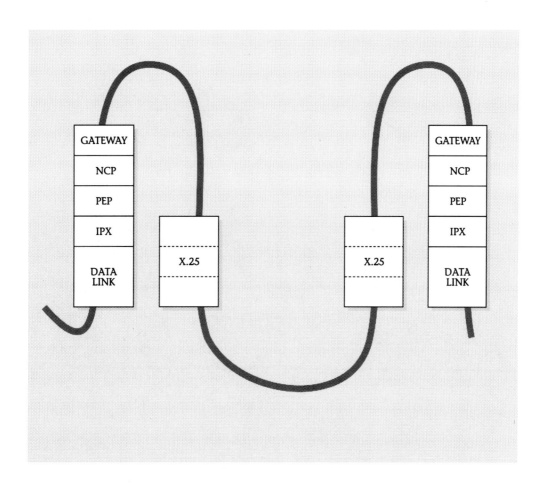

CHAPTER 12

X.25 and Wide Area Networks

Wide Area Networks

Chapters 3, 4, and 5 dealt with how to configure a network and how to connect those networks together using the IPX protocols. The focus was on the local area network. This is because the vast majority of Novell networks are local workgroup configurations.

This chapter looks at how to connect different LANs together into a wide area internetwork. It also looks at how to connect a Novell environment to other resources such as remote hosts. In both cases, a wide area data link protocol will be used.

This chapter looks at two types of data links. First, there are asynchronous links using standard telephone lines or leased lines. If the link is being used by the network layer of NetWare, then each end of the link has a Novell router. Another form of asynchronous link allows a remote workstation to become part of a Novell network. Workstations access an asynchronous server, which in turn provides access to a high-speed data link such as Ethernet.

The reverse is to allow a Novell workstation to use the asynchronous link to access remote, non-Novell servers. Typically, these servers are a remote mini-computer, such as a DEC VAX or a Sun workstation. An asynchronous link allows a Novell workstation to emulate a terminal, which is quite useful when the server does not have a NetWare implementation.

Next, this chapter will discuss another form of data link, the X.25 network. X.25 is an international protocol specified by the CCITT (the same committee that specified the X.400 protocols). X.25 allows a virtual circuit to be established to a remote X.25 destination. This virtual circuit is then used for the transfer of data.

Asynchronous Bridges

In Novell terminology, a bridge is a server that has links to two or more different data links. This is usually called a router in most other networks.

Figure 12-1 shows two networks connected together using wide area links. On the left, a dial-up telephone line is being used to connect two networks together. Novell IPX programs on either end of the link are able to send data across the line to their peer server.

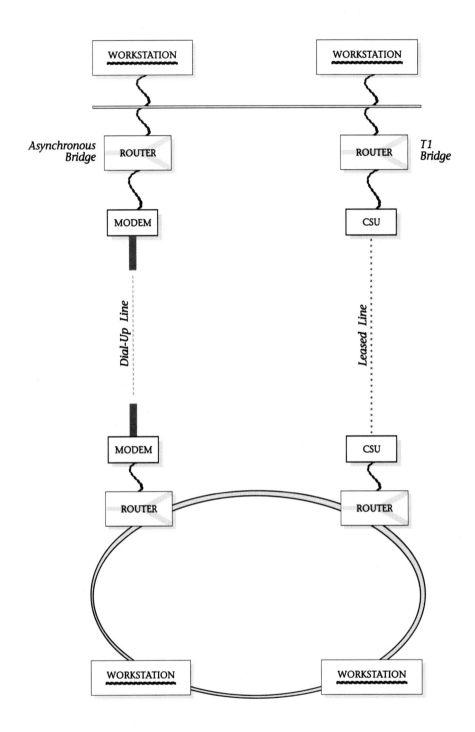

Fig. 12-1 Asynchronous Bridges (Routers)

To the IPX program, this link appears in the routing table as a series of remote networks and a port. The port, the asynchronous link, accepts data and sends it to the router on the other end, which is then responsible for sending the packet on to its eventual destination.

An asynchronous link such as this can transmit data over normal telephone lines at speeds of up to 19.2 Kbps, which is too slow for high volumes of data. An alternative is to use third-party solutions that support synchronous communications over high-speed leased lines.

In Figure 12-1, one of the links shows a T1 line connecting the two networks. A T1 line is a leased digital line that sends data at speeds of 1.544 Mbps. Since the line is digital, it does not use a modem (which modulates and demodulates analog signals into digital and vice versa). Instead, the T1 link uses an access device known as a Channel Service Unit (CSU). The CSU is then connected to a card in the server. The vendor provides a device driver so the link appears to NetWare as a communications link. The link can then be used with either the asynchronous or X.25 bridge products from Novell.

Asynchronous Gateways

Figure 12-1 shows how to transparently connect two Novell networks using a wide area link. In many environments, it is necessary to access non-Novell resources, such as a remote workstation or minicomputer.

Figure 12-2 shows two kinds of specialized Novell servers that are using asynchronous lines for access to remote resources. In both cases, the computers are dedicated 80386 PCs with the Novell Wide Area Network Interface Module (WNIM+) communications boards in them.

The NetWare Access Server is used to allow a remote workstation to become part of a Novell network. The workstation can be a PC or Macintosh (with a terminal emulation package) or a plain terminal.

Users dial into the NetWare Access Server, just as they would a remote bulletin board or other computer. The server has a dial-back feature, which provides an additional layer of security. It takes an incoming call and records the username. Then the server breaks the connection and checks its database to see the phone number of this particular user. It then dials the user back and establishes the connection. The dial-back feature helps ensure that somebody does not impersonate the user.

The server uses software developed jointly by Quarterdeck Office Systems and Dynamic Microprocessor Associates. It combines Quarterdeck's DESQview 386, DMA's pcAnywhere, and the Novell WNIM+ boards. The server is able to maintain several simultaneous connections at once, making the server appear to the rest of the Novell network as a series of workstations.

DESQview 386 provides the multitasking capability for the server. This software spawns "virtual" PCs, using the protected mode of the 80386 processor. Each virtual computer has MS-DOS, applications, and the remote server software.

The pcAnywhere software is an efficient user of the asynchronous link. The software controls data transfer by receiving screen information and keyboard

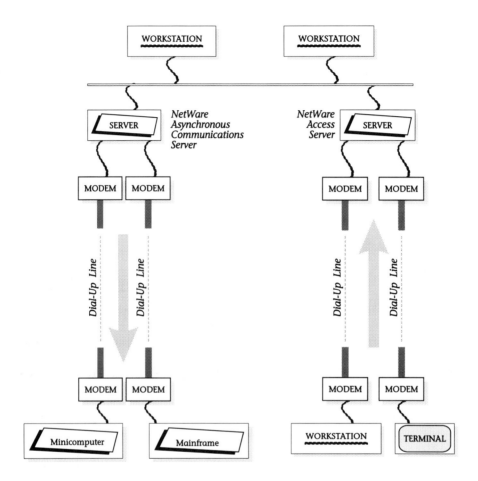

Fig. 12-2 Asynchronous Gateways

signals from the remote user. When the screen changes, the software only sends back the changes instead of the whole screen.

The NetWare Asynchronous Communications Server (NACS) allows a Novell workstation (which could be a remote workstation) to access asynchronous resources. This server is again a dedicated PC and uses the services of the Service Advertisement Protocol to broadcast its availability to the rest of the network.

Attached to the NACS are a series of asynchronous resources which could be cables to the asynchronous terminal ports of a minicomputer, or a series of modems, printers, or any other asynchronous devices.

On the workstation, a terminate and stay resident (TSR) utility is installed that traps all data intended for the COM1 port of the PC. The utility then takes that outgoing data and sends it to the NACS, which in turn sends it through one of its ports.

To the workstation, the NACS looks like an extension of the local serial port. Software, such as a print spooler or terminal emulator, uses the virtual serial port to access a remote device.

The TSR utility is known as NetWare Asynchronous Services Interface (NASI). In the basic mode, NASI is a transparent extension of the serial port. An extended mode allows a program specially written to use it to do more complex operations. For example, the extended mode allows the program to dynamically change the speed of the connection or the parity of a port. Other extended function calls allow access to name services to find specific ports on the NACS.

Using a specific port is useful when the workstation is expecting an incoming call and needs to know which modem will be receiving the call. This data might then be sent over the Novell network to the workstation, which would act as a host for a remote user.

X.25 Bridges

X.25 is a packet-switched network that allows the user to send data transparently to a remote host on the network. X.25 defines a standard interface to a wide area network. This standard interface includes the method used to specify which remote destination is needed.

Once data is received at the X.25 network, it is the responsibility of that network to decide how to get it to the remote host. This internal routing of data is not defined in X.25 and is transparent to the user.

X.25 is an important protocol because of its wide acceptance internationally. Many national and commercial data networks are based on X.25. In addition, many countries have connected separate X.25 networks together using the X.75 protocols, providing connections across national boundaries.

Figure 12-3 shows how X.25 can be used to connect two Novell networks together into an internet. An X.25 bridge (i.e., a Novell router with one connection on the LAN and the other on X.25) is used on each of the networks. The network manager establishes a virtual circuit between the two sites.

Once the virtual circuit is in place, IPX uses it as a path between the two networks. In this case, the X.25 network is transparent to the user and is used solely by IPX. A special case is the point-to-point X.25 bridge. Here, instead of a public or private X.25 network with many hosts on it, the connection is a point-to-point link between two Novell routers.

Instead of using an asynchronous protocol to transfer data one character at a time, the X.25 protocols are used to move data across the telephone link. X.25 puts the data in packets, allowing for more efficient use of the telephone line.

Novell X.25 Gateway

An alternative to using X.25 as an internal routing mechanism for a Novell network is to use the X.25 network to access remote devices. Figure 12-4 shows

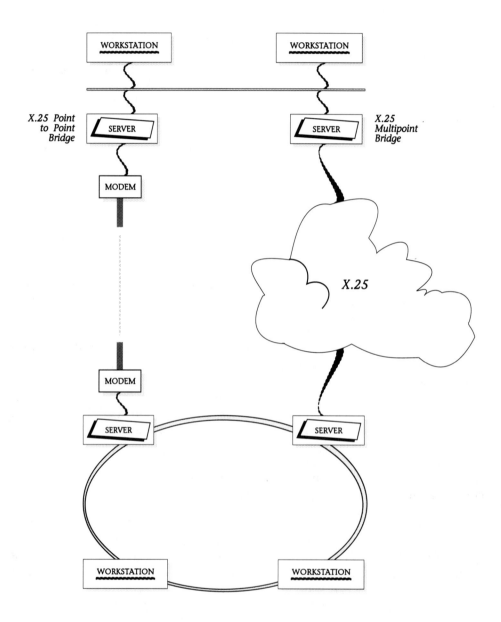

Fig. 12-3 X.25 Bridges (Routers)

such a configuration, which allows a workstation to appear as a locally connected terminal to some remote resource. In this configuration, the user logs onto the X.25 gateway. Then, a call is placed to a remote host, such as a minicomputer or mainframe. The data goes from the user workstation to the gateway using the IPX protocols.

When the data reaches the X.25 gateway, it is repackaged as an X.25 packet and sent to the X.25 network. X.25 then delivers the data to the remote destination.

Figure 12-4 shows a device called a PAD, for Packet Assembler/Disassembler. The PAD allows a terminal, which is an asynchronous device, to use the synchronous X.25 network.

The Novell X.25 gateway looks like a PAD to the X.25 network. It has a series of terminals attached to it, which happen in this case to be workstations on a Novell network. The PAD allows the remote computer to control certain aspects of the virtual circuit. In addition, the terminal (workstation) is able to change how the PAD operates for this session.

An example of changing characteristics is deciding when a packet of data should be sent out. The workstation appears to the PAD as an asynchronous terminal—data is delivered one character at a time. It doesn't make sense to put each character into a separate X.25 packet.

Instead, the X.25 PAD uses a series of rules to decide when a packet should be sent. Obviously, when enough data is received to fill up a packet, the PAD will have to send the data out. However, it could be that the user types a single character that is a command for the remote host. Normally, the PAD will wait for a specific period of time before sending out a character of data. It is also possible to tell the PAD to send out data when certain characters, such as a carriage return, are received.

In addition to controlling the PAD operation, the Novell X.25 gateway supports a variety of other features supported in the standard. Most of these are options provided by a specific X.25 service provider. For example, a PAD can be programmed to bar outgoing calls or to bar reverse charging acceptance. Reverse charging is used so that the workstation instead of the host bears the charges for the call.

Integrating Novell and WANs

Wide area networks (WANs) can be used to access non-Novell resources as well as to connect Novell networks together into an internetwork. In both cases, a dedicated PC is used as a gateway or router for the remote resources.

Asynchronous and X.25 links are the two forms of data links provided for this remote access. Note that in the case of connecting networks together, the MAC-layer bridge provides an alternative strategy.

An important use of both X.25 and asynchronous links is to access non-Novell resources. Workstations can dial into a LAN and become part of the network, using any servers or other resources available on the network. Similarly, local workstations can use the gateway to dial out to remote resources, such as a minicomputer.

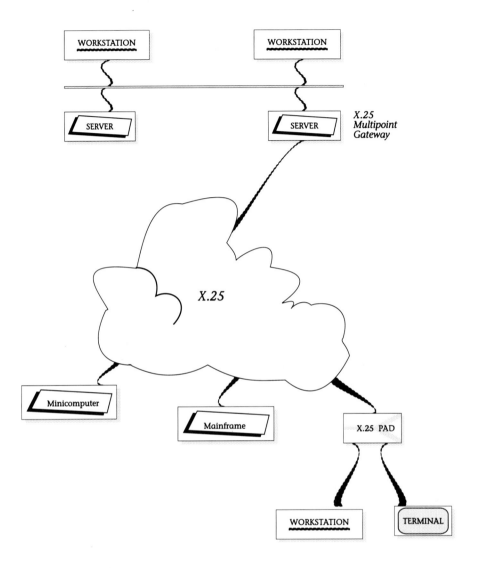

Fig. 12-4 X.25 Gateways

Key Points in This Chapter

- Novell supports both X.25 and asynchronous wide area connections.
- X.25 is a packet-switching standard, widely implemented on public wide area networks.
- An X.25 gateway allows the NetWare workstation to appear as a terminal on the X.25 network. The user can then set up an X.25 virtual call to any host on the network.

- The X.25 "bridge" allows two Novell networks to use X.25 as a data link. X.25 bridges tie the two networks (or more) together into an internetwork.
- The NetWare Asynchronous Communications Server allows a workstation to access remote, asynchronous resources. For example, a pool of modems can be attached to a NACS to allow workstations to initiate remote connections with bulletin boards for downloading more games.
- The NetWare Access Server allows remote computers to dial into a Novell network and become part of it. Instead of just emulating a terminal, the workstation uses the IPX/SPX protocols to access servers on the network.
- A variety of third-party products are available that allow wide area communications lines to be used to connect different Novell networks.

CHAPTER 13

Gateways to Other Networks

NFS	APPLICATION		NAU Services Manager
XDR	PRESENTATION	SMB	FI.FMD Presentation Services
RPC	SESSION		Data Flow Control
TCP/UDP	TRANSPORT	NetBIOS	Transmission Control
IP	NETWORK		Path Control
DATA LINK	DATA LINK	DATA LINK	DATA LINK

TCP/IP   *OSI*   *NetBIOS*   *IBM SNA*

CHAPTER 13

Gateways to Other Networks

Gateways

We saw in the chapter on Portable NetWare and DECnet support that a DEC environment can be closely integrated with Novell in two different ways. First, the Portable NetWare actually makes a VAX part of the Novell environment. The second method used is a virtual terminal service to log a user onto the VAX. Once on the VAX, the user becomes a member of the DECnet and has full access to those resources. Data goes from the workstation to the VAX using IPX and then is forwarded out to the eventual destination using DECnet.

This method of connectivity works for practically any two environments. As long as there is a method of connecting the user to the edge of the network as if they were a local terminal, the user can then access remote resources.

The disadvantage of this method is the level of integration. The user must know the location of the gateway computer, how to log into it, and how to use the resources of that network. A true gateway allows the user to use local commands to access remote resources transparently.

In this chapter, we will look at different levels of connectivity to different networking environments. The simplest case of a remote log in can be achieved using the asynchronous servers discussed in the previous chapter. Here, we look at how the user can achieve a more sophisticated type of remote log in, as well as higher levels of connectivity to three key environments: TCP/IP, IBM's SNA, and NetBIOS. In addition, the OSI networking protocols and their impact on interconnectivity are briefly discussed.

TCP/IP

TCP/IP is a network architecture sponsored by the Defense Advanced Research Projects Agency (DARPA) and subsequently adopted by a large number of vendors. TCP/IP is particularly important in Unix-based computers and for large wide area networks.

Unix-based computers, such as Sun, DEC, and Hewlett-Packard/Apollo, provided a strong boost for TCP/IP. Since many of their sales are to the government, these companies have to provide TCP/IP support. The nonproprietary nature of the protocols allows many different brands of computers to work together, hence a wide acceptance by users.

TCP/IP also forms the basis for the Internet, a collection of different networks that are able to exchange mail and other information. The National Science Foundation's NSFnet, for example, uses TCP/IP to provide American and international researchers access to computing resources.

The basic TCP/IP protocols are shown in Figure 13-1. Like Novell, the architecture begins at the network layer. Several different data links are supported in this environment, including Ethernet, token ring, X.25, and synchronous wide area links.

The Internet Protocol (IP) is used at the network layer and provides a very similar service to IPX. A variety of support protocols are used for the maintenance of routing tables and for finding the remote network address.

The Transmission Control Protocol (TCP) is a reliable data transfer protocol, similar to SPX. The User Datagram Protocol (UDP) provides best-effort delivery service and is a very simple form of a transport protocol. Built on top of TCP or UDP are three standard services: remote log in, file transfer, and a simple messaging service. Note that these are very simple services. For example, the file transfer is nontransparent—the user must transfer the file to the home computer before using it. No provision is made for record-level access or mapping of disk drives to local drives.

Figure 13-2 shows the configuration of a simple gateway between Novell and TCP/IP. The user logs into the gateway, which is running both Novell and TCP/IP networking software. This makes the remote user appear to be a local user who has full access to software on the system. In this case, the software that is run happens to be TCP/IP instead of word processing or some other local application.

The NCP protocols are responsible for delivering data to the TCP/IP software program. TCP/IP then picks that data up and performs operations on remote TCP/IP resources. In the case of a remote log in, the virtual terminal service

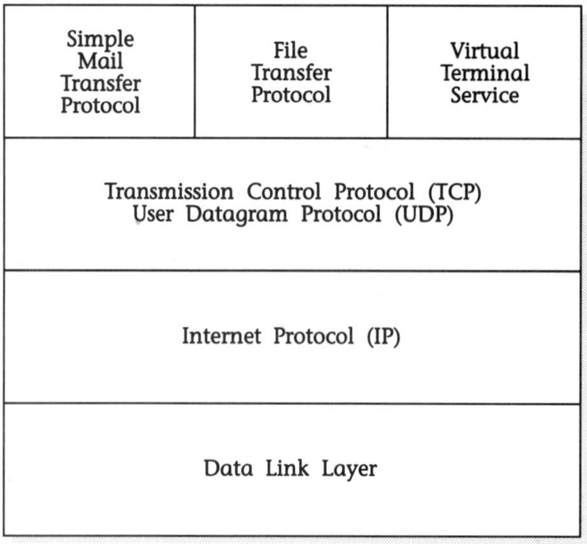

Fig. 13-1 TCP/IP Protocol Stack

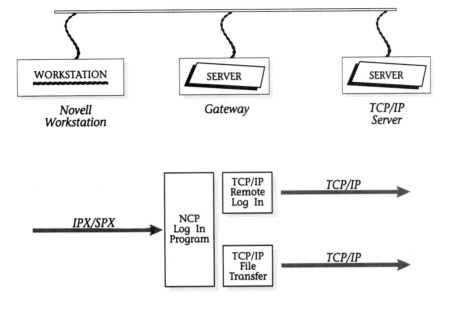

Fig. 13-2 Simple TCP/IP Gateway

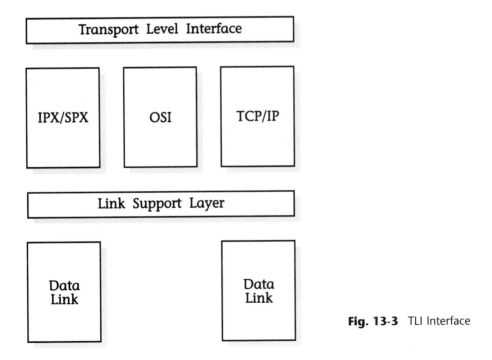

Fig. 13-3 TLI Interface

would simply deliver the data onto the remote host. In the case of a file transfer, the TCP/IP program takes a remote file and moves it to the gateway. The user then uses the Novell NCP protocols to move that file from that gateway to the local workstation.

The STREAMS interface discussed in Chapter 10 provides a more integrated solution to this type of connectivity. The Transport Level Interface provides a standard way for a network service to move data on the network (see Fig. 13-3). Underneath the Transport Level Interface can be a variety of transport stacks.

Novell has publicly committed to supporting three sets of transport stacks. First, IPX and SPX will, of course, be supported. In addition, there will be support for OSI and TCP environments. As long as there is a similar program at the destination, the underlying network becomes transparent.

Network File System

An important addition to the TCP/IP protocols is the Network File System (NFS), developed by Sun Microsystems and licensed to most other vendors in the computer industry. NFS builds on top of the basic TCP/IP protocol stack to provide a more sophisticated level of service (see Fig. 13-4).

The first thing that NFS does is provide a session-level protocol to support remote procedure calls. This RPC mechanism is supported in the NetWise RPC Tool and is used to allow a program to execute commands on another computer.

Figure 13-5 shows the RPC header for a packet being used by NFS. Notice that the packet includes a transaction ID and a program number. In this envi-

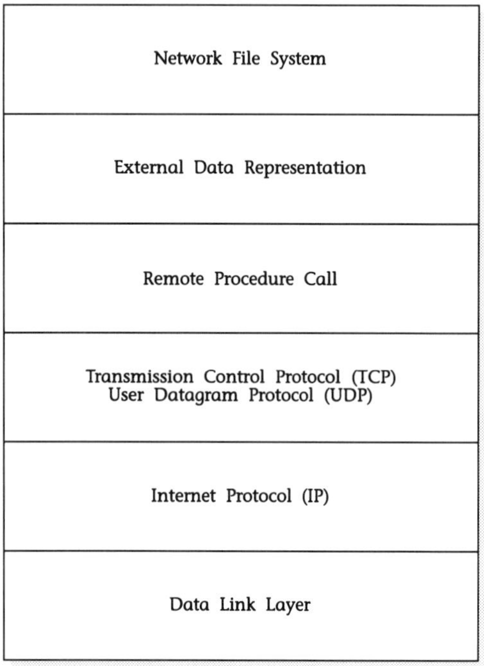

Fig. 13-4 Network File System Protocol Stack

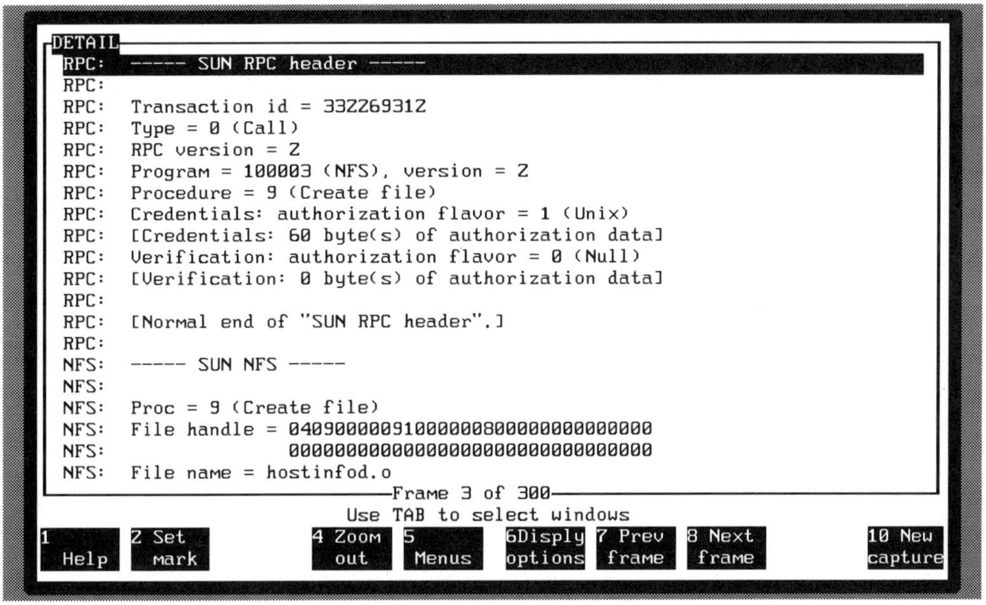

```
┌DETAIL─────────────────────────────────────────────────────┐
│RPC:    ----- SUN RPC header -----                         │
│RPC:                                                       │
│RPC:    Transaction id = 332269312                         │
│RPC:    Type = 0 (Call)                                    │
│RPC:    RPC version = 2                                    │
│RPC:    Program = 100003 (NFS), version = 2                │
│RPC:    Procedure = 9 (Create file)                        │
│RPC:    Credentials: authorization flavor = 1 (Unix)       │
│RPC:    [Credentials: 60 byte(s) of authorization data]    │
│RPC:    Verification: authorization flavor = 0 (Null)      │
│RPC:    [Verification: 0 byte(s) of authorization data]    │
│RPC:                                                       │
│RPC:    [Normal end of "SUN RPC header".]                  │
│RPC:                                                       │
│NFS:    ----- SUN NFS -----                                │
│NFS:                                                       │
│NFS:    Proc = 9 (Create file)                             │
│NFS:    File handle = 040900009100000080000000000000000    │
│NFS:                  00000000000000000000000000000000     │
│NFS:    File name = hostinfod.o                            │
│                        ─Frame 3 of 300─                   │
│                    Use TAB to select windows              │
│ 1      2 Set          4 Zoom  5       6Disply 7 Prev  8 Next         10 New   │
│ Help   mark           out     Menus   options frame   frame          capture  │
└───────────────────────────────────────────────────────────┘
```

Fig. 13-5 Remote Procedure Call

ronment, programs can be registered to provide a general service to a variety of users. Here, the program is the Network File System.

The packet also includes a particular procedure number within that program. When a program is ready to provide service to remote users, it registers itself with the RPC program on its computer. It tells the RPC program which number it will use and what procedures it has available.

For well-known programs like NFS, the numbers are static. It is also possible to have dynamically assigned numbers. These are assigned as the remote program is created and are used for subsequent calls during the same session.

Like the NetWise RPC Tool, there needs to be a standard method of representing data across the network. Therefore, the next layer that Sun added was the External Data Representation (XDR). XDR is a format for the presentation of data and does not show up as a separate layer in a network analyzer. Support for XDR is provided by local pack and unpack procedures.

The XDR standard provides a standard method of representing primitive data types, such as integers and characters. In addition, there is support for a wide variety of data structures, such as arrays, unions, and other structures commonly found in the C programming language.

The next level of the network is the application layer. The main application provided by Sun is the Network File System itself. In addition, there are other services available, such as messaging and time synchronization.

NFS allows a computer to mount a remote file system as if it were local. This service is similar to that offered by the NetWare Core Protocols in mapping a server drive to a local drive. It is then up to the server to coordinate access and security to that device.

Figure 13-6 shows an NFS packet on the network. In this case, the user is attempting to create a file. The local shell saw that this was a remote operation and handed it off to NFS. NFS then sent a packet to the file server to have a file created. Notice that the *create file* packet includes a value of –1 for several of the attributes of the file, such as the creation time. This tells the file server that it should use its own default values.

Notice also that the packet includes a UID (user identification) and GID (group identification), along with security permissions based on those IDs. These security attributes are characteristic of the Unix file system, where many of the NFS implementations exist.

It is the responsibility of the local file system to map these attributes to the local file system. In the case of a Unix-based computer, the mapping is quite simple. For other file systems, such as an IBM mainframe, the mapping can be a little more difficult.

Figure 13-7 shows some typical NFS traffic on an Ethernet. The first exchange of data was a request for 4096 bytes to be read. The server sent back a positive acknowledgment but with 0 bytes of data. This means that the file existed but was empty.

The next exchange, including the packet shown in the detail section of the screen, shows a write operation to a file. Notice that some of the data is missing in the first packet. The NFS operation is to write 4096 bytes of data, but the underlying data link, network, and transport protocols are limited to under 1600 bytes per packet. The next two packets contain the rest of the data, followed by an acknowledgment from the remote side that it has received all three packets.

By transparently mounting remote file systems on a user's workstation, NFS makes the network a transparent resource. Since NFS is supported by many vendors, it provides an easy way of sharing data among different brands of computers.

NFS is used, among other things, for remote booting of diskless workstations. The NFS protocols are built into the ROM of a computer (actually, just a subset used for remote booting is built in—not the full protocol set).

When the diskless computer is turned on, it uses NFS to receive the operating system. Then it mounts remote file systems so they appear local. This method works so well that it is possible to store one computer's operating system on another brand of computer. For example, Sun workstations can use a DEC VAX for remote booting.

NFS is particularly useful in a university-type environment, where there are many users and no guarantee which computer a user will be on at any one time. No matter which workstation users are on, NFS is used to get their files and make them available.

NFS is also used to share an expensive resource. For example, help files can take up a considerable amount of disk space. Instead of giving each user a copy of the help files, a single machine acts as the help server. When a user types *help*, the help command will start searching files on a portion of the file system that is actually resident on the help server.

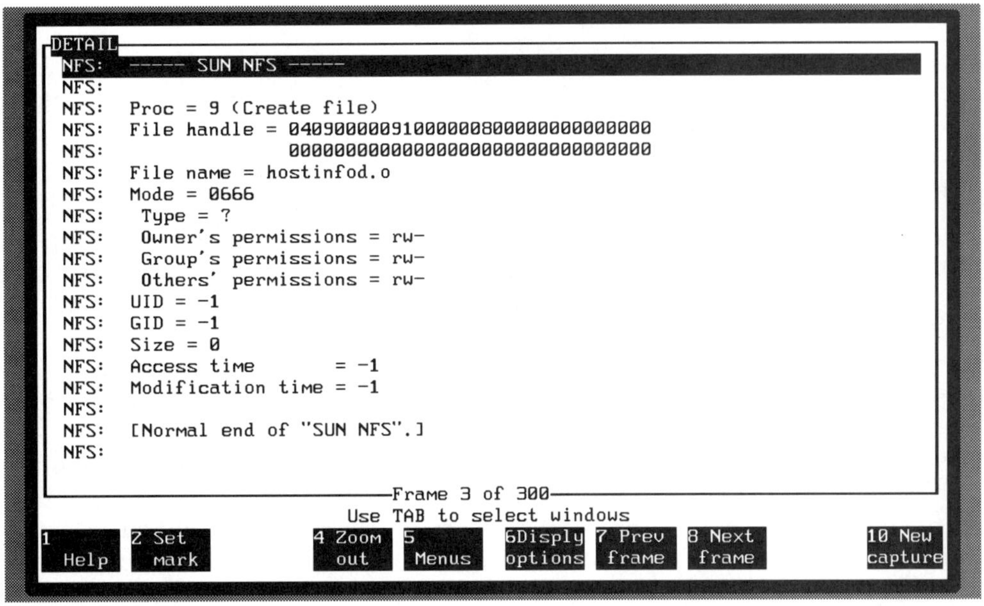

```
┌DETAIL─────────────────────────────────────────────────────────┐
│NFS: ───── SUN NFS ─────                                       │
│NFS:                                                           │
│NFS: Proc = 9 (Create file)                                    │
│NFS: File handle = 040900009100000080000000000000000           │
│NFS:               00000000000000000000000000000000            │
│NFS: File name = hostinfod.o                                   │
│NFS: Mode = 0666                                               │
│NFS:   Type = ?                                                │
│NFS:   Owner's permissions = rw-                               │
│NFS:   Group's permissions = rw-                               │
│NFS:   Others' permissions = rw-                               │
│NFS: UID = -1                                                  │
│NFS: GID = -1                                                  │
│NFS: Size = 0                                                  │
│NFS: Access time       = -1                                    │
│NFS: Modification time = -1                                    │
│NFS:                                                           │
│NFS: [Normal end of "SUN NFS".]                                │
│NFS:                                                           │
│                    ─Frame 3 of 300─                           │
│                 Use TAB to select windows                     │
│ 1      2 Set        4 Zoom  5        6Display 7 Prev  8 Next       10 New  │
│ Help   mark         out     Menus    options  frame   frame        capture │
└───────────────────────────────────────────────────────────────┘
```

Fig. 13-6 NFS Create File Packet

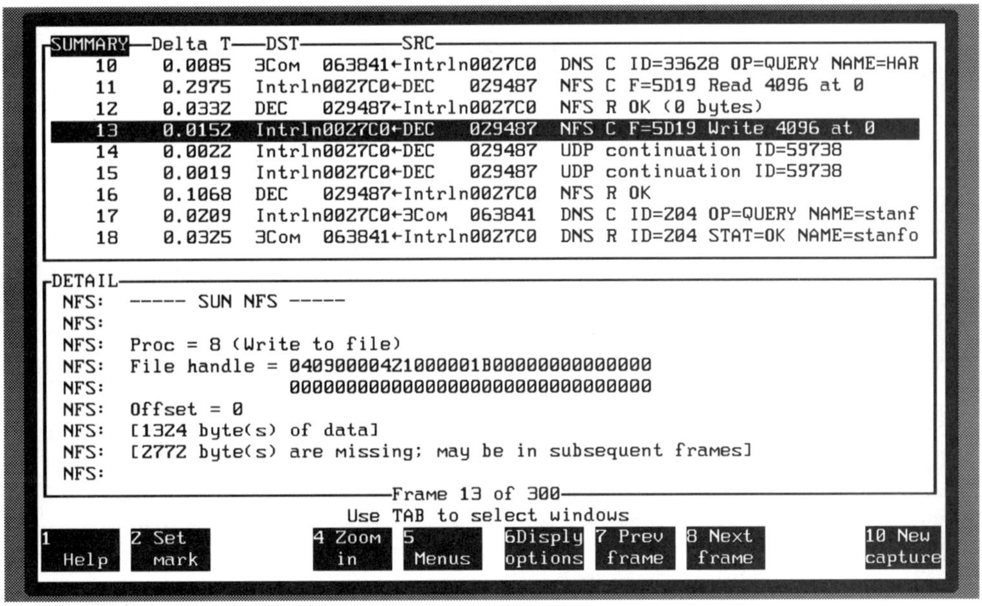

```
┌SUMMARY──Delta T────DST────────SRC─────────────────────────────────────┐
│   10     0.0085   3Com   063841←Intrln0027C0  DNS C ID=33628 OP=QUERY NAME=HAR│
│   11     0.2975   Intrln0027C0←DEC   029487   NFS C F=5D19 Read 4096 at 0 │
│   12     0.0332   DEC    029487←Intrln0027C0  NFS R OK (0 bytes)       │
│   13     0.0152   Intrln0027C0←DEC   029487   NFS C F=5D19 Write 4096 at 0│
│   14     0.0022   Intrln0027C0←DEC   029487   UDP continuation ID=59738│
│   15     0.0019   Intrln0027C0←DEC   029487   UDP continuation ID=59738│
│   16     0.1068   DEC    029487←Intrln0027C0  NFS R OK                 │
│   17     0.0209   Intrln0027C0←3Com  063841   DNS C ID=204 OP=QUERY NAME=stanf│
│   18     0.0325   3Com   063841←Intrln0027C0  DNS R ID=204 STAT=OK NAME=stanfo│
├DETAIL─────────────────────────────────────────────────────────────────┤
│NFS: ───── SUN NFS ─────                                               │
│NFS:                                                                   │
│NFS: Proc = 8 (Write to file)                                          │
│NFS: File handle = 04090000421000001B0000000000000000                  │
│NFS:               00000000000000000000000000000000                    │
│NFS: Offset = 0                                                        │
│NFS: [1324 byte(s) of data]                                            │
│NFS: [2772 byte(s) are missing; may be in subsequent frames]           │
│NFS:                                                                   │
│                      ─Frame 13 of 300─                                │
│                   Use TAB to select windows                           │
│ 1      2 Set        4 Zoom  5        6Display 7 Prev  8 Next    10 New│
│ Help   mark         in      Menus    options  frame   frame     capture│
└───────────────────────────────────────────────────────────────────────┘
```

Fig. 13-7 NFS Traffic on an Ethernet

NFS thus offers an alternative to the NetWare Core Protocols but in a multi-vendor environment. Several versions of NFS are available for the PC, along with TCP/IP and Ethernet support.

IBM and SNA

Another networking environment, not quite as nonproprietary as TCP/IP, is IBM's System Network Architecture (SNA). SNA is particularly important to a Novell environment because many organizations use SNA for central data processing and Novell for workgroup computing.

Novell markets a variety of different gateways into an IBM environment (see Fig. 13-8). It is possible to access the SNA network either by directly accessing it from a workstation or through the services of a dedicated gateway.

Many IBM devices, such as the 37x5 communications controllers or the 3x74 cluster controllers, have token ring support. The NetWare TR Workstation software allows a workstation user to access one of these devices and then get access to an IBM mainframe. IBM minicomputers, such as the 9370 series, also offer token ring support.

The other approach is the SNA gateway. Here, a dedicated PC is used to access the SNA environment. The gateway can be linked to the communications or cluster controllers with either a token ring or a point-to-point link using the SDLC synchronous data protocols.

The highest-capacity gateway is the High-Speed Remote option, which uses a 56-Kbps synchronous link to the 37x5 communications controller. The upper limit on this configuration is 128 concurrent mainframe terminal emulation sessions. The real limit on performance here is the ability of the PC acting as the gateway to keep up with all the requests.

A lower-performance (and hence lower-cost) solution is to use a coaxial cable SDLC connection to a 3x74 cluster controller (the IBM equivalent of the DEC terminal server). This solution supports up to 40 mainframe terminal sessions.

The token ring solution is the most flexible, allowing up to 128 host and terminal sessions concurrently. The gateway provides services for up to 97 workstations on the token ring. Since a large variety of IBM devices are token ring compatible, this solution offers the most flexibility.

Solutions are also available for single computers or gateways to connect to other IBM devices, such as the System/36, System/38, and AS/400 minicomputers. To reach one of these systems, the gateway or workstation emulates an IBM 5250 terminal, which uses a synchronous data link to the IBM minicomputer.

The SNA gateway just provides the base level of service. It simply takes an IPX/SPX packet and reformulates it as an IBM packet. To do any useful work, the workstations have to be running a software program that makes use of the gateway.

The most common application is to emulate an IBM 3270 terminal. The workstation in Figure 13-8 is using the NetWare 3270 LAN Workstation Software, via the gateway, to log onto an IBM mainframe or minicomputer. This software allows the user to maintain a DOS session on the local workstation and up to five host sessions in the SNA environment. Running concurrent sessions

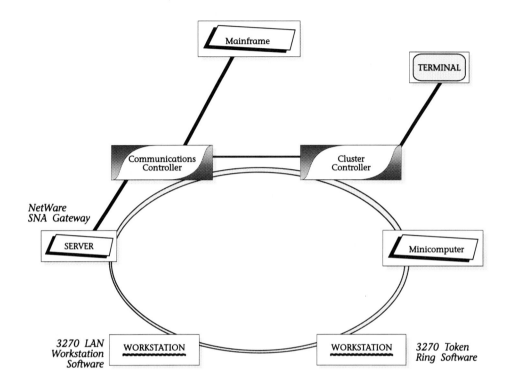

Fig. 13-8 IBM Connectivity Options

is quite useful when response time is slow on the mainframe, allowing the user to keep doing local work while the mainframe is processing.

In addition to the basic 3270 terminal emulator, it is possible for a programmer to use the 3270 protocols to communicate with a mainframe program. This 3270 Application Programming Interface (API) might be used to automatically log in in a particular environment for the user.

Several other programming interfaces are available that support other IBM protocols. Particularly important is the LU (Logical Unit) 6.2 programming interface. LU 6.2 is a standard for a particular set of capabilities present on an SNA node that allow program-to-program communication. Another term for this is Advanced Program to Program Communications (APPC).

Novell supports a subset of the APPC standard, including most of the major operations, in their API. This standard is used for communicating with advanced IBM programs such as the DB2 database management system or the DISOSS library and messaging system.

NetBIOS

The Network Adapter Basic Input/Output System (NetBIOS) is a standard originally set out by IBM for their IBM PC LAN network. Because of the IBM imprint, many software vendors have written programs that are compatible with NetBIOS. Since so many vendors sell software that uses NetBIOS, most networking vendors, including Novell, provide NetBIOS support.

NetBIOS was originally formulated as a direct user of the data link and was thus limited to the capacity of a single token ring or other data link (such as the IBM PC LAN). Very few other vendors actually directly implement NetBIOS this way.

Instead, the vendor provides an interface for the workstation and the servers that emulates NetBIOS—it acts as a true NetBIOS implementation would. Then, the messages are passed over the vendor's own network.

This is what Novell has done with their NetBIOS implementation (see Fig. 13-9). Underneath the NetBIOS emulation package, the real network transport is done by the Packet Exchange Protocol (which performs the same task for the NetWare Core Protocols).

What vendors provide in the NetBIOS emulator is the session management capacities of NetBIOS. Programs in this environment are given names. Users initialize a session with a specific named program and then transfer data.

Figure 13-10 shows an example of this traffic on an Ethernet that is using Novell's version of NetBIOS. Notice that the summary section of the screen shows that a packet was sent over the network asking for a particular name of a service. After the name was found by the server responding to the broadcast, a session was initiated (see Fig. 13-11).

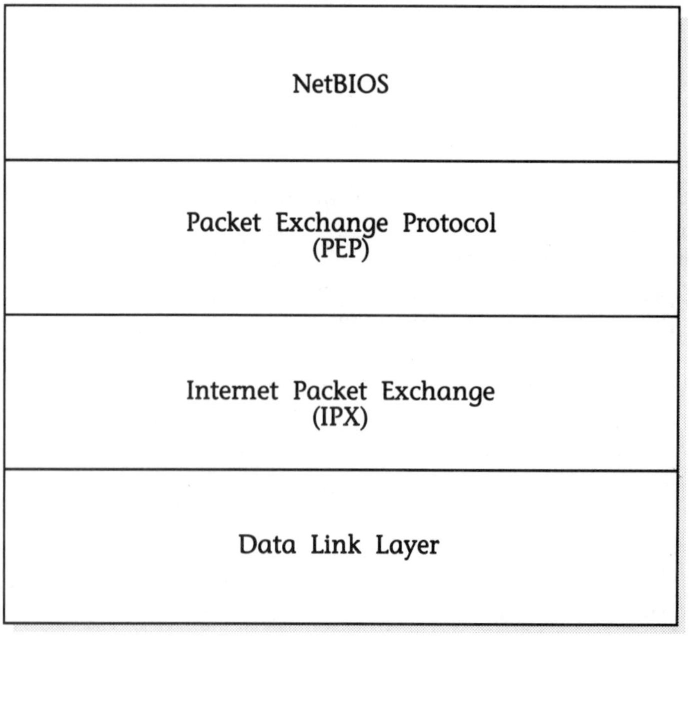

Fig. 13-9 NetBIOS Protocol Stack

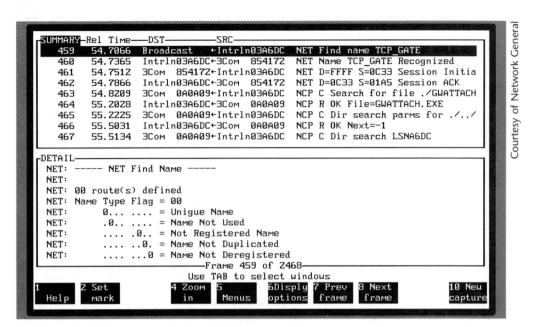

Fig. 13-10 NetBIOS Traffic on an Ethernet

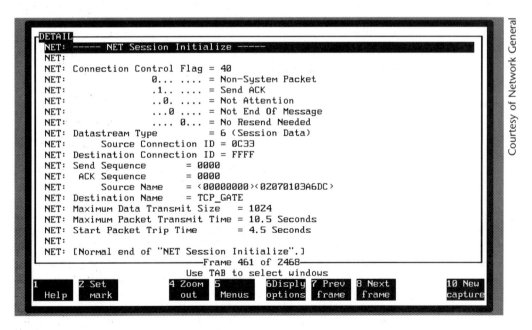

Fig. 13-11 NetBIOS Session Initialization

Since Novell's NetBIOS is built on top of IPX, the NetBIOS servers are not limited to a single data link as in the original implementation by IBM. Of course, there is no name management capability in NetBIOS, so users must administer a wider namespace in the internet.

Many third-party software programs for Novell use NetBIOS. This is because they can write a software program that can be easily ported to different networks. NetBIOS thus plays a role that is similar to the Transport Level Interface examined earlier in the book.

NetBIOS is also the basis for the Microsoft LAN Manager, a strong competitor to the Novell protocols. For this reason, Novell continues to support a NetBIOS emulator on their workstations and servers (including the Portable NetWare servers).

OSI

Novell has committed to supporting the Open Systems Interconnect (OSI) networking protocols, at least at the transport and network layers. This would, like TCP/IP, be provided as a STREAMS module under the Transport Level Interface. A number of vendors provide OSI gateways. The user logs onto the gateway and then accesses OSI-based resources.

OSI support is particularly important for sharing resources among different organizations. Many organizations, or even departments, have different kinds of networks: DECnet, TCP/IP, SNA, Banyan, Novell, 3Com, AppleTalk, and a host of proprietary environments.

OSI provides the glue that allows these different environments to work together. In addition, many organizations are rapidly migrating toward internal OSI-based networks. Many vendors, such as DEC, are also moving away from their proprietary architectures and offering OSI solutions.

One reason for OSI's broad support is that it uses existing technologies at the lower layers of the network. Token ring, Ethernet, and X.25, for example, are all supported as OSI data link providers. On top of that is a series of network and transport options that provide support for a broad class of networking applications.

However, although two vendors both support OSI at the lower layers, they don't necessarily support the same subset. For example, one vendor may support the IEEE Ethernet, while another might support token ring.

Where OSI becomes useful is at the upper layers of the network. Rather than taking existing protocols and adapting them, OSI provides a variety of advanced services. For example, standards exist for basic services such as virtual terminal, remote data access, and messaging. Other standards are used for remote job management, remote database access, directory services, and other advanced methods of exchanging information between different computing environments.

Key Points in This Chapter

- Gateways allow a workstation to take advantage of services that reside on other network architectures.
- A simple gateway makes the workstation appear as a terminal to a device on the remote network. A more complex gateway allows the workstation to take advantage of remote services transparently.
- TCP/IP and NFS are an alternative to NetWare. A gateway allows the workstation to do file access, mail transfer, and emulate a terminal. An alternative to the gateway is to use TCP/IP on all nodes on the network.
- SNA gateways allow a Novell workstation to emulate an IBM 3270 terminal. The gateway can also emulate an IBM printer, allowing mainframe data to be downloaded.
- SNA gateways are a server on the Novell network. They are connected to the IBM with a direct SDLC connection or with a token ring data link.
- A variety of Application Programming Interfaces (APIs) are available to allow development of NetWare programs that interact with the IBM SNA network.
- NetBIOS support is a part of all NetWare environments. Novell emulates the NetBIOS protocols on both the workstation and the server, allowing programs that have been written for NetBIOS to work on a Novell network.
- Novell has said they will support both TCP/IP and OSI network and transport layers using the STREAMS mechanism.

Bibliography

By the Same Author

Malamud, Carl. *DEC Networks and Architectures.* New York: McGraw-Hill, 1989.

———. *INGRES: Tools for Building an Information Architecture.* New York: Van Nostrand Reinhold, 1989.

Novell Documents

Novell. *Ethernet Supplement.* Provo, Utah: Novell, rev. 1.01, part no. 100-000547-001, May 1988.

———. *IBM Token-Ring Network Supplement.* Provo, Utah: Novell, rev. 1.02, Manual Revision Preliminary, Dec. 1988.

———. *IBM PC Network Supplement.* Provo, Utah: Novell, rev. 1.01, part no. 100-000544-001, May 1988.

———. *NetWare Buyer's Guide.* Provo, Utah: Novell, Sept. 1989.

———. *NetWare Internetwork Packet Exchange Protocol (IPX) for OS/2 Clients.* Provo, Utah: Novell, Manual Revision Preliminary, May 1989.

———. *NetWare NetBIOS Reference for OS/2 Clients.* Provo, Utah: Novell, Manual Revision Preliminary, May 1989.

———. *NetWare RPC Users Manual.* Provo, Utah: Novell, Manual Revision Preliminary, May 1989.

———. *NetWare RX-Net Supplement.* Provo, Utah: Novell, part no. 100-000546-001, May 1989.

———. *Netware Sequenced Packet Exchange Protocol for OS/2 Clients.* Provo, Utah: Novell, Manual Revision Preliminary, May 1989.

———. *NetWare System Call Reference for OS/2 Clients.* Provo, Utah: Novell, rev. 1.01, Manual Revision Preliminary, Feb. 1989.

———. *NetWare 386 Btrieve Technical Overview.* Provo, Utah: Novell, Manual Revision Preliminary, May 1989.

———. *NetWare 386 Interprocess Communication Facilities.* Provo, Utah: Novell, rev. 1.00, part no. 100-000554-001 Jan. 1989.

———. *NetWare 386 SQL Technical Overview.* Provo, Utah: Novell, Manual Revision Preliminary, May 1989.

———. *Standard ARCNET Packet Header Definition (Proposal).* Version 3.0 Draft. Provo, Utah: Novell, March 24, 1989.

———. *STREAMS Programmer's Guide.* Provo, Utah: Novell, May 1989 (originally published by Prentice-Hall).

Other Documents

Action Technologies. *MCB Programmer's Reference Manual.* Emeryville, California: Action Technologies, Inc., Oct. 1989.

———. *Message Handling Service Installation and Operation Guide.* Emeryville, California: Action Technologies, Inc., May 1989.

———. *SMF Programmer's Reference Manual.* Emeryville, California: Action Technologies, Inc., Oct. 1989.

Addison, Skip. "Introduction to the NACS," *NetWare Technical Journal,* vol. 1, no. 2, pp. 27–30, April 1989.

Anderson, Milton. "Using AFP for DOS Clients," *NetWare Technical Journal,* vol. 1, no. 3, pp. 63–68, July 1989.

Andrus, David L. "Netwise Remote Procedure Call Application Development Tools," *NetWare Technical Journal*, Premier Issue, pp. 28–31, Oct. 1988.

ANSI. *American National Standard Code for Information Interchange (ASCII)*, ANSI X3.4-1966. New York: American National Standards Institute, 1966.

Black, Uyless. *Physical Level Interfaces and Protocols.* New York: Computer Society Press, IEEE, 1988.

Burdge, Joni, and Tim Bird. "Cracking the NetWare Shell," *NetWare Technical Journal*, vol. 1, no. 1, pp. 46–54, Jan. 1989.

CCITT. *Data Communication Networks: Message Handling Systems, Recommendations **X.400-X.430**,* vol. VIII - Fascicle VIII.7 (Red Book), VIIIth Plenary Assembly, Malaga-Torremolinos, 8-19 Oct. 1984. Geneva, Switzerland: International Telecommunication Union, 1985.

———. *Data Communication Networks: Services and Facilities, Interfaces, Recommendations **X.1-X.32**,* vol. VIII, Fascicle VIII.2 (Blue Book), IXth Plenary Assembly, Melbourne, 14-25 Nov. 1988. Geneva, Switzerland: International Telecommunication Union, 1989.

Comer, Douglas. *Internetworking with TCP/IP, Principles, Protocols, and Architecture.* Englewood Cliffs, New Jersey: Prentice-Hall, 1988.

———. *Operating System Design, Volume II: Internetworking with XINU.* Englewood Cliffs, New Jersey: Prentice-Hall, 1987.

Crocker. *Standard for the Format of ARPA Internet Text Messages.* Request for Comment 822. Stanford, California: Stanford Research Institute (Network Information Center), Aug. 1982.

Datapoint. *ARCNET Cabling Guide.* Dallas, Texas: DATAPOINT Corporation, doc. no. 51087, ed. 02, 1988.

———. *ARCNET Designer's Handbook.* Dallas, Texas: DATAPOINT Corporation, doc. no. 61610, ed. 02, 1988.

Date, C. J. *An Introduction to Database Systems,* vol. 1, 3rd ed. Reading, Massachusetts: Addison-Wesley, 1981.

———. *An Introduction to Database Systems,* vol. 2. Reading, Massachusetts: Addison-Wesley, 1983.

Davis, Dwight. "Benchmarking the Impacts of Distributed Database Architecture," *NetWare Technical Journal,* Premier Issue, pp. 41–45, Oct. 1988.

Digital Equipment Corporation. *DECnet DIGITAL Network Architecture (Phase IV) General Description,* part no. AA-N149A-TC. Maynard, Massachusetts: Digital Equipment Corporation, May 1982.

———. Networking Products (Special Issue). *Digital Technical Journal,* Number 3, Sept. 1986.

———. VAX Cluster Systems (Special Issue). *Digital Technical Journal,* Number 5, Sept. 1987.

———. Intel Corporation, and Xerox Corporation. *The Ethernet: A Local Area Network (Data Link Layer and Physical Layer Specifications)*, Version 2.0. Palo Alto: Xerox, Nov. 1982.

Dixon, Drew C. "NetWare 386 in the LAN Driver's Seat," *NetWare Technical Journal*, vol. 1, no. 3, pp. 73–87, July 1989.

Durfey, Douglas C. "Functionality Overview of NetWare APIs, Part 1," *NetWare Technical Journal*, Premier Issue, pp. 82–89, Oct. 1988.

———. "Functionality Overview of NetWare APIs, Part 2," *NetWare Technical Journal*, vol. 1, no. 1, pp. 68–74, Jan. 1989.

———. "Functionality Overview of NetWare APIs, Part 3," *NetWare Technical Journal*, vol. 1, no. 2, pp. 53–60, April 1989.

Haugdahl, Scott J. *Inside NETBIOS,* 2d ed. Minneapolis, Minnesota: Architecture Technology Corporation, 1988.

———. *Inside SAA,* 2d ed. Minneapolis, Minnesota: Architecture Technology Corporation, 1989.

———. *Inside the Token Ring,* 2d ed. Minneapolis, Minnesota: Architecture Technology Corporation, 1988.

Horton. *UUCP Mail Interchange Format Standard.* Request for Comment 976. Stanford, California: Stanford Research Institute (Network Information Center), Feb. 1986.

Humphries, Kyle. "Database Programming with XQL/NetWare SQL, Part 1," *NetWare Technical Journal*, vol. 1, no. 3, pp. 21–30, July 1989.

IEEE. *Carrier Sense Multiple Access with Collision Detection (CSMA/CD)*, ANSI/IEEE Std. 802.3-1985 (ISO/DIS 8802/3), dist. by Wiley-Interscience.

———. *Logical Link Control,* ANSI/IEEE Std. 802.2-1985 (ISO/DIS 8802/2), dist. by Wiley-Interscience.

———. *Token-Passing Bus Access Method and Physical Layer Specifications,* ANSI/IEEE Std. 802.4-1985 (ISO/DIS 8802/4), dist. by Wiley-Interscience.

———. *Token Ring Access Method and Physical Layer Specifications,* ANSI/IEEE Std. 802.5-1985 (ISO/DIS 8802/5), dist. by Wiley-Interscience.

International Organization for Standardization (ISO). *Information Processing Systems, Open Systems Interconnection, Basic Reference Model*, Geneva, Switz.: International Organization for Standardization, ISO 7498, Oct. 1984.

———. *Information Processing Systems, Open Systems Interconnection, Specification of Basic Encoding Rules for Abstract Syntax Notation One (ASN.1)*, Geneva, Switz.: International Organization for Standardization, ISO 8825, Nov. 1987.

———. *Information Processing Systems, Open Systems Interconnection, Transport Service Definition*, Geneva, Switz.: International Organization for Standardization, ISO 8072, June 1986.

Johannessen, Paul. "Implementation of NetWare LU6.2," *NetWare Technical Journal,* Premier Issue, pp. 47–52, Oct. 1988.

———. "Writing Applications for NetWare LU6.2," *NetWare Technical Journal,* Premier Issue, pp. 53–55, Oct. 1988.

Kingdon, Kevin. "The NetWare Requester: Functionality Overview," *NetWare Technical Journal,* Premier Issue, pp. 23–26, Oct. 1988.

Knightson, K. G., T. Knowles, and J. Larmouth. *Standards for Open Systems Interconnection.* New York: McGraw-Hill, 1987.

Knutson, Charles D. "Working on the Pipeline," *NetWare Technical Journal,* vol. 1, no. 3, pp. 91–99, July 1989.

Koontz, Michael. "Chatting with IPX and SPX," *NetWare Technical Journal,* vol. 1, no. 2, pp. 79–86, April 1989.

Major, Drew. "The Architecture of NetWare 386," *NetWare Technical Journal,* vol. 1, no. 3, pp. 35–44, July 1989.

Martin, James, and K. K. Chapman. *SNA: IBM's Networking Solution.* Englewood Cliffs, New Jersey: Prentice-Hall, 1987.

Mason, Jack. "APIs of the NetWare Requester," *NetWare Technical Journal,* vol. 1, no. 1, pp. 76–79, Jan. 1989.

McCann, John T. "A Bindery Tale," *NetWare Technical Journal*, vol. 1, no. 3, pp. 115–120, July 1989.

———. "Skeleton Programming with IPX/SPX," *NetWare Technical Journal,* vol. 1, no. 2, pp. 111–116, April 1989.

Network General. *Ethernet Network Portable Protocol Analyzer, Operation and Reference Manual (Series 402 and 502).* Mt. View, California: Network General Corporation, 1988.

———. *Token-Ring Network Portable Protocol Analyzer, Operation and Reference Manual (Model PA-301).* Mt. View, California: Network General Corporation, 1988.

Partridge. *Mail Routing and the Domain System.* Request for Comment 974. Stanford, California: Stanford Research Institute (Network Information Center), Jan. 1986.

Postel, J. *File Transfer Protocol (FTP).* Request for Comment 959. Stanford, California: Stanford Research Institute (Network Information Center), Oct. 1985.

———. *Internet Control Message Protocol.* Request for Comment 792. Stanford, California: Stanford Research Institute (Network Information Center), Sept. 1981.

———. *Internet Protocol.* Request for Comment 791. Stanford, California: Stanford Research Institute (Network Information Center), Sept. 1981.

———. *Telnet Protocol Specifications.* Request for Comment 854. Stanford, California: Stanford Research Institute (Network Information Center), May 1983.

———. *Transmission Control Protocol.* Request for Comment 793. Stanford, California: Stanford Research Institute (Network Information Center), Sept. 1981.

Schwaderer, W. David. *C Programmer's Guide to NetBIOS,* Indianapolis, Indiana: Howard W. Sams and Company, 1988.

———. "NetBIOS Services and Ncb Fields," *NetWare Technical Journal,* vol. 1, no. 2, pp. 65–75, April 1989.

Scribner, Tom. "Using Semaphores," *NetWare Technical Journal,* vol. 1, no. 3, pp. 123–124, July 1989.

Sidhu, Gursharan S., et. al. *Inside AppleTalk.* Reading, Massachusetts: Addison Wesley, 1989.

Sidhu, Gursharan S., and Richard Andrews. "AppleTalk Filing Protocol Login and Security," *LAN Times,* vol. VI, no. III, pp. 108–115, March 1989.

———. "Bridging the Design of Diverse File Systems," *LAN Times,* vol. VI, no. II, pp. 99–102, Feb. 1989.

———. "File System Incompatibilities Between Three Operating Systems," *LAN Times,* vol. VI, no. I, pp. 90–91, Jan. 1989.

Siegel, John A. "Using Novell's 3270 APIs," *NetWare Technical Journal,* Premier Issue, pp. 33–38, Oct. 1988.

Sondej, Vince. "A Look at NetWare Loadable Modules," *NetWare Technical Journal,* vol. 1, no. 3, pp. 49–60, July 1989.

Sparks, Bryan. "Building Software Servers: Advertising and Locating Services," *NetWare Technical Journal,* vol. 1, no. 2, pp. 119–124, April 1989.

———. "Connectivity and Freedom of Choice, An Introduction to Portable NetWare," *NetWare Technical Journal,* vol. 1, no. 3, pp. 101–106, July 1989.

Stallings, William. *Department of Defense (DOD) Protocol Standards,* Handbook of Computer-Communications Standards, vol. 3. New York: Macmillan, 1988.

———. *Local Network Standards,* Handbook of Computer-Communications Standards, vol. 2. New York: Macmillan, 1987.

Sun Microsystems. *External Data Representation Protocol Specification.* Mt. View, California: Sun Microsystems, Feb. 1986.

———. *Network File System Protocol Specification.* Mt. View, California: Sun Microsystems, Feb. 1986.

———. *Remote Procedure Call Protocol Specification.* Mt. View, California: Sun Microsystems, Feb. 1986.

———. *Yellow Pages Protocol Specification.* Mt. View, California: Sun Microsystems, Feb. 1986.

Xerox. *Courier: The Remote Procedure Call Protocol,* XSIS 038112. Stamford, Connecticut: Xerox, Dec. 1981; with Appendix F: *Bulk Data Transfer,* XSIS 038112, Add. 1, Oct. 1982.

———. *Internet Transport Protocols* (Xerox System Integration Standard), XSIS-028112. Stamford, Connecticut: Xerox, Dec. 1981.

———. *Introduction to Xerox Network Systems,* XNSG 058504. Sunnyvale, Calif: Xerox Systems Institute, April 1985.

———. *Xerox Network Systems Architecture General Information Manual,* XNSG 068504. Sunnyvale, Calif: Xerox Systems Institute, April 1985.

Glossary

10BASE2 — *10 Mbps/baseband/200 meters.* IEEE standard for thinwire Ethernet.

10BASE5 — *10 Mbps/baseband/500 meters.* IEEE standard for "thickwire" coaxial Ethernet.

10BASET — *10 Mbps/baseband/twisted pair.* IEEE standard for twisted pair Ethernet.

3+ — 3Com networking products.

3270 Display Stations — Terminals for IBM mainframe computers.

370 architecture — IBM architecture for mainframe computers, including the 3090 processors.

3Com — A leading competitor to Novell.

4GL — *See fourth-generation language.*

5250 — IBM terminal used on the System/3X line.

802.2 — IEEE standard for the Logical Link Control.

802.3 — IEEE standard for CSMA/CD (Ethernet) medium access method.

802.4 — IEEE standard for the token bus medium access method.

802.5 — IEEE standard for the token ring medium access method.

80x86	Family of microprocessors made by Intel used in the PC line. The PC/AT uses the 80286 chip. More modern systems, including the PS/2, use the 32-bit 80386 chip.
AC	*Access control.* Token ring field that holds the priority and reservation bits for a token or data packet.
access method	A means of accessing information in a file. Btree is an example of an access method.
ACK	*Acknowledge.* A network packet acknowledging the receipt of data.
Action Technologies	Makers of the Message Handling Service bundled into Novell as NetWare MHS.
active hub	ARCNET component used to connect workstations into a star topology.
active monitor	A computer on a token ring that acts as the controller for the ring—regulating the token and other performance aspects.
Active Monitor Present	Packet issued every 3 seconds by the active monitor on a token ring.
ad hoc	Latin phrase meaning for a specific instance. Used in computing to refer to functions not previously planned.
address space	A collection of addresses that form a unified collection such as an internetwork.
Advanced NetWare	A version of Novell's software.
Advanced Program to Program Communications	Protocol used for peer-to-peer communication in IBM's System Network Architecture.
AFP	*See AppleTalk Filing Protocol.*
Agenda	Lotus software used for time management.

aggregate	A function in a query language used to perform an operation on several rows of data. Sum is an example of an aggregate.
All-In-One	DEC's office automation shell, consisting of a menu driver, a mail user interface, a calendar manager, and a file manager.
allocation	Concept used in the SPX transport layer protocol. An allocation is the amount of unacknowledged traffic that may be outstanding at one time.
American National Standards Institute	Private organization that coordinates some United States standards-making. Represents the United States to the International Standards Organization.
AMP	*See Active Monitor Present.*
ANSI	*See American National Standards Institute.*
API	*See application programming interface.*
APPC	*See Advanced Program to Program Communication.*
Apple	Maker of AppleTalk and the Macintosh.
AppleShare	Program that allows different kinds of computers to provide or take advantage of AppleTalk resources such as printing.
AppleTalk	Apple's network protocol.
AppleTalk Filing Protocol	The protocol in AppleTalk used for remote access to data.
AppleTalk Session Protocol	AppleTalk session layer protocol.
AppleTalk Transaction Protocol	AppleTalk transport layer protocol.

application

A program that performs functions for a user. Order entry system or word processors are both examples of applications.

application layer

The top layer of the network protocol stack. The application layer is concerned with the semantics of work. For example, getting a certain record from a file by key value on a foreign node is an application layer concern. How to represent that data and how to reach the foreign node are issues for lower layers of the network.

application programming interface

A set of services available to a programmer for performing certain tasks. Network APIs are the programmer's interface to the network.

architecture

A set of plans that allow different components to work together. A network architecture allows different computers on a network to communicate. An information architecture allows different users to access a variety of data repositories.

ARCNET

Hardware and software data link components manufactured by Datapoint and other companies that allows computers to form a 2.5-Mbps local area network with a star topology.

ARCNET fragmentation layer

A sublayer between the ARCNET Medium Access Control and the network layer (i.e., Novell's IPX). The fragmentation layer to submit packets that are larger than the 508-byte ARCNET maximum packet length.

ARCNET Plus

20 Mbps version of ARCNET.

array

A data structure used in programming.

ASCII

American Standard Code for Information Interchange. A standard character set that assigns an octal sequence to each letter, number, and selected control characters. The other major encoding standard is EBCDIC.

Ashton-Tate — Makers of dBase and Framework data management products.

Ashton-Tate/Microsoft SQL Server — Database server marketed by Ashton-Tate and Microsoft but really made by Sybase.

ASN.1 — *Abstract Syntax Notation One.* OSI presentation layer protocol.

ASP — *See AppleTalk Session Protocol.*

asynchronous communication — Communication in which every byte is sent individually. Synchronous communication (i.e., X.25 or Ethernet) bunches several pieces of data into a frame or packet.

asynchronous event — Events occur asynchronously on a system when you cannot predict which one will happen next.

ATP — *See AppleTalk Transaction Protocol.*

attenuation characteristic — As a signal propagates on a cable, it gets weaker, or attenuates. The attenuation characteristic of the medium is the rate at which it gets weaker.

attribute — This term has a variety of meanings. In a relational database, attribute is another name for a column in a table. In a data dictionary or other information model, an attribute is attached to a relationship or entity. Number of times modified is an example of an attribute for the entity "User_Name."

back end — A general term used to denote all the programs in a database system that get data for a user. An application is a front end and it dispatches SQL statements to a back end data server, which in turn returns rows of data.

bandwidth — The amount of data that can be moved through a particular communications link. Ethernet has a bandwidth of 10 Mbps.

Banyan Maker of VINES, a competing network to NetWare.

BASIC *Beginner's All-purpose Symbolic Instruction Code.* A programming language.

beacon A token ring packet that signals a serious failure on the ring.

best-effort delivery service A network module, such as the network layer IPX, will attempt to deliver data but will not try to recover if there is an error such as a line failure.

binary tree Often referred to as a Btree. A storage structure with a dynamic index used for environments with frequent updates to data.

bindery A file on the NetWare operating system used to store management information such as user passwords.

binding Concept used in remote procedure calls. Two remote programs bind with each other by starting a connection and then exchanging command requests.

bit mapped A graphics term in which all bits of a display station are controllable in contrast to a character-oriented terminal.

BNC *Bayonet nut connector.* Connecter type used for 10BASE5 coaxial cable. The term *bayonet* refers to the way the connector slides in and then twists to lock the connection.

bridge Term used by Novell to denote a computer that accepts packets at the network layer and forwards them to another network. Bridge usually means a MAC-layer bridge, operating at the data link layer.

broadband	A high-bandwidth communication system used to carry radio frequency signals on coaxial cable. Carrier signals at various frequencies are modulated by data signals, and the cable can carry many different channels of voice, data, video, or other signals.
broadcast	Sending information to all users of a particular service. An Ethernet broadcast, for example, sends an Ethernet packet to every address on the network.
BROUTER	Program on the NetWare operating system that manages Btrieve access among multiple computers.
brouter	*Bridge/router.* Device that forwards messages between networks at both network and data link levels.
BSERVER	Program on the NetWare operating system that retrieves data for Btrieve users.
Btree	*See binary tree.*
Btrieve	Novell programs that allow use of the Btree access method to retrieve data from servers.
buffer	A portion of main memory on a computer used to hold data.
bus	The part of a computer that connects peripheral devices so that they may communicate with the CPU and memory. IBM's Micro Channel Architecture is an example of a peripheral bus architecture.
C	A programming language. Often used with computers running the Unix operating system.
cached	A piece of information that is retained in main memory instead of being flushed to disk. Keeping information cached alleviates the need to go to the disk to retrieve the data.

Carrier Sense–Multiple Access/Collision Detect The methodology used in Ethernet to mediate access to a single physical medium among multiple computers.

Castelle Makers of a fax gateway for Message Handling Service users.

CCITT *Comité Consultatif International Télégraphique et Téléphonique International.* Standards-making body administered by the International Telecommunications Union.

cluster A file system concept. A disk is made up of a series of clusters. The clusters are dynamically allocated to files and directories as needed. Similar to a block.

CRC *See cyclical redundancy check.*

credit A flow control mechanism used in DEC's LAT protocols. A node is allowed to send a packet only if it has a credit available. If not, it must wait for the remote node to send one.

cyclical redundancy check A number derived from a set of data that will be transmitted. By recalculating the CRC at the remote end and comparing it to the value originally transmitted, the receiving node can detect some types of transmission errors.

DA *Destination address.*

DAP *Data Access Protocol.* DECnet protocol for access to remote data.

DCE *Data circuit–terminating equipment.* Term used in X.25 networks for the device on the edge of the network that accepts and initiates calls. The DCE is in turn connected to a DTE which communicates with the user.

DDP *Datagram Delivery Protocol.* AppleTalk network-level protocol.

Delta T	*Delta time.* Sniffer Analyzer indication of time elapsed between consecutive packets on the network. Contrast to relative time, which is the time that has elapsed since a particular anchor packet was sent.
distributed database	Looks to the user like a single database but is in fact a collection of several different data repositories.
Distributed File Service	DEC product to make files on the network all appear local. Similar to the Network File System.
distributed naming service	Network-based service to allow a user to find the current address of a given resource, such as a printer or file system.
DLC	*Data Link Control.* Sniffer Analyzer notation for data link layer information.
DNA	*Digital Network Architecture.* A network architecture developed by DEC that allows large networks of computers to be connected together.
domain	An area within which a particular service is performed. In a messaging domain, a message transfer agent for that domain is able to deliver a message. Splitting a namespace into domains allows easier management.
DRP	*Digital Routing Protocol.*
DSAP	*Destination service access point.* The address for the destination user of a service. A remote IPX process would be considered the DSAP from the point of view of the local data link module.
DST	*Destination address.* Sniffer Network Analyzer abbreviation for destination address.
DTE	*Data terminal equipment.* An X.25 term for a device or peudo-device that interacts with the user of the service. The DTE uses the DCE to request X.25 circuits.

dual-porting Making a disk drive available to two different computers, as in the case of SFT Level III in NetWare or in a VAX Cluster.

EBCDIC *Extended Binary Coded Decimal Interchange Code.* A character code scheme used in IBM environments. See ASCII.

Echo A maintenance protocol in XNS. Used to echo information back across the network and thus test the connection.

ECONFIG Novell utility to force NetWare drivers to conform to the standard operation of Ethernet.

electronic mail Collection of programs that allow users to exchange messages across a network.

enumerator Concept used in AppleTalk Name Binding Protocol searches. The enumerator value is used to distinguish among several instances of an entity on a single socket.

Error XNS protocol used to report errors across a network.

Etherlink Ethernet controller made by 3Com.

Ethernet A data link protocol jointly developed by Intel, Xerox, and DEC and subsequently adopted by the IEEE as a standard. Several upper-layer protocols, including DECnet, TCP/IP, and XNS, use the Ethernet as an underlying transport mechanism. Ethernet is to be contrasted with other data link protocols such as the token ring, DDCMP, and SDLC.

Ethernet controller A device controller that gives the computer access to the Ethernet services. Typically, the CSMA/CD protocols are built into the controller so the CPU doesn't have to worry about the details of the protocol.

Ethernet Version 2.0	The second version of the original specification for Ethernet, which differs slightly from the IEEE 802.3 standard.
Ethertype	Field in Version 2.0 of Ethernet that indicates the type of user (DECnet, NetWare, or TCP/IP, for example).
exclusive lock	A lock on data that prevents other users from accessing it. Used for write operations. In contrast to a shared (read) lock.
executable image	A program that is ready to run on an operating system. A program starts as source code and gets compiled to generate object code. The object code is then linked to form an executable image.
External Data Representation	Presentation layer protocol developed by Sun Microsystems as part of NFS.
FAL	*File access listener.* Software program that implements the DECnet Data Access Protocols. The listener accepts remote requests for data from DAP-speaking processes.
fault tolerance	An attribute of a computer system that reflects its degree of tolerance to hardware and software failures while continuing to run.
fax	*Facsimile.* A messaging service based on transmitting bit maps of 200 dots per inch across dial-up telephone lines.
FaxPress	A fax gateway for the Message Handling Service made by Castelle.
FC	*Frame control.* Token ring field that indicates whether the packet is a MAC-layer management packet (i.e., a token, beacon, AMP, or SMP) or is carrying LLC data.
FCS	*Frame check sequence.* A mechanism like a CRC or checksum to guarantee the integrity of a packet of data.

FDDI   *See Fiber Distributed Data Interface.*

FFFF   *16 16 16 16.* A hexadecimal number. Hexadecimal is base 16 numbering in which the symbols A through F are used to represent the digits 10 through 16.

Fiber Distributed Data Interface   A 100-Mbps fiber optic local area network standard based on the token ring.

fiber optic hub   ARCNET hub used for sites with up to several thousand meters of separation between them.

field   An area on a display for user input and the display of data.

file cache   Keeping portions of files in main memory. When the computer requests data, if it is in the cache, it alleviates the need to refetch it from the much slower disk drive.

file system   The portion of an operating system that is responsible for storing and retrieving pages of data onto a disk.

finder   *See Macintosh Finder.*

floating point   A native data type on most operating systems. A floating point number is one that can have numbers after the decimal point, in contrast to an integer, which cannot.

fourth-generation language   A group of new languages often linked with database packages such as Ingres or Oracle. In contrast with Fortran and other third-generation languages.

fragmentation header   The sublayer on ARCNET networks between the ARCNET header and the IPX header. Used to allow IPX to transmit packets of 576 bytes, which is larger than the 508-byte ARCNET maximum.

Framework   Data management program sold by Ashton-Tate.

free buffer enquiry An ARCNET packet type. Used by a node to ensure that there is buffer space available on the receiving node before sending the data packet. Alleviates the possibility of a "deaf" controller as in Ethernet.

front end A program with which a user interacts. The front end sends off requests to the back end for data.

FS *Frame status.* Token ring field that indicates if the address on a packet has been recognized by a station and if the data has been copied.

function Takes a piece of data as input and returns a value. For example, the query language has functions that can accept a date and return the day of the week that the date falls on.

gateway A computer connected to two different network architectures that allows users to access services in the remote environment. A Novell SNA Gateway, for example, allows a NetWare user to access SNA resources.

GID *Group identification.*

gigabytes *Billion bytes of data.*

granularity A term used in the lock manager. It refers to the amount of information that a lock affects. A database lock has a very coarse granularity, while a page-level lock is of fine granularity.

Gupta Technologies Maker of a database server that competes with Novell's NetWare SQL.

handle A number used to refer to a file or directory that is being remotely accessed on the network.

heap A storage structure for data where data is not placed in any particular order, requiring a scan of the entire table for every retrieval.

heterogeneous Different.

heterogeneous network	A network consisting of different network protocols or kinds of computers. A network combining SNA and DNA protocols using an SNA gateway to connect the two is a heterogeneous network.
Hewlett-Packard/ Apollo	The workstation division of Hewlett-Packard.
hierarchical database	A database that structures data as a hierarchy instead of in tables. Programmers then navigate the hierarchy to retrieve a particular row of data. IMS is an example of a hierarchical database system.
hierarchical routing	Routing based on domains. Interdomain routers are responsible only for getting data to the right domain. There, an intradomain router takes responsibility for routing within the domain.
Hierarchical Storage Controller	Stand-alone disk and tape controller used in clusters using the CI bus. The HSC is actually a modified PDP computer that has been optimized as a mass storage controller.
homogeneous	The same.
hooks	Programming technique. Allows a programmer to add new code to an existing program. The existing program has hooks that execute any additional code.
hop	A single data link. The link could be a dial-up line, an Ethernet, an X.25 virtual circuit, or any other mechanism that will move data for the network layer.
HP DeskManager	Hewlett-Packard office automation software.

HSC	*See Hierarchical Storage Controller.*
hub	A device connected to several other devices. In ARCNET, a hub is used to connect several computers together. In a message handling service, a hub is used for the transfer of messages across the network.
IBM 8228 Multistation Access Unit	A MAU sold by IBM.
IBM PC LAN	IBM PC network using broadband.
IBM Token-Ring	IBM token ring network.
IBM Token-Ring Adapter	Token ring controller card sold by IBM.
icon	A small pictorial object on a workstation used to represent a closed window. The user points to the icon, clicks the mouse button, and a window opens.
IDP	*See Internetwork Datagram Protocol.*
IEEE	*Institute of Electrical and Electronics Engineers.* A leading standard-making body in the United States, responsible for the 802 standards for local area networks.
IEEE 488	IEEE standard for real-time data acquisition.
IMS	*Information Management System.* Old database system software from IBM based on the hierarchical data management model.
index	A direct access method to data. An index has a key value and a pointer to the row of the table that contains data with the key value. An index can be a primary index, where the index is part of the storage structure of the actual table, or a secondary index, which is a separate table in the database with pointers to the base table.

Informix	A relational database management system.
Ingres	A popular relational database management system that runs on a variety of operating system platforms. Considered to be the most powerful of the major database systems.
initialization packet	A token ring packet used when a node joins the network.
INPOST	A utility program in the Message Handling Service used for transferring messages from an application to MHS.
Intel	Makers of the 80x86 microprocessors used in the IBM PC.
intelligent hub	ARCNET device used for the connection of computers.
International Organization for Standardization	International standards-making body, responsible for the Open System Interconnect network architecture.
International Telegraph and Telephone Consultative Committee	English name for the CCITT.
internet	*See internetwork.*
Internet	A collection of networks that share the same namespace and use the TCP/IP protocols. The Internet consists of at least 400 connected networks. The Internet should not be confused with the internet (lowercase) which refers to all networks that have a path between them. All members of the Internet use TCP/IP.
internetwork	A collection of data links and the network layer programs for routing among those data links.

internetwork address	An address consisting of a network number and a local address on that network. Used by the network layer for routing packets to their ultimate destination.
Internetwork Datagram Protocol	Network layer protocol in XNS.
Internetwork Packet Exchange	Network layer protocol in Novell NetWare.
Internetwork Protocol	Network layer protocol in TCP/IP.
Interpress	Page description language in XNS used for driving laser printers.
interprocess communication	Communication between two processes by passing parameters and return values. Remote calls are a special case of an interprocess communication mechanism.
Invitation to Transmit	Name for the token packet in an ARCNET network.
I/O	*Input/Output.* The process of moving data from disk to main memory and back again.
IOCTL	*I/O Control.* Unix function call used to control a device.
IP	*See Internet Protocol.*
IPC	*See Interprocess Communication.*
IPX	*See Internetwork Packet Exchange.*
ISDN	*Integrated Services Digital Network.* An emerging international communications standard that allows the integration of voice and data on a common transport mechanism.

ISO	*See International Organization for Standardization.*
ITT	*See Invitation to Transmit.*
job queue	A method of letting multiple requests for a scarce resource queue up, as in the case of a print queue.
join	A term used in relational databases to denote two or more tables being combined together.
Kbps	*Thousand bits per second.*
keep alive message	A message sent over a network link during periods when there is no traffic between users. The message tells the remote node that this computer is still in operation.
LAN Manager	A competing network to Novell advocated by companies such as Microsoft.
large non-moveable cabling system	Another great product name from IBM. *See small moveable cabling system.*
LAT	*See Local Area Transport.*
latency buffer	Token ring concept. The buffer is maintained by the active monitor and is used to compensate for variations in the speed of data on the network.
Link Support Layer	Interface standard developed by Novell and Apple for interconnection of various data link device drivers and various network layers.
LLC	*See Logical Link Control.*
Local Area Transport	Protocol developed by DEC for communication between terminal servers and hosts on an Ethernet.
LocalTalk	Data link developed for AppleTalk that uses ordinary twisted pair cabling.

lock manager	Part of the operating system that ensures that multiple requests for the same data are not serviced in a way that will damage the integrity of the data.
locking	Preventing another user from accessing a piece of data.
logical	Without reference to physical details. Asking for data in a logical manner, for example, means not having to know where the data is located or how to get it.
Logical Link Control	The upper portion of the data link layer, defined in the IEEE 802.2 standard.
Lotus	Maker of the popular 1-2-3 spreadsheet program.
LSL	*See Link Support Layer.*
LU 6.2	*Logical Unit 6.2. See APPC.*
MAC	*See Medium Access Control.*
MacAccess	Electronic mail package made for the Macintosh by Action Technologies.
Macintosh	A computer made by Apple Computer that is characterized by the graphical, intuitive user interface.
Macintosh Finder	The portion of the Macintosh operating system that manages the desktop.
MAC-layer bridge	A device that connects two or more similar data links in a way that is transparent to the user of the data link service (the network layer).
MAILbridge Server/MHS	A SoftSwitch product used for connecting Action Technologies' MHS to other message handling environments.

MAU	*See multistation access unit.*
Mbps	*Million bits per second.*
MCI Mail	Commercial electronic messaging service.
medium	The physical cable, such as coaxial cable, used on a network.
Medium Access Control	The bottom half of the ISO data link layer.
Message Handling Service	Action Technologies' product for message handling, bundled into Novell networks as NetWare MHS. To be contrasted with the generic message handling service, which includes X.400 and other standards.
Message Router	DEC's message handling service.
Message Transfer Agent	The portion of a message handling system responsible for getting the message to its final destination.
MHS	*See Message Handling Service.*
Microsoft Windows	Control program developed by Microsoft to allow several programs to be active at once. One of the reasons for the success of the Macintosh.
Microsoft Word	Word processor developed by Microsoft for the Apple and the PC.
MicroVAX	A series of DEC processors usually used as workstations or small servers that compete in the marketplace with Sun and Hewlett-Packard/Apollo.
MIP	*Million instructions per second.* A measure of the speed of a CPU.
mirrored	A disk drive is mirrored when two identical copies of the data are kept on two different disk drives. If one fails, the other can keep on operating.

MIS	*Management Information System.* A database system used to provide information to managers in an organization. The term has come to refer to the department in an organization responsible for computing.
MIT	*Massachusetts Institute of Technology.* Developers of the X Windows System. Also a university.
MLI	*See Multiple Link Interface.*
MLID	*See Multiple Link Interface Driver.*
monitor bit	Token ring concept. The monitor bit is flipped by the active monitor to prevent a frame of priority greater than 0 from circulating continuously.
MOP	*Maintenance Operation Protocol.* Special-purpose DECnet protocol used for remote booting on the node and attaching a console onto a station remotely.
mount	Term used in the Network File System for making a remote file system appear as if it were a local disk drive.
mouse	A pointing device used on workstations.
MPI	*See Multiple Protocol Interface.*
MPR	*See multiport repeater.*
MPT	*See multiport transceiver.*
MS-DOS	*Microsoft-Digital Operating System.* Microsoft's version of the DOS operating system for the IBM PC.
multicast	An address to which several nodes will respond. Contrast to broadcast, where all nodes on a network will respond.

Multiple Link Interface The bottom portion of the Link Support Layer standard from Novell and Apple. This interface specifies how device drives interact with the Link Support Layer.

Multiple Link Interface Driver A network device driver that conforms to the Link Support Layer specification.

Multiple Protocol Interface The upper portion of the Link Support Layer standard from Novell and Apple. This interface describes how transport service providers interact with the Link Support Layer.

multiport repeater An Ethernet repeater, typically for thinwire networks, that connects several segments together into a multisegment Ethernet.

multiport transceiver Several Ethernet transceivers built into one device. Can operate as a concentrator on a cable or as a stand-alone Ethernet (known as "Ethernet in a can").

multisegment Ethernet Several segments of Ethernet connected together with repeaters. All signals broadcast on a multisegment Ethernet are received by all other nodes. This is in contrast to the extended Ethernet, where the MAC-layer bridge forwards only those packets destined for the other Ethernet.

multistatement transaction Several different interactions with the database that are grouped into a single transaction. If any one of the operations is not carried out because of a user abort or system crash, the entire transaction is rolled back. In a multistatement transaction all or none of the operations are carried out.

multistation access unit Token ring device used to connect several stations to the ring. Similar to the multiport transceiver for the Ethernet.

multitasking   When an operating system (and microprocessor) maintains its position in several tasks simultaneously. The microprocessor alternates between the different tasks under control of the operating system scheduling process. Unix is an example.

multithreaded   An operating system feature that allows a process to maintain several threads of execution, each under the control of the parent process. OS/2 is an example.

MVS/TSO   *Multiple virtual storage/time sharing option.* MVS is an IBM operating system. TSO is the interactive subsystem, as opposed to a system like JES used for batch processing.

NACS   *See NetWare Asynchronous Communications Server.*

Name Binding Protocol   AppleTalk protocol for mapping logical names to network addresses. Similar to SAP in NetWare.

Named Pipes   A process-to-process protocol that allows a full-duplex communication path to be maintained. The "pipe" is the endpoint of the communication path, through which a process gains entry to the function. Names are maintained and registered on the network, allowing a pipe to access services.

namespace   The collection of names in a computing environment. A data dictionary in a database is an example of a namespace.

NASI   *See NetWare Asynchronous Services Interface.*

native NetWare   The version of NetWare marketed by Novell for 80386 computers. In contrast to Portable NetWare, which is a guest on another operating system.

NBP *See Name Binding Protocol.*

NCP *See NetWare Core Protocols.*

NCPMux *NetWare Core Protocols Multiplexor.* A software module in Portable NetWare that maintains connections between a single NetWare engine and several clients.

NET *NetBIOS.* Sniffer Analyzer abbreviation for NetBIOS packets.

NetBIOS *Network Adapter Basic Input/Output System.* A Network protocol that allows a client program to find a server process and communicate with it. Similar to Named Pipes.

NetWare The networking components sold by Novell. A collection of data link drivers, a transport protocol stack, workstation software, and the NetWare operating system.

NetWare Access Server A server that allows dial-in asynchronous access from a workstation to a NetWare network.

NetWare Asynchronous Communications Server Server software that allows a workstation to use outside asynchronous resources such as hosts or modem pools.

NetWare Asynchronous Services Interface An API that allows a program to control the function of the NetWare Asynchronous Communications Server (NACS).

NetWare Core Protocols Protocols used to obtain the core services offered by a NetWare file server. Includes a variety of facilities such as file access, locking, printing, and job management.

NetWare for VMS Program for DEC's VMS operating system that makes the VAX look like a NetWare server. Ancestor of Portable NetWare.

NetWare MHS	Novell's product name for Action Technologies' Message Handling Service.
NetWare Name Service	Distributed naming service introduced by Novell in 1990 to replace the bindery mechanism.
NetWare SQL	Software for a NetWare server to allow it to service incoming SQL requests from clients.
NetWare SQL Requester	Workstation software for accessing a database server running NetWare SQL.
NetWare 3270 LAN Workstation Software	Software that sits on a workstation and emulates an IBM 3270 terminal. The workstation uses the services of an SNA gateway.
NetWare Token-Ring Gateway	Allows Novell workstations to access devices compatible with the IBM Token-Ring, such as IBM minicomputers or cluster controllers.
NetWare 286	NetWare Operating System for the 80286-based computer.
Netwise	Maker of the Netwise RPC Tool, remarketed as NetWare RPC by Novell.
network address	The number of the network that the user is on. Each network (data link) in an internetwork has a number assigned to it. The full address of a station is the network address plus the local address of the node on that network.
Network File System	A distributed file system developed by Sun Microsystems and widely used on TCP/IP systems.
network library	Software module that comes with the Netwise RPC Tool. The network library is added to the code generated by the RPC Compiler to form a complete program. The library masks access to network communications from the rest of the program.

Network Loadable Module	Program on NetWare 386 that when loaded becomes a part of the operating system.
Network Services Protocol	DECnet transport layer protocol.
NFS	*See Network File System.*
nibble	Half a byte.
NLM	*See Network Loadable Module.*
node	An individual item in a set. An Ethernet node, for example, is a device attached to the cable with a transceiver, including a repeater, bridge, or computer. A file system node is a directory or individual file.
nonexclusive (read) lock	A type of lock on a file that permits other users to read information but prevents any write operations.
Nonpersistent binding	A style of binding in remote procedure calls where the connection is set up and torn down every time the remote procedure is called.
Novell	Makers of NetWare software for networks.
Novell Wide Area Network Interface Module	A Novell hardware board that allows several asynchronous connections to be maintained at the same time.
N(R)	*Receive sequence number.* LLC field that indicates the sequence number of the last packet received.
N(S)	*Send sequence number.* LLC field that indicates the sequence number of the packet being sent.
NSFnet	*National Science Foundation network.* A research network established by the NSF to give access to supercomputer and other computing facilities.

NSP	*See Network Services Protocol.*
object	NetWare bindery concept. A bindery consists of a series of objects that have properties. A user is an example of an object, which would have the property password.
ODLI	*See Open Data-Link Interface.*
ONC	*See Open Network Computing.*
Open Data-Link Interface	Another way of referring to data link devices that conform to Novell's Link Support Layer specification. ODLI is synonymous with the Multiple Link Interface Driver (MLID).
Open Network Computing	Sun marketing term for the family of protocols that include the Network File System.
OSI	*Open Systems Interconnect.* A set of standards developed by ISO that allow many different vendors' equipment to communicate.
OS/2	*Operating System/2.* Successor to DOS for the IBM PC (assuming anybody wants it, that is).
OUTPOST	Utility program on the Message Handling Service for taking messages out of the MHS environment into another application.
Pack	Term used in remote procedure calls for translating data from the machine-dependent format into a machine-independent format.
packet	A general term used in networking to refer to a message sent to a peer entity in the network.
Packet Assembler/ Disassembler	Special-purpose computer on an X.25 network that allows asynchronous terminals to use the synchronous X.25 network by packaging asynchronous traffic into a packet.

Packet Exchange Protocol An XNS transport protocol that requires each packet to be separately acknowledged. A PEP-like protocol forms the foundation of the NetWare Core Protocols.

packet switching A network that has packaged data into packets. A computer can handle many more virtual connections with packets than it can with dedicated connections (known as circuit switching). Packet switching forms the basis for X.25, as well as most network-layer protocols.

PAD *See Packet Assembler/Disassembler.*

PAP *See Printer Access Protocol.*

Paradox Popular database program for the IBM PC.

PARC *See Xerox Palo Alto Research Center.*

passive hub ARCNET hub for connecting up to four computers. *See also active hub.*

path A file system concept. The path indicates what set of folders or subdirectories a file is stored in.

PBX *Private branch exchange.* A telephone switch which is installed at the customer premises. Allows the organization to take control of many of their telecommunications functions.

PC *Personal computer.* A desktop computer developed by IBM or a clone developed by a third-party vendor. PC is sometimes used more generically to refer to other desktop systems, such as the Apple Macintosh.

PDU	*See Protocol Data Unit.*
PEP	*See Packet Exchange Protocol.*
piggybacked	Added on to. A term used in protocols that require the acknowledgment of prior packets. The acknowledgment can often be "piggybacked" into the same packet as data that is headed in that direction.
ping-pong	A type of transport protocol that requires each packet to be individually acknowledged. Before a node can send another packet, it must wait for an acknowledgment. PEP is an example of this, as opposed to SPX, which allows a window of unacknowledged packets to be outstanding.
pipe	*See Named Pipes.*
Portable NetWare	Software that resides on a guest operating system and allows NetWare workstations to treat the host as a NetWare server.
Portable Streams Environment	A generic version of STREAMS that is packaged into the source code for Portable NetWare.
PostScript	A page description language used on printers such as the Apple LaserWriter and on computer displays used in workstations from companies such as NeXT and Sun Microsystems. Similar in function to Xerox's Interpress.
Preimaging	Making a copy of a piece of data just before it is changed. The copy is stored on the disk in case the computer fails in the middle of the update operation and corrupts the file. The preimage is then used to return the data to its previous state.
presentation syntax	A standard method of representing data in a heterogeneous environment. The Abstract Syntax Notation 1 (ASN.1) is an example of a presentation syntax.

print spooler A software program that accepts several jobs at once for printing. The spooler controls access to the printer and queues incoming jobs for execution.

Printer Access Protocol AppleTalk protocol for accessing printers.

PROFS IBM office automation package for the VM/CMS operating system.

propagation velocity The rate at which a signal propagates on a wire. Signals travel over a wire much like ripples in a pond after a stone is thrown in.

property NetWare bindery concept. The bindery is organized around objects that have properties. Each property has a name (such as password) and a current value (such as the current value for password).

protocol data unit A layer communicates with its peer by sending packets. Each packet has a header that contains information that the peer will work with, such as addresses or acknowledgment requests. It also contains data, the protocol data unit, that is passed up to the client of the layer.

protocol stack A set of functions, one at each layer of the protocol stack, that work together to form a set of network services. Each layer of the protocol stack uses the services of the module beneath it and builds on that service.

PSE *See Portable Streams Environment.*

public domain Intellectual property available to people without paying a fee. Most computer software developed at universities is in the public domain.

QMS *See Queue Management Services.* Also a company that makes laser printers and accessories.

Quarterdeck Office Systems	Makers of Desqview/386, a program that allows the 80386 computer running DOS to perform several different tasks.
Queue Management Services	Part of the NetWare operating system used by programs to manage a queue of several incoming requests.
R	*Reply.* Sniffer Analyzer label for a packet that is a reply. C stands for command.
RAM	*Random access memory.* Dynamic memory, sometimes known as main memory or core.
RDA	*Remote Data Access.* An international standard for access to databases in a heterogeneous computing environment.
Rdb	DEC's relational database management system.
reconfiguration burst	A term used in ARCNET. When a node wishes to initiate a network reconfiguration, it starts transmitting a long burst of data, thereby clearing the network of any other data.
REM	*See Remote Electronic Mail.*
Remote Electronic Mail	An MCI Mail account used by companies that have several users.
remote procedure call	A set of network protocols that allow a node to call procedures that are executing on a remote machine. The Netwise RPC Tool is an example of such a protocol.
repeater	An Ethernet device used to connect two or more segments of cable together. The repeater retimes and reamplifies the signal received on one segment before resending it on all other segments.
request bitmap	An AppleTalk Transaction Protocol field used to keep track of which pieces of a reply have been sent or received.

reservation field	A field in token ring packets that allows a node to inform the active monitor that it has data of a certain priority to send.
resource fork	The second half of a file on a Macintosh file system. The resource fork contains the executable code while the data fork has user data.
RG-62	Grade of coaxial cable.
ring purge	A token ring packet that clears the network of data, similar in function to the ARCNET reconfiguration burst.
RIP	*See Routing Information Protocol.*
RISC	*Reduced instruction set computer.* Generic name for CPUs that use a simpler instruction set than more traditional designs. Examples are the IBM PC/RT, Pyramid minicomputers, and the Sun 4 (SPARC) Workstations.
RLogin Mux Module	A portion of Portable NetWare that allows multiple remote workstations to emulate a terminal on the host operating system.
Router Hello	DECnet packet used by routers to let other nodes on the network know they are operating.
routing directory	A database maintained by the network layer to determine which paths to use to get to particular networks.
Routing Information Protocol	Protocol used in Novell's NetWare and Xerox's XNS to inform computers on a network of any changes in the topology of the network.
Routing Table Maintenance Protocol	AppleTalk protocol for the maintenance of routing tables. Similar to RIP in Novell's NetWare and XNS.
routing tables	A directory maintained by the network layer that contains the address of nodes on the internetwork and how to reach them.

RPC	*See remote procedure call.*
RPC Compiler	Product sold by Netwise. Allows programs written for a single computer to be distributed on the network.
RPC specification	The information prepared by a programmer as input to the RPC Compiler. The specification informs the compiler which procedures will be distributed.
RPC Tool	The RPC mechanism sold by Netwise, including the RPC compiler.
RR	*Receive ready.* An LLC field indicating that the sending node is ready to receive data.
RTMP	*See Routing Table Maintenance Protocol.*
RX-Net	Novell's version of ARCNET.
SAP	*See Service Advertisement Protocol.* Also means Service Access Point, which is the address of the user of a service. *See DSAP or SSAP.*
SCP	*See Server Control Procedure or Session Control Protocol.*
search index	A method used in NetWare to keep track of the results of a request that returns more than one value. When one value is returned, as in the case of a directory search for file names, the packet also contains a search index value. The search index value is submitted with the next search request, and the next file name will be returned. A value of –1 means no more data.
search path	A mechanism in DOS, Unix, and other operating systems that allows a user to specify a command without knowing which directory it is stored in. The operating system will search each of the directories in the search path for the command until it finds the file.

Semaphore	A synchronization mechanism on NetWare and other operating systems.
sequence number	A unique number for every packet on a particular connection maintained by a reliable transport layer service. The sequence number allows the transport layer to see if any packets were lost or delivered out of sequence by the underlying network and data layers.
Sequenced Packet Exchange	Novell implementation of the XNS Sequenced Packet Protocol.
Sequenced Packet Protocol	XNS protocol for reliable transfer of data at the transport layer.
server	A program on a computer that provides services to workstations. File, database, print, and communications are just a few kinds of servers.
Server Control Procedure	Program used in Netwise RPC.
server stub	A piece of software generated by the RPC Tool. The server stub emulates the calling application program to the remote procedure on the server.
Service Advertisement Protocol	NetWare protocol for publicizing the current network address of services.
Session Control Protocol	DECnet session layer protocol.
shell	A program that provides a user environment. The DOS shell, for example, accepts user requests and translates them into the appropriate low-level DOS calls.
slot	An entry in a fixed-size table. For example, the NetWare table that holds the mapping of resources to local drive letters has 26 slots.

small moveable cabling system	IBM cabling system. Contrast with the "large, non-moveable" system sold by the same company.
SMP	*See Standby Monitor Present.*
SNA	*See System Network Architecture.*
snail mail	The traditional postal service.
Sniffer Network Analyzer	Network General product used to monitor many different upper- and lower-layer network protocols.
socket	An entry point to a program. User programs communicate with IPX by means of sockets. Each user typically has a separate socket.
Softswitch	Company that makes gateways between different message handling services.
source address	The origin of a data packet on a network.
spool	A place for a fast device (such as a software program) to leave data for later processing on a slow device (such as a printer).
SPP	*See Sequenced Packet Protocol.*
SPX	*See Sequenced Packet Exchange.*
SQL	*Structured Query Language.* ANSI-standard data manipulation language used in most relational database systems.
SRC	*Source address.* Sniffer Analyzer abbreviation for the source data link address.
SSAP	*Source service access point.* Address of the user of a service. *See also DSAP.*
SSS	*Server session socket.* AppleTalk Session Protocol field that contains the socket number to which session level packets are sent.

standard — A standard interface for two components. The nice thing about standards is there are so many to choose from.

Standard Micro Systems — Makers of ARCNET hardware.

standby monitor — Token ring term for a computer that is waiting for the active monitor to fail and is ready to step in if that happens. Kind of like a vice president.

Standby Monitor Present — Packet sent out by a standby monitor every 7 seconds to advertise its presence.

stored upstream address — Token ring concept. Each node on the token ring stores the address of the neighbor from which it receives data.

stream head — The entry point to a stream, a series of software modules connected with the STREAMS mechanism.

stream-oriented — A type of transport service that allows its client to send data in a continuous stream. The transport service will guarantee that all data will be delivered to the other end in the same order as sent, and without duplicates. Also known as a reliable transport service.

STREAMS — An AT&T mechanism developed for the Unix operating system and adopted by Novell for NetWare. STREAMS is a way of connecting a series of software modules, letting them send messages to each other.

Structured Query Language — International standard language for communicating with relational database systems.

subvector — Portion of a MAC frame. For example, the token ring command to request initialization on the ring contains subvectors with the adapter software level, upstream neighbor address, and several other fields.

Sun Microsystems	Makers of workstations and the Network File System.
SUPERVISOR	The network manager on a NetWare network.
synchronization	Coordination of tasks among multiple users. Synchronization mechanisms include locking and semaphores.
syscode	ARCNET concept. Indicates which network layer user the packet is intended for.
System Network Architecture	IBM's networking architecture.
System/3X	IBM minicomputers including the System/36 and System/38. Replaced by the AS/400 line.
T1	Digital telephone line operating at 1.544 Mbps.
table	Relational database term for data grouped into rows and columns.
TCP	*See Transmission Control Protocol.*
TCP/IP	*Transmission Control Protocol/Internet Protocol. Non-proprietary network architecture used extensively in Unix and heterogeneous environments.*
Telex	Messaging mechanism that predates fax or electronic mail.
terminal emulator	A program that allows a computer to emulate a terminal. The workstation thus appears as a terminal to the host.
terminate and stay resident	DOS program that is loaded before application programs. The TSR programs are activated by a specific keystroke. Borland's Sidekick is an example of a TSR.

termination expression Term used in the Netwise RPC Tool. The termination expression is included in structures when there is less data than the data structure could have held. The termination allows the RPC mechanism to send only the real data instead of transmitting blank cells for unused portions of the data structure.

terminator Device on each end of an Ethernet cable to prevent reflections.

The Coordinator User interface made by Action Technologies for the Message Handling Service.

thickwire Another name for the 10BASE5 standard for coaxial cables and Ethernet.

thinwire Thinner, and cheaper, version of baseband coaxial cable used for Ethernet networks. Also called cheapernet or 10BASE2.

tickle An AppleTalk packet that is sent periodically to keep a connection alive.

TLI *See Transport Level Interface.*

token bus A medium access method where nodes are not allowed to transmit until they receive a token. The token is broadcast on the medium, as in Ethernet, and gives each successive node permission to use the medium.

token ring A medium access method where nodes are not allowed to send until they receive a token, which is a series of bits that are passed from one node to its physical neighbor. *See 802.5.*

topology A network topology shows the computers and the links between them. A network layer must stay abreast of the current network topology to be able to route packets to their final destination.

transaction	A series of one or more operations that form a logical whole. The entire transaction or none of it must take effect.
Transaction Tracking System	Novell software to maintain the integrity of file operations in the case of system failures.
transceiver	The device that is physically attached to the Ethernet cable.
transceiver cable	A cable of up to 50 meters between the transceiver and the Ethernet controller.
Transmission Control Protocol	The transport protocol in TCP/IP used for the guaranteed delivery of data. Similar to Novell's SPX.
Transport Level Interface	AT&T-developed specification for the interface between the transport layer and upper-layer users.
trap	Programming concept for a block of code that is executed whenever a specific condition occurs, usually an error.
trunk cable	Used to distinguish the coaxial Ethernet cable (the trunk) from the attachment to the individual node (the transceiver cable).
trustee	NetWare security concept. Trustees have certain specified privileges for file access, in contrast to the general public. Trustees can be individual users or groups of users.
TSR	*See terminate and stay resident.*
TTS	*See Transaction Tracking System.*
tuple	A term used in relational database systems. A tuple is the equivalent of a record in a file management system and corresponds to one row of data in a table.

twisted pair A pair of wires (or several pairs of wires) such as is used to connect telephones to distribution panels. Twisted pair is also being used as a physical transmission medium for Ethernet, token ring, and other forms of data links.

UAM *See User Authentication Method.*

UDP *See User Datagram Protocol.*

UID *User identification.*

Ultrix Version of Unix sold by DEC for VAX computers.

Unix Operating system developed and trademarked by American Telephone and Telegraph. Unix is a pun on the Multics operating system.

unpack Term used in remote procedure calls for translating data from the machine-independent form into the form used on a particular computer.

User Authentication Method AppleTalk concept for the way that users are identified to a file server before they can access resources.

User Datagram Protocol Part of the TCP/IP protocol suite. UDP operates at the transport layer and, in contrast to TCP, does not guarantee the delivery of data.

VAP *See value-added process.*

value-added process An optional program for older versions of NetWare. Replaced by the Network Loadable Module in NetWare 386.

VAR *Value-added reseller.* Company that embeds another company's products into a more sophisticated product.

VAX *Virtual address extension.* Hardware series made by DEC.

VAX Cluster	High-speed DEC network used to supplement DECnet for highly integrated systems.
view	A database construct that makes a collection of one or more tables appear as a single database table.
VINES	Network architecture made by Banyan in direct competition with Novell's NetWare.
virtual circuit	A service offered usually at the transport layer. The user of a virtual circuit is able to send data to a remote user and not worry about putting data in packets, error recovery, missing data, or routing decisions.
Virtual Terminal	DECnet protocol to allow a user on one DECnet node to emulate a locally attached terminal on a remote node.
VM	*Virtual machine.* An IBM operating system that permits guest operating systems, such as MVS, to reside on top of it. Usually used in conjunction with the CMS user interface.
VMS	*Virtual memory system.* A DEC proprietary operating system for VAX computers.
VMS Mail	DEC electronic mail utility on the VMS operating system.
VT200	Type of terminal developed by DEC for use on VAX computers.
Wang	Maker of a popular word processing system. Maker of a less popular general-purpose computer.
Wang Office	Wang software for electronic mail.
watchdog program	A program, not associated with a user, that watches for specific events. A typical watchdog program looks for idle terminals and logs the user off.

wide area bridge A MAC-layer bridge that works on wide area communications links such as T1 and dial-up lines.

WNIM+ *See Novell Wide Area Network Interface Module.*

workgroup Trendy term for people who work together. Several computers may be isolated on a small network, known as a workgroup network. Whether anything is accomplished is another matter.

write lock Also known as an exclusive lock. Prevents others from reading or writing the locked data.

WSS *Workstation session socket.* AppleTalk Session Protocol field for the socket on the workstation that will receive session-level packets. *See also SSS.*

X.121 CCITT addressing standard.

X.21 CCITT standard for circuit-switched networks.

X.25 CCITT standard for packet-switched networks.

X.25 Bridge Novell product to allow an X.25 network to be used to route information between two NetWare networks.

X.400 CCITT standard for message handling services.

X.500 CCITT standard for directory information on an X.400 network.

XDR *See External Data Representation.*

Xerox Maker of a variety of products.

Xerox Network System The network architecture that forms the basis for Novell's NetWare.

Xerox Palo Alto Research Center Xerox research laboratory that led the development of many current technologies including PostScript, the Apple Macintosh, and Ethernet.

XNS	*See Xerox Network System.*
XNS Mail Transport Protocol	Message handling service in XNS.
XQL	*Xtructured Query Language.* Novell's subset of the SQL standard. *See NetWare SQL, the database server.*
XQLM	*See XQL Manager.*
XQL Manager	High-level library of calls to Novell's XQL.
XQLP	*See XQL Relational Primitives.*
XQL Relational Primitives	Low-level library of calls to Novell's XQL.
ZIP	*See Zone Information Protocol.*
zone	An AppleTalk concept. A zone is a collection of computers, which together make up an internetwork. Isolating operations within a zone limits the number of devices, such as printers, that the user has to choose from.
Zone Information Protocol	AppleTalk protocol for the maintenance of zones.

Index

Abstract Syntax Notation One Basic Encoding Rules. *See* ASN1
Access rights, 127, 129–132
Access Server, 259
Accounting services, 143–144
Action Technologies, 13, 81, 147
Active hub, 55, 56, 58
Active monitor, 68–71
Addresses, 30, 59, 71, 73, 80, 83, 90
Advanced Program to Program Communications. *See* APPC
AFP (AppleTalk Filing Protocol), 230, 232–234
Allocation number, 100, 102
American National Standards Institute. *See* ANSI
AMP (Active Monitor Present) frame, 70–71
Analysis, definition of, 22
ANSI (American National Standards Institute), 31, 64
API (Application Programming Interface), 277
APPC (Advanced Program to Program Communications), 277
AppleShare, 225
AppleTalk, 16, 225–237
   basic configuration, 226
   filing protocol, 230, 232–235
   lower-level protocols, 227
   miscellaneous features, 237
   names and zones, 227–228
   network, transport, and session protocols, 228, 230–233
   Novell and, 225
   Printer Access Protocol, 235–237
AppleTalk Filing Protocol. *See* AFP
AppleTalk Session Protocol. *See* ASP
AppleTalk Transactions Protocol. *See* ATP
Application layer, 186, 273
Application Programming Interface. *See* API
Architecture, network, 3–4, 6–8, 81
ARCNET, 6, 8, 9, 53–64, 66–67
   cables, 55–58
   error recovery, 59–62
   fragmentation header, 62–64
   hubs, 55–56, 58
   and IPX, 86–89
   local address, 83
   packets, 54–55, 58–59, 62
Arrays, 192
Ashton-Tate/Microsoft SQL Server, 181
ASN1 (Abstract Syntax Notation One Basic Endcoding Rules), 200
ASP (AppleTalk Session Protocol), 230–231
Asynchronous bridges, 257–259
Asynchronous gateways, 259–261, 263
Asynchronous processing, 198
AT&T, 15, 207, 241

335

ATP (AppleTalk Transactions Protocol), 230–231
Attachments, MHS, 152

Bandwidth, 54, 60, 79
Beacon, 71, 74
Binary tree (Btree), 170–174
Bindery, 115–120, 132, 143
Binding, 193
BNC port, 43
Body, message, 150, 151–152
Bridges, 8, 82
   asynchronous, 257–259
   Ethernet, 43–48
   MAC-layer, 8, 37, 79, 82, 244, 263
   multiple, 46
   wide area, 48, 79
   X.25, 261, 262
   See also Routers
Broadcast, 92, 104, 120–121, 124
BROUTER process, 173
BSERVER process, 173
Btree. *See* Binary tree
Btrieve utilities, 13, 170, 173–174

C programming language, 243
Cable
   ARCNET, 55–58
   coaxial, 6, 38, 40, 43, 58
   fiber optic, 40, 55, 58
   See also Wire
Captured data, 18–20
Carrier Sense-Multiple Access/Collision Detect. *See* CSMA/CD
CCITT (International Telephone and Telegraph Consultative Committee), 161
Cheapernet. *See* Thinwire
Checksum field, 85
Clearinghouse protocol, 81
Clients, 4–5, 103, 105, 111–112
Client stub, 189, 194–196
Clocks, 120–121, 124
Coaxial cable, 6, 38, 40, 43, 58
Comment keyword, 151
Commercial gateways, 160–161

Communications utilities, 120–121
Compaq, 246
Compiler, 189, 191
Connectivity manager, 156–158
Create file packet, 274, 275
CSMA/CD (Carrier Sense-Multiple Access/Collision Detect), 32, 43
Custom procedures, 197–198, 200

DAP (Data Access Protocol), 248
DARPA (Defense Advanced Research Projects Agency), 269
Data, captured, 18, 19, 20
Data access, 169–182
   Btree file, 170–174
   Btrieve, 173–174
   database security, 178–179
   flat versus structured, 169–170
   locking and data integrity, 179–181
   SQL and databases, 174–176
   XQL, 176–177
Data Access Protocol. *See* DAP
Databases, 175–176
Data collision, 32
Data fork, 234
Data links
   ARCNET, 53–64
   asynchronous, 257–261, 263
   Ethernet, 29–49
   extended LAN, 75
   IPX and SPX, 79–106
   MAC and LLC sublayers, 29–31
   and networks, 6, 8–9, 11
   nodes, 53–55, 57–62
   token ring, 64–74
   X.25 network, 261–265
Data manipulation, 13
Datapoint Corporation, 54
Data structures, 192
DDCMP protocol, 246
Deadlock detection algorithms, 138
DEC network, 17, 31, 36, 92, 243, 245–248, 251, 253
Defense Advanced Research Projects Agency. *See* DARPA

Delta time, 127
Desktop database, 234
DESQview, 259
Destination node, 6, 67–68, 80, 98
Destination socket, 93
Device driver, 208–210
DFS (Distributed File Service), 248, 251
Directory access rights, 127, 129–132
Directory nodes, 127
Directory services, MHS, 165
Disk drives, 10, 12, 115, 121, 125, 208, 251
Distributed File Service. See DFS
Duplicate address, 71, 73
Dynamic Microprocessor Associates, 259

Echo protocol, 10, 93–94, 95
ECONFIG utility, 36, 85
Electronic mail, 13–14, 22, 147–166
Encoding, MHS, 152
Error protocol, 10, 93–94, 95
Error recovery
  ARCNET, 59–62
  token ring, 67, 71–74
Ethernet, 5–9, 15, 29–49, 62, 66–67, 83
  and AppleTalk, 225
  basic service, 32–33
  bridges, 43–48
  extended, 44
  and IEEE 802.3, 30–37, 84, 246
  and IPX, 84–89
  and LAT, 248, 250
  MAC and LLC sublayers, 29–31
  multisegment, 39–42
  NetBIOS traffic on, 278–279
  NFS traffic on, 274, 275
  and Novell, 48–49
  server, 244
  thickwire networks, 38
  Version 2.0, 31, 34, 246
Execute-only attribute, 131
External Data Representation. See XDR

Fax gateways, 159–160
FDDI (Fiber Distributed Data Interface), 74
Fiber Distributed Data Interface. See FDDI
Fiber optic cable, 40, 55, 58
Fiber optic hub, 55
File access, 121, 125–127
File attributes, 131, 133
File nodes, 127
File operations, 132–133
File servers, 10, 12, 16, 103–104, 120, 125, 225, 234–235
Filtering, 18, 20, 46
Flat file, 169–170
Flat network topology, 92
Fragmentation header, 62–64
Free Buffer Enquiry, 59

Gateways
  AppleTalk, 225–237
  asynchronous, 259–261
  commercial, 160–161
  fax, 159–160
  MHS, 158–161
  networks, 16–17, 269–281
  STREAMS and protocol stacks, 207–222
  X.25 and wide area networks, 257–265
Gupta Technologies, 181

Handle, 125, 128
Header, message, 148–151
Hierarchical Storage Controller. See HSC
Hops, 89–92
Hosts, MHS, 156–158
HSC (Hierarchical Storage Controller), 251
Hubs
  active, 55–56, 58
  ARCNET, 55–56, 58
  fiber optic, 55
  intelligent, 55, 56
  MHS, 156–158
  passive, 55, 56, 58

IBM System Network Architecture (SNA), 276
IBM token ring, 66, 74
IDP (Internetwork Datagram Protocol), 81, 82
IEEE (Institute of Electrical and Electronics Engineers), 30–31, 64
Indexed file, 170–171, 173
Initialization, 71–74
Institute of Electrical and Electronics Engineers. *See* IEEE
Intel, 31
Intelligent hub, 55, 56
Intended destination node, 6
International Standards Organization. *See* ISO
International Telegraph and Telephone Consultative Committee. *See* CCITT
Internet, 270
Internet Protocol. *See* IP
Internetwork, 8, 11, 79, 80, 82–84, 87–88, 101
Internetwork Datagram Protocol. *See* IDP
Interpress, 81
Interprocess communication. *See* IPC
IP (Internet Protocol), 35, 36, 270
IPC (interprocess communication), 187–188, 190
IPX (program), 10, 11, 30, 34, 45, 66, 81–100
  and ARCNET, 62–63
  and asynchronous bridges, 257, 259
  clients, 103, 105
  and communications services, 121
  Error and Echo protocols, 93–94, 95
  local address, 29, 83, 90, 95
  NetWare Core Protocols, 94–100
  packets, 5, 36, 63, 82–83, 85–87, 95, 244
  and Portable NetWare, 241
  and RIP, 89–93
  and SAP, 102–103
  sockets, 83–89
ISO (International Standards Organization), 6, 7, 30, 31, 64, 200

Job servers, 141–143

Keep alive message, 99, 100
Keywords, 151

LAT (Local Area Transport), 248–251
Length field, 85
Library, network, 189–190, 193–195
Link Support Layer. *See* LSL
LLC (Logical Link Control), 29–31, 34, 36, 66, 68, 218
Local address, 29, 80, 83, 90, 95
Local Area Transport. *See* LAT
LocalTalk, 225, 227
Locking, 133, 135, 137–138, 179–181
Logical Link Control. *See* LLC
LPT port, 5
LSL (Link Support Layer), 16, 208, 213, 217–219

MAC (Medium Access Control), 29–31, 34, 36, 218
Macintosh. *See* AppleTalk
MAC-layer bridge, 8, 37, 66, 79, 82, 84, 244, 263
MAILbus, 14
MAU (multistation access unit), 65–66
MCI MAIL, 147, 160–161
Menu operation, 18, 19, 21
Message continuation fragments, 64
Message Handling Service. *See* MHS
Message Router, 14, 248
Message transfer agent, 153–154, 156
MHS (Message Handling Service), 13–14, 81, 147–166, 185
  commercial gateways, 160–161

connectivity manager and hubs, 156–158
directory services, 165
fax gateways, 159–160
gateways, 158–161, 162
message attachments and encoding, 152
message body, 151–152
message header, 148–151
message transfer agent, 153–154, 156
services, 147–148
structure, 148–149
user interface, 152–153
X.400 and, 161, 163–165
Mirrored volume, 115
MLI (Multiple Link Interface), 217
MLID (Multiple Link Interface Driver), 217
Modules, 209–212, 241–243
Monitor, active, 68–71
MPI (Multiple Protocol Interface), 217
MPT (multiport receiver), 6, 37, 38
Multiple Link Interface. *See* MLI
Multiple Link Interface Driver. *See* MLID
Multiple Protocol Interface. *See* MPI
Multiplexing modules, 242
Multiplexing protocol, 37
Multiport receiver. *See* MPT
Multistation access unit. *See* MAU

NACS (NetWare Asynchronous Communications Server), 260–261
NAK (negative acknowledgment), 102
Name Binding Protocol. *See* NBP
Named Pipes, 208, 213, 219–221
Name Service, 104
NASI (NetWare Asynchronous Services Interface), 261
National Science Foundation, 270
NBP (Name Binding Protocol), 227–229

NCP (NetWare Core Protocols), 23, 111–144, 241, 270, 272
accounting services, 143–144
attributes and access rights, 127–132
basic services, 10, 12–14, 113
bindery, 115–120
communications utilities, 120–121
and Ethernet, 34
file access, 121–127
file operations, 132–133
and IPX, 86, 94–100
job servers, 141–143
locking and synchronization, 133–138
operating system, 113–115
and PEP, 105
print services, 140–141
and SAP, 102–104
semaphores, 138–140
and servers, 111–113
traffic, 18
and XNS, 22
NCPMux module, 242
Negative acknowledgment. *See* NAK
NetBIOS, 105, 241, 278–280
NetWare
architecture, 3, 6–8
Asynchronous Communications Server. *See* NACS
Asynchronous Services Interface. *See* NASI
Core Protocols. *See* NCP
data access, 169–182
and data links, 8
file server, 16, 103–104, 234–235
MHS, 147–166
Name Service, 104
operating system, 5, 16, 111, 113–115, 119
Portable, 16, 241–243, 248
and servers, 111–112, 244
shell, 5, 10, 111
and STREAMS, 221, 243
supplements to, 14–16
for VMS, 244–245
workstation, 5, 132–133

Network Adapter Basic Input/Output System. *See* NetBIOS
Network address, 30
Network File System. *See* NFS
Network General, 18
Network library, 189–190, 193–195
Network Loadable Module. *See* NLM
Networks
  analyzing, 3–24
  architecture, 3–4, 6–8, 81
  cheapernet, 42–43
  clients and servers, 4–5
  data links and LLC, 29–49
  gateways, 16–17, 269–281
  integrating subnetworks, 74–75
  layers, 8, 45, 79–81
  protocol stack, 5–8, 12
  Sniffer Analyzer, 18–22, 24, 34, 127
  TCP/IP, 36, 46, 90, 269–272
  thickwire, 38
  TOPS, 225
  transport layer, 8, 10
  see also specific networks
Network Services Protocol. *See* NSP
NFS (Network File System), 272–276
NLM (Network Loadable Module), 113–114, 180, 235
Nodes
  ARCNET, 53–55, 57–62
  destination, 67–68, 80, 98
  directory, 127
  Ethernet, 45, 83
  file, 127
  and IPX, 82, 95
  and network transport layers, 79–80
  Novell, 40
  remote, 102
  routing, 89
  token ring, 68, 74
  trustee, 127, 130
NSFnet, 270
NSP (Network Services Protocol), 246
NWDAEMON, 242

ODLI (Open Data-Link Interface), 217
OLI (Open Link Interface), 221
ONC (Open Network Computing), 200–201
Open Data-Link Interface. *See* ODLI
Open Link Interface. *See* OLI
Open Network Computing. *See* ONC
Open Systems Interconnect. *See* OSI
Operating system, 5, 16, 111, 113–115, 119, 207–208
OSI (Open Systems Interconnect), 280

Packet Assembler/Disassembler. *See* PAD
Packet Exchange Protocol. *See* PEP
Packets, 18, 21, 22, 23, 29, 30
  ARCNET, 54–55, 58–59, 62
  create file, 274, 275
  error recovery, 67
  Ethernet, 33, 35–37, 45, 48
  fragments, 64
  initialization, 71–72
  IPX, 5, 36, 63, 82–83, 85–87, 95, 98, 244
  NCP, 252
  and network transport layers, 80
  RIP, 90–92
  token ring, 66–68
  types, 86
  X.25, 263
PAD (Packet Assembler/Disassembler), 263
PAP (Printer Access Protocol), 235–237
Passive hub, 55, 56, 58
Passwords, 115–118, 178, 232
PC (personal computer), 5
  AppleShare, 225
  and asynchronous gateways, 259, 260
  disk drives, 10
  and IBM SNA, 276
  and LAT, 249
  and MHS, 152

print services, 140
"virtual", 259
pcAnywhere, 259
PDU (protocol data unit), 196
PEP (Packet Exchange Protocol), 10, 23, 81, 94, 241, 278
Peripherals, 115
Personal computer. See PC
Portable Netware, 16, 241–243, 248
Ports, 66
PostScript, 81
Preimaging, 179
Presentation layer, 185
Printer Access Protocol. See PAP
Printing, 5, 12, 140–141
Process binding, 193
Programs. See Software; specific programs
Propagation velocity, 57
Protocol data unit. See PDU
PROTOCOL messages, 211
Protocol stack, 6–8, 12, 207–208, 243, 245, 278
Public network, 46
Put procedure, 213

Quarterdeck Office Systems, 259
Queue management program, 13, 142

Random number exchange, 232
Read-only file, 131
Reflections, 38
Remote node, 102
Remote Procedure Call Tool. See RPC Tool
Remote time, 127
Research network, 46
Resource fork, 232
Respond-by keyword, 151
Ring-in ports, 66
Ring-out ports, 66
Ring purge, 71, 72
RIP (Routing Information Protocol), 10, 80, 86, 89–93, 95, 103
RLogin module, 242, 245

Routers, 257–258
  AppleTalk, 228
  definition, 82
  and network layer, 8, 80
  and RIP, 89–90, 92
  see also Bridges
Routing Information Protocol. See RIP
Routing Table Maintenance Protocol. See RTMP
RPC (Remote Procedure Call) Tool, 14–15, 81, 185–202, 241
  client stub, 189, 194, 195–196
  custom procedures, 197–198, 200
  interprocess communication, 187–188
  ISO and Sun mechanisms, 200–201
  and Network File System, 272–273
  procedure declarations, 191–192
  process binding, 193
  role of, 201–202
  Server Control Procedure, 196–197
  upper layers, 185–186
RTMP (Routing Table Maintenance Protocol), 228

SAP (Service Advertisement Protocol), 10, 14, 80, 81, 100, 102–105, 219, 228
SCP (Server Control Procedure), 196–197
Screen dumps, 22
Security, 12, 127, 133, 178–179. See also Locking
Semaphores, 138, 140
Sequenced Packet Exchange. See SPX
Sequenced Packet Protocol. see SPP
Sequence number, 87, 89, 98, 100
Server Control Procedure. See SCP
Servers, 4–5, 103
  asynchronous, 257, 259–260
  components of, 114–115
  and data links, 8, 47, 88
  Ethernet, 87

Servers (*continued*)
   job, 141–143
   Netware, 111–112, 244
   transport, 157
   See also File servers; Routers
Server stub, 189–190, 195
Service address, 30
Service Advertisement Protocol. *See* SAP
Session layer, 185, 230, 246
Seven-layer model, 6
SFT (System Fault Tolerance), 115, 251
Shareable attribute, 131
Shell, NetWare, 5, 10, 111
SMP (standby monitor present) frame, 70–71
SNA (System Network Architecture), 276
SNA Distribution Services (SNADS), 14
Sniffer Network Analyzer, 18–22, 24, 34, 127
Sockets, 83–89, 90, 93, 101
Software
   C programming language, 243
   interprocess communication, 187–188
   module, 209
   and NetWare Core Protocols, 12
   NetWare TR workstation, 276
   obtaining, 24
   programming interfaces, 277
   see also specific programs
Splicing, 42
SPP (Sequenced Packet Protocol), 81
SPX (Sequenced Packet Exchange), 81, 100–102
   clients, 103, 105
   and Portable NetWare, 241
   and program communication services, 121
   transport layer, 10, 11
SQL (Structured Query Language), 13, 175–182
Standby monitor, 69–71

Star topology, 55, 60
Stream head, 209–211
STREAMS, 15, 16, 207–222, 272
   basic components, 209
   character I/O mechanisms, 208–209
   flow control, 213
   Link Support Layer, 217–219
   message queues, 211–213
   message types, 209–211
   multiplexor, 213–215
   Named Pipes, 219–221
   and NetWare environments, 221, 243
   protocol stacks and operating system, 207–208
   Transport Level Interface, 215–216
Structured access, 13
Structured Query Language. *See* SQL
Subnetworks, 74–75
Sun Microsystems, 225, 272, 273
Sun Open Network Computing, 200–201
Synchronization, 12, 133, 135, 137–138
System Fault Tolerance. *See* SFT
System Network Architecture. *See* SNA

TCP (Transmission Control Protocol), 270
TCP/IP networks, 36, 46, 190, 269–272
TechWriter, 228
Terminate and stay resident utility. *See* TSR utility
Terminators, 38
Thickwire, 38
Thinwire, 32, 41–42
TLI (Transport Level Interface), 15, 207–208, 210, 213, 215–216
Token, 59, 60, 67, 68
Token ring, 6, 8, 9, 15, 83
   active and standby monitors, 68–71
   basic operation, 66–68, 70

error recovery and initialization, 67, 71–74
extensions, 74
and IPX, 87–88
ISO/IEEE standard, 64–66
TOPS network, 225
Trademarks, xiii
Traffic, 18, 22, 33, 245, 274, 275, 278–279
Transaction Tracking System. *See* TTS
Transmission Control Protocol. *See* TCP
Transparency, 121, 189
Transport control field, 86
Transport layer, 8, 10, 79–81, 87
Transport Level Interface. *See* TLI
Transport servers, 157
Trunk cable. *See* Coaxial cable
Trustee node, 127, 130
Trustee rights, 130
TSR (terminate and stay resident) utility, 260–261
TTS (Transaction Tracking System), 115, 179–181
Twisted pair cable, 32, 43
2-repeater limitation, 40
2.5-meter separation rule, 38

UAM (User Authentication Methods), 232
UDP (User Datagram Protocol), 270
Unions, 192
Unix, 8, 197, 207, 211, 241, 242, 269, 274
User Authentication Methods. *See* UAM
User Datagram Protocol. *See* UDP
User interface, MHS, 152–153

Value-Added Process. *See* VAP
VAP (Value-Added Process), 113–114, 180
VAX minicomputer, 16–17, 244, 245, 246, 248, 249–252
Virtual circuit, 10, 11, 101
Virtual terminal service, 248

VMS product, 16–17, 243, 244–245, 248
Volumes, 115, 123

WANs (wide area networks), 257, 263
Wide area bridges, 48, 79
Wide Area Network Interface Module. *See* WNIM
Wide Area Networks. *See* WANs
Wire
  thickwire, 38
  thinwire, 32, 41–42
  see also Cable
WNIM (Wide Area Network Interface module), 259
Workgroup-wide router, 156
Workstations
  Apple, 225
  ARCNET, 8, 55
  as client of network, 4
  and data links, 9
  and Ethernet, 7
  IPX, 83, 86–88, 95
  NetWare, 5, 132–133
  NetWare TR software, 276
  and token ring, 8

X.25 network, 257
  bridges, 261, 262
  gateway, 261, 263
X.400-based messaging systems, 161
XDR (External Data Representation), 273
Xerox, 31
XNS (Xerox Network System), 22, 23
  broadcast, 92
  header, 22, 90
  and Novell, 81
XQL products, 13, 176–177

Zero priority token, 68
ZIP (Zone Information Protocol), 228
Zone Information Protocol. *See* ZIP

Ordering the Software

A demonstration version of the Sniffer Network Analyzer software is available to readers of this book. Simply send in the order form to Network General Corporation and they will send you the software. You need not purchase this book to obtain the software.

Free Software Offer
Network General Corporation
4200 Bohannon Drive
Menlo Park, California 94025

ANALYZING NOVELL NETWORKS

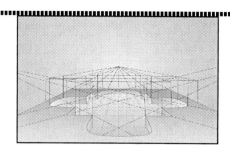

Please send me a demonstration version of the Sniffer Network Analyzer.

PLEASE PRINT CLEARLY

Name		Title	
Name of Company			
Mail Stop			
Address			
Town		State	Postcode
Country	Telephone		Telex